Reading Old English Texts focuses on the critical methods currently being used and developed for reading and analyzing writings in Old English. It is the first collection of its kind in the field and is a timely book, given the explosion of interest in the theory, method, and practice of critical reading in recent years.

Each chapter engages with current work on Old English texts from a particular methodological stance. The authors are all expert, but are also concerned to explain their method and its application to a broad undergraduate and graduate readership.

The chapters include a brief historical background to the approach; a definition of the field or method under consideration; a discussion of some exemplary criticism (with a balance of prose and verse passages); an illustration of the ways in which texts are read through this approach, and some suggestions for future work. The larger issues raised by the interactions between the separate chapters are a major focus of the Introduction.

Reading Old English texts

Reading Old English texts

Edited by

Katherine O'Brien O'Keeffe

University of Notre Dame

•

CAMBRIDGE
UNIVERSITY PRESS

PUBLISHED BY THE PRESS SYNDICATE OF THE UNIVERSITY OF CAMBRIDGE
The Pitt Building, Trumpington Street, Cambridge CB2 1RP, United Kingdom

CAMBRIDGE UNIVERSITY PRESS
The Edinburgh Building, Cambridge CB2 2RU, United Kingdom
40 West 20th Street, New York, NY 10011-4211, USA
10 Stamford Road, Oakleigh, Melbourne 3166, Australia

First published 1997

Printed in the United Kingdom at the University Press, Cambridge

Typeset in Concorde BQ 9.25 on 13.75 pt

A catalogue record for this book is available from the British Library

Library of Congress cataloguing in publication data
O'Keeffe, Katherine O'Brien.
Reading Old English texts / edited by Katherine O'Brien O'Keeffe.
p.   cm.
Includes bibliographical references and index.
ISBN 0 521 46575 3 (hardback). – ISBN 0 521 46970 8 (paperback)
1. English literature–Old English, ca. 450–1100–History and
criticism–Theory, etc. 2. Civilization, Anglo-Saxon, in
literature. 3. Civilization, Medieval, in literature. I. Title.
PR173.038   1997
829–dc21   96–47374 CIP

ISBN 0 521 46575 3 hardback
ISBN 0 521 46970 8 paperback

829
0412

CONTENTS

CONTRIBUTORS

PETER S. BAKER
University of Virginia

DANIEL DONOGHUE
Harvard University

NICHOLAS HOWE
Ohio State University

MICHAEL LAPIDGE
University of Cambridge

CLARE A. LEES
University of Oregon

KATHERINE O'BRIEN O'KEEFFE
University of Notre Dame

ANDY ORCHARD
University of Cambridge

CAROL BRAUN PASTERNACK
University of California, Santa Barbara

D. G. SCRAGG
University of Manchester

PAUL E. SZARMACH
Western Michigan University

ABBREVIATIONS

ASPR	Anglo-Saxon Poetic Records
ASE	*Anglo-Saxon England*
BL	British Library
Bosworth-Toller	Joseph Bosworth, *An Anglo-Saxon Dictionary*, ed. and enlarged by T. Northcote Toller (Oxford, 1898); T. Northcote Toller, ed., *An Anglo-Saxon Dictionary: Supplement*, with revised and enlarged addenda by Alistair Campbell (Oxford, 1972).
Catalogue	N. R. Ker, *Catalogue of Manuscripts Containing Anglo-Saxon* (Oxford, 1957; suppl. 1990)
CL	*Comparative Literature*
EEMF	Early English Manuscripts in Facsimile
EETS	Early English Text Society (os = original series; ss = supplementary series)
JEGP	*Journal of English and Germanic Philology*
MÆ	*Medium Ævum*
MLN	*Modern Language Notes*
NM	*Neuphilologische Mitteilungen*
OE	Old English
OEN	*Old English Newsletter*
PBA	*Proceedings of the British Academy*
PMLA	*Publications of the Modern Language Association*
PQ	*Philological Quarterly*
SN	*Studia Neophilologica*
TRHS	*Transactions of the Royal Historical Society*

Old English verse is quoted throughout from the Anglo-Saxon Poetic Records, unless otherwise specified. Prose texts are quoted from the standard editions and are cited in the notes.

Introduction

KATHERINE O'BRIEN O'KEEFFE

•

This is a book about ways of reading Old English, each of which presupposes a set of interpretative practices. Each of the essays which follow undertakes to describe and argue for a specific current approach (= a set of practices) with the understanding that reading within that approach produces a particular kind of outcome. In this sense, each approach might be imagined as a different sort of lens (perhaps even, at times, a filter) which permits the reader to visualize and comprehend differentially particular objects in a complex field. Each approach, whether it be through, for example, oral traditional criticism, source work, feminist criticism, or historicist analysis, constructs itself within two sets of conversations, one with the past from which it wishes to be distinguished, and one with the present, where it wishes to differentiate itself from other contemporary approaches. Thus, to understand an argument *for* something, it is necessary to understand the often unspoken conversations and quarrels that argument assumes. The most pressing among these exchanges concern the proper approach to and utility of the past, broadly conceived.

We might begin with two contemporary, but complementary, notions of engagement with the past, whose complex negotiations of objectivity and desire have, in their own ways and at different times, shaped our interpretation of the past. The first must be envisioned as a scene: the public funeral in 1870 of a leader of the French resistance during the Franco-Prussian War. In the crowd the young historian Gabriel Monod displays a banner whose message, 'History is the master science', proclaims the undertaking of history as partner to a nationalist agenda.[1] Monod, whose graduate training was in the German seminar system, appropriated (while apparently misconstruing) the German approach to historical researches and adopted 'scientific' history as the necessary tonic to revive a defeated and dispirited France in the aftermath of the Franco-Prussian War. In this view, the future lay in proper attention to the past, an attention to be paid in the form of positivist histories. The other form of engagement appeared as part of a published critique of the role of history in contemporary German culture. In the second of his *Untimely Meditations* (February 1874), Friedrich Nietzsche addresses the use of history in what he saw as its three modes: antiquarian, monumental, and critical. His opening, monitory observation, 'Insofar as it stands in the service of life, history stands in the service of an unhistorical power, and, thus subordinate, it can and should never become a pure science . . .', follows from his conviction that complete knowledge of a historical phenomenon kills it.[2] For Nietzsche, the posture of critical objectivity is a deadly illusion, which produces only more written history and cannot lead to living events themselves. In contradistinction to Monod, one of Nietzsche's antidotes to a suffocating history is the art of forgetting. Born in the same year (1844), Monod the historian and Nietzsche, the philosopher and quondam classical philologist, wrote and worked in a period of consolidation and institutionalization of their respective disciplines. But their antithetical views, in unequal measure, figure for us two different takes on the past that emerge and reemerge in various forms in the approaches of this volume. In the space between Monod's banner and Nietzsche's critique stand a variety of ways to read and use the texts of the past. And if now we can read back into Monod's banner the extension of positivism into history and literature, with its emphasis on the individual's trans-historical access to the past and its unproblematic alliance with nationalism, we must allow Nietzsche's protest to be proleptic of the ways in which his discourses on power and knowledge, relational analysis, the subject and desire have come to shape the academic discourses of our own fin-de-siècle.

Our questions, then, are how do we read the texts of the past, how do we gain access to them, and to what uses are they put. To put these questions in focus, we might begin with a description of access to and use of the OE past contemporary with Monod and Nietzsche. Henry Sweet's 1871 introduction to his edition of Alfred's translation of Gregory the Great's *Regula pastoralis* will concern us for what it says and for what it does not. His claim for the text itself, 'Of all the unpublished Old

English texts, the present is perhaps the most important. . . . It affords data of the highest value for fixing the grammatical peculiarities of the West-Saxon dialect of the ninth century . . .', gives and takes away at the same time.[3] Sweet has nothing to say about the king's project of translation, the significance of the translation, the importing of ideas from the continent to England, or the king himself. The text's importance lies solely in the 'data' it provides for determining Early West Saxon. The context for this valuing of 'data' emerges at various points in the Preface.

Throughout, the Preface is dedicated to outlining Sweet's method in establishing the text. 'All additions of my own in either text [i.e. Oxford, Bodleian Library, Hatton 20 and Cambridge, Corpus Christi College 12] are enclosed in parentheses, and are intended solely to assist the beginner. From a strictly scientific point of view such additions are hardly advisable, as tending to bias the reader's judgment; but in an edition like the present, which endeavours to supply a variety of wants, they are less objectionable.'[4] Such a 'scientific' viewpoint seeks to maintain the posture of objectivity (avoiding 'bias') and focus on verifiable textual evidence. In such a perspective, the text functions as a specimen in a case. Any attempt to repair a cracked tooth or supply a missing wing on the specimen transforms it from an object of scientific study into an exhibition for amateurs to gawk at. Indeed, the problem of audience for this edition surfaces disturbingly here: the scientific interest of this philological exercise is threatened by the 'variety of wants' it must address. The Early English Text Society (under whose auspices Sweet was publishing the edition) specifically addressed itself to a general audience, and advertised as its purpose, from its inception in 1864, 'bringing the mass of Early English Literature within the reach of the ordinary student, and . . . wiping away the reproach under which England had long rested, of having felt little interest in the monuments of her early language and life'.[5] But the needs of the 'ordinary student' and the professional researcher are far apart, and Sweet chafes at the requirement to supply a translation: 'I look upon a translation to a text like this, which is of exclusively philological interest, as so much waste paper, utterly useless except to the merest tyro – useless even to him, if he wishes to acquire a sound knowledge of Old English, a language, which, like all others, ought either to be studied properly with grammar and dictionary, or else let alone.'[6] While Sweet and the directors of EETS agreed on the national importance of producing reliable editions of venerable English texts, they appeared to diverge on audience, use, and approach.

What is assumed yet unstated in Sweet's Preface is that there is one overriding reason to retrieve the written monuments of the past, that is, to recover the earliest state of the nation's language. That other interests in the text may exist, Sweet (at least for Alfred's translation) is unwilling to concede. For Sweet, there is but one approach (philology in its narrow definition as a science of language) and one method (the scientific method of objectivity). His introduction is a paradigm of scientific method: laying out the assumptions of his research, his method, his principles for selection, and analysis of the language. His palpable regret at the necessity of including a translation stems from his understanding of the membership and goals of the community of scientific scholarship.

My purpose here is not to rehearse a history of the enterprise, but to look rather at the frameworks within which work in the discipline may be conceived. Sweet's invocation of science, philology, and history is one such framework, and the trio has combined *in bono et in malo* in the 125 years of work in Old English since. While Sweet's 1871 Preface marks neither a beginning nor a point of perfection for the various configurations of such a framework, it nonetheless offers a provocative moment of combination for such ideas. As Monod's banner suggests, the possibilities for such frameworks were developing in France at about this time. In 1876 Monod and Gustave Fagniez launched *Revue historique*, a journal dedicated to a scientific point of view and scholarly objectivity. But it was through the collaboration of two younger French historians, Charles-Victor Langlois and Charles Seignobos, that the scientific method in historical studies was most productively disseminated. Their *Introduction aux études historiques*, published in 1898 and translated into English that same year, was enormously influential in France, England, and the United States. As a manual for the production of 'good' history, the *Introduction* offered a method of historical research designed to ensure both an objective heuristic and an objective narrative. It is this manual which codifies much of the process of what is called positivist history.[7] And while there was a reaction in the community of historians, certainly by the close of the First World War, against the dead ends of positivist history, many of the presuppositions of such history – the stance of objectivity, the importance of the individual, the unmediated access to the past, the construction of the monuments of the past within a nationalist context – remained part of the ways in which Old English texts were edited and read.

Sweet, of course, did not envision his task as presenting Alfred's translation as a work of historical literary criticism. His job was that of textual editor, and his methodology was supplied by philology. 'Philology' is a term with a long history and for this reason is a moving target for definition. In pragmatic terms, 'philology' describes a set of practices for establishing reliable texts given difficult conditions of textual transmission: numerous manuscripts, high variance, scribal ignorance, damaged copies, etc. Under these circumstances, the 'making' of texts requires a fairly wide range of knowledge, including paleography, history, language, and stylistic criticism (see chapter 6). As such, philology, as it developed in the previous century, encompassed both the study of language and, more broadly, culture. In the nineteenth century, philology, as a study of languages, particularly as they related to each other in 'families', aspired to a scientific precision under the influence of nineteenth-century positivism.[8] So we see Sweet in his Preface to Alfred's *Pastoral Care* referring to his practice within a very specific context: his making of this particular text was in aid of the study of OE language, which, it is clear, also had nationalist political ramifications. Philology of the sort practiced by Sweet produced over the next century extremely important resources for our understanding of the language: grammars, dictionaries, and syntax (see chapter 3 below). But, it should be remembered, in his emphasis on 'science' and on the national importance of studying OE Sweet is very much a man of his time, practicing a philology remade under the aegis of positivism. The later, larger aspiration of philology as a cultural study of texts (as practiced, for example, by Leo Spitzer, Ernst Robert Curtius, and Erich Auerbach) sought to offer critical readings attentive to the historical language of the text. But this sensitivity to language still retained a vision of the transparent readability of the past which jars with most current understandings of the difficulties inherent in bridging the gulf between the past and the present and in representing that past. There is much, indeed, that is familiar, as well as disturbing, in Curtius's identification of the philological entrée to the trans-historical nature of literature:

The 'timeless present' which is an essential characteristic of literature means that the literature of the past can always be active in that of the present. . . .

But historical investigation has to unravel it and penetrate it. It has to develop analytical methods, that is, methods which will 'decompose' the material (after the fashion of chemistry with its reagents) and make its structures visible.... Only a literary discipline which proceeds historically and philologically can do justice to the task.[9]

The implications of his desire to 'penetrate' a text and 'decompose' it with 'reagents' certainly unsettle the feminist and the materialist textual critic in me. And while those of us practicing various forms of historicist scholarship today might recognize here the desire to engage the past, we would certainly foreground our own roles in the construction of it (see chapter 4).

The attacks on philology (in Old English as well as in other medieval disciplines) in the past decade or so have often proceeded metonymically. In attacking philology, its critics at times point to deadening pedagogy (all those paradigms), blaming the theory for failures of its practitioners. But the most telling criticisms focus on the theoretical shortcomings of the philological procedures assumed in the description by Curtius quoted above: that readers in the present have unmediated access to the texts of the past (in part from the notion of a 'timeless present' of the text); that the vision of the reader's relationship to the text and its author recapitulates the stance of an exhausted humanism (where an ideal reader encounters the intentions of an ideal author); that the stance of objectivity inherited from the nineteenth-century reconstruction of philology is either a naive or even irresponsible avoidance of the political elements in any reading or a tacit acceptance of the politics of the status quo. Another way to state this last critique is to describe such philology as a hermeneutics without a politics (or with a covert or unconscious politics).[10] In recent years, the attempt to refurbish philology as a modern critical practice (the so-called 'New Philology') recognizes the need for a responsible criticism of medieval texts to be grounded in an understanding of certain technical fundamentals: among them language, history and manuscripts as full partners to current theoretical practices. It reflects as well the perception that informed readings of medieval texts (in the present instance, OE texts) are cultural readings, broadly construed (see chapter 3).

In explicit reaction to the philological approaches of the earlier part of the century, the two dominant modes of reading OE literary texts in the third quarter of the century were formalism (in the US 'New

Criticism', 'practical criticism' in the UK) and patristic exegesis.[11] Individually, and in dialogue with each other, these approaches to reading did much to enliven the subject, and, as even a cursory glance at annual bibliographies will indicate, were responsible for explosive growth in the production of articles and books on Old English. The differences between them are instructive, and while the theories behind them have ceased to generate productive critical conversation, the problems they set out to address are still with us.

The operative points of difference between these two approaches may be highlighted as the relationship of text and context (at issue is the way in which the text under consideration is seen within history), and the importance of the individual in both the writing and the reading of the text (at issue are humanist values in the critical approach). In the relation of text to context the problem of history and philology reemerge. Although in its purest state, formalism is an ahistorical practice which assumes immediate access of the reader to the text, in general OE formalist reading carefully discriminated appropriately historical meanings for individual words and paid homage to the artistic 'intentions' of their individual authors (despite the anonymous state of nearly all OE verse and much OE prose). Where history was invoked, it remained a context essentially separable from the text at hand. So, for example, Stanley Greenfield attempts to modify extreme formalism in his description of a 'valid' criticism:

If we respect and make clear in our criticism the various sets of expectations that impinge upon a particular poem, if we are aware of the limitations imposed upon those expectations by formal relationships within a text and of the possible implications those relationships generate, if we work outwards from a poem to its contemporary cultural environment – we are more likely to achieve a larger consensus of agreement about meaning than we will by pursuing 'typical' approaches on the one hand or purely 'internalist' analyses on the other.[12]

The 'internalist' analyses to which Greenfield refers were the shibboleths of the New Criticism. In reaction both to Romanticism and positivism, practitioners of New Criticism held up the work of art as a verbal icon; their concerns were the work as an integral whole. Interested primarily in image and symbol (the optimal text for analysis was a lyric poem), they pursued analysis with rigorous attention to the unique, internal workings of the language of the poem and with little interest in questions of referentiality. (For observations on the effects of New Criticism on comparative work in Old English, see chapter 1 below.)

In vivid contrast, patristic exegesis (Greenfield's 'typical' approach) is rigorously (one might even say rigidly) historicist in its reading.[13] Its earliest theoretical position was that all medieval literary texts were read contemporaneously in terms of Augustine's doctrine of charity. The job of the medieval and contemporary reader was to interpret the hidden allegorical meaning lying behind the husk of the letter. Later refinement softened and extended this fundamental position to include an emphasis on the method of reconstructing the patristic context for vernacular literature. In its purest form, patristic exegesis applied a totalizing historicist frame to all medieval literature, essentially razing differences among them in its allegiance to the doctrine of charity (see chapter 4). To the degree that it does so, such an approach is essentially anti-humanist in its leveling of difference and its promotion of adherence to Augustinianism above the possibilities of individual creativity so championed by the New Critics.[14]

If these critical positions have lost their hold on us, the issues of text and context, the involvement of the reader, and the use of history still remain problems on which we must take stands. In various ways, the essays in this volume, in their conversations with each other, offer redescriptions of earlier practices, rethink positions, make fresh syntheses and negotiate a second challenge from the continent, this time as Nietzsche appears in and is reinterpreted by the thought of French poststructuralists.[15] (See especially chapters 7 and 8.) The concerns of their work in deconstruction, discourse analysis, semiotics, and psychoanalysis productively reconfigure questions of language, power, desire, and the subject, and in so doing, offer readers of Old English challenging avenues of approach.

The contemporary engagement with the issues presented in this book opens with an analysis of the role of comparative method in the interpretation of OE texts. In chapter 1 Michael Lapidge shows how the comparative approach to literature in Old English has been fundamental to the discipline since its inception. While the specifics of method have varied since the early days of the dominance of Germanic philology, a comparative perspective, broadly construed, underlies many of the different approaches in this volume. For example, Lapidge shows how Henry and Nora Chadwick used a comparative method in their monumental study of heroic literatures, and this kind of work would be extended to include study of oral tradition.[16] Similarly, many maneuvers in source criticism work hand in hand with comparative method (see chapter 2).

Lapidge's essay shows how the development of comparative method involves more than placing two texts side by side. While the essentially generic approach of formalism fostered an ahistorical vision of texts (insofar as work in a dead language can ever be divorced from history) to focus on the 'verbal icon', much early work (done under the banner of a Germanic hypothesis) and some mid-century work (done under the banner of patristics) performed particular comparative maneuvers within specific historical visions. In the wake of formalism, however, comparative work in Old English has taken more culturally informed directions. Current comparative work (for example, reading *The Battle of Maldon* in the light of the *Männerbund*, or together with the Old High German *Das Ludwigslied* or the Latin *Bella Parisiacae urbis*) combines textual and cultural analysis.[17]

As illustration, Lapidge offers an intriguing demonstration of comparative method in his reading of two apparently dissimilar epic moments: Grendel's descent into fear at the recognition of Beowulf's grip and Turnus' realization that he is about to lose his battle against Aeneas. Lapidge's comparison of the monster's reflection to that of Turnus provides scope for speculating on the significance of this unique manifestation of interiority in the Old English poem. It also opens the door to the larger question of the dimensions of the subject in early England, showing in passing the continued flexibility of the comparative approach.

Source study is connected conceptually to the comparative approach in that both approach their goal through the tropes of similarity and difference. What separates them, it would seem, is that the approach through comparison ultimately looks at similarities. The approach through source study, finally, looks at differences.[18] In chapter 2, D. G. Scragg shows how source study works in a textual culture in which borrowing ideas (or phrasing or even appropriating whole passages — what we would call 'plagiarism') was the dominant intellectual practice. Such a culture did not have 'authors' in the sense that Foucault has defined them, nor a concept of ideas in the way that international copyright law construes them as intellectual property. In this milieu source study seeks to make discriminations. Its goal is to establish levels of borrowing for further analysis of the stylistic difference of a particular Anglo-Saxon text, or, as Scragg puts it, 'the distinctive contribution of Anglo-Saxon authors' to intellectual history.

In method, source study is essentially historical, constructing genealogies (in the pre-Foucaultian sense) of ideas. Order of ideas is of primary importance, since in such genealogical thinking, the earlier writer cannot be borrowing from the later one. In its early, nineteenth-century phases, source study aspired to ultimate sources (what Allen Frantzen has analysed as 'origins')[19] and was wedded to a rather mechanical reflex of positivism, but in its current form, source study is most interested in proximate forebears, what Scragg defines as 'immediate' sources. In this way, source study can be attentive to the material inflections of cultural studies, looking for the vehicles for transmissions of ideas, the manuscripts moving to and from the continent, or the traces of intellectual exchange with the Irish. Current work on inter-textuality in Anglo-Saxon England or on the OE archive uses the fruits and occasionally some of the methods of source study, though with a different aim in mind.

Chapters 3 and 4 look both backward and forward in their analyses of approaches to OE texts. Daniel Donoghue, in his survey of language-based approaches, looks at the claims of philology and linguistics in their study of Old English and the apparent divide between these disci-plines. Viewed as a study of language, philology is a practical and empirical discipline. Its purview includes grammar, dictionary-making, and textual editing, though the latter activity extends philology into an interpretative discipline: as we have seen, in some definitions 'philology' is a discrete practice of literary criticism, laying heavy emphasis on the interpretation of language. Linguistics, often seen as the more 'scientific' of the two approaches to OE language, is interested in higher level theory, less the explication of specific OE texts then the framing of rules for the operation of language in general.

While the purview of linguistics (as a relatively recent discipline) seems fairly clear, the purview of philology is haunted by its history and by some of the claims made for it. Whose philology is it, when someone claims to do (or accuses someone else of doing) philology? What is increasingly clear, from the number of books, special issues, collections, and essays devoted to 'philology' which have appeared in the present fin-de-siècle, is that philology cannot sustain the mantle of objectivity it borrowed from science when it constituted itself as an academic field in the late nineteenth century. (Recall Sweet's project cited above.) However, Donoghue points out that current practitioners of philology consciously distance themselves from the claims of positivism, erecting, testing, and modifying their hypotheses with clear understanding of the subjectivity involved. Donoghue proceeds to deconstruct this dichotomy between philological and linguistic approaches to OE language and OE texts, illustrating how both combine in contemporary writing on Old English and how both, in the process, continue to renew and reinvent their engagements with the subject. In this process, Donoghue works through an argument on Kuhn's Law both to illustrate the specific process of thinking in an approach through language, and to demonstrate some ways in which such an approach connects itself with current questions in paleography and editing.

For sheer slipperiness of definition, 'historicism' can match 'philology' at every turn of the road.[20] In chapter 4 Nicholas Howe negotiates the difficult twists in the definition of 'historicism' and the various ways in which scholars of OE literature have used history in the service of their reading. As with the case of philology, the question 'whose history?' is apposite when examining the methodical application of historical studies to the reading of OE texts, for 'top-down' and 'bottom-up' models will produce widely different outcomes. Howe examines historicist approaches, broadly conceived, in two planes: the kinds of narratives they use and the ways in which they deploy their evidence. To set the stage, Howe uses two classic studies as stalking horses: Girvan's *Beowulf and the Seventh Century* and Huppé's *Doctrine and Poetry*. In Girvan's 'bottom-up' model, the programmatic application of social conditions in the seventh century to *Beowulf* produces a circular (and self-confirming) argument. In Huppé's top-down application of totalizing Augustinianism, history disappears, paradoxically, like the Cheshire cat behind his grin. If the study of Old English is wedded to history, the matchmaker is concern for the language itself. In Howe's analysis, claims of language study on historicism in Old English are paramount (though they themselves must be historicized!). We might compare here the contrasting priorities of history and language in Howe's and Donoghue's approaches.

To illustrate his contentions about the ways in which historicist reading can illuminate an OE text, Howe reads Ælfric's *Colloquy*. In the process, he must necessarily 'unread' a number of previous assumptions and editorial conventions, and his illustrative reading shows the ways in which historicism attempts to negotiate the gap between past and present, while acknowledging the resistance of past texts to current interpretation. His tongue-in-cheek concluding reversal of the 'New Historicist two-step' offers as well a cautionary tale, illustrating what can be at stake in the misappropriation of scholarship and the ways in which an engaged historicism might counter it. In such a stance we see a modern reflex of Nietzsche's protest against 'dead' history.

In a number of senses, three chapters (5, 'Oral tradition', 6, 'The recovery of texts', and 9, 'Old English and computing') carry on a three-way conversation, insofar as they all treat technologies of transmitting OE texts. A consideration of oral tradition in Anglo-Saxon England must examine the delicate interplays of oral and literate modes of thinking, remembering, and transmitting information. In an oral culture, memory is a bodily practice of preserving information. Manuscript culture makes memory bodily in a different way: the scribe's body copies information onto parchment, the dead skin of an animal. With print culture and beyond, memory becomes increasingly disembodied; with the computer, it approaches the virtual. From this perspective, the recovery of OE texts is an exercise in looking both backward and forward. The powerful techniques of print culture have made available for study almost all the surviving texts from Anglo-Saxon England. However, in the process it has re-presented these texts in a particular, authorial mode, leveling the variance inherent in a residually oral culture. While computer technology can now essentially restore that variance, making available (theoretically) every surviving record of a particular text, and offering readers the option of remaking their own, the price tag may be a different, quiet sort of authority − that of the textual editor.

Andy Orchard examines various models for approaching the distinction between 'oral' and 'written' elements in Old English. The 'strong' hypothesis for orality in OE argued on the basis of Homeric and South Slavic poetry that formulas were the guarantee of oral origin. Orchard shows the ways in which this hypothesis has been challenged and modified over the years as 'orality' and 'literacy' have been demonstrated not to be dichotomous states in Anglo-Saxon England, but rather to interact in subtle ways. Establishing the initial hypothesis and modifying it, one might note, were essentially products of comparative method, as oral studies in OE modeled themselves from the start on Parry and Lord's work on Homeric epics and South Slavic poetry. Orchard brings oral-traditional studies considerably farther by illustrating how the method can be extended to OE prose texts. In his study of Wulfstan's sermons, Orchard shows how repetition occurs at the level of phrase, theme, and larger passage, and he extends his study to a comparison of Wulfstan's technique with that of several African-American preachers. In so doing, he makes possible a number of intersections of oral-traditional studies with interests in vocality and performance. His further examination of repetition in several Exeter Book riddles highlights the difficulties in determining how repetition and variance function in a scribal culture. These difficulties offer textual editors either noisome headaches or attractive opportunities, depending on their points of view and on the technologies available to them.

Reading OE texts, whether prose or verse, involves more than simply accepting the words as they appear on the page. Engaged reading (and hence critical reading) requires an understanding of how any text we read has come into being in the way we read it. It requires some under-standing of the manner in which texts came to be preserved, how they were transmitted, the circumstances under which they were copied, and the circumstances under which they received the printed form which aids our reading. Paul E. Szarmach addresses these issues and their importance for reading OE texts in his essay, 'The recovery of texts'. Szarmach shows how the various choices an editor can make in pre-paring an edition affect what we can read in the text and how the text means.

Playing on the words of the Johannine Gospel ('and the Word was made flesh'), Szarmach contrasts two approaches to recovering an Old English text. Editing, which hitherto has operated tacitly under a set of essentially Neoplatonic rubrics, often seeks to reclaim an 'ideal' text (a maneuver, effectively, to efface the operation of history). Szarmach shows, however, that the 'ideal' is only one possible goal in editing and that methods of textual recovery are driven by editorial desire – that is, particular goals, expectations, and audiences which affect the choice of editorial procedure and often base text. The 'ideal' text, governed by the purity of the 'word', is countered by a different conception of text, its materiality, determined by the 'body' in which it travels. The word committed to the flesh of the parchment takes on a body, and the material conditions of the book embodying the text are integral parts of its historicity and its meaning. The difference between attempting an 'ideal' (or 'authorial') version and pursuing a material text (with some, at least, of its warts intact) is in part a function of the editor's (and the reading community's) judgment on the value of variance. Szarmach's survey of the range of editorial choices shows how editors may affect the meaning of the texts they edit on the grand level of version or on the local textual level of word choice. Nor is the latter a trivial matter: as the case of Modþryð illustrates, editorial choice determines whether we read a female character at that point in *Beowulf* or not. This realization forefronts not simply editorial theory but editorial desire in the making of a text.

Peter Baker's 'guided tour' of the on-line resources for students and scholars of Old English includes a stop at the Internet and the material available on it. As he points out the wealth of material available (and emerging) on-line, he notes the problem of quality: free editions are almost always the ones out of copyright, nineteenth-century editions long superseded. The warning *caveat lector* is only useful if the reader already knows how to judge an edition in terms of its working principles and its adherence to them. For the wary user, however, electronic resources promise to remake the field in various important ways. Baker guides us through the most important of these resources: the ongoing *Dictionary of Old English* and the Old English Corpus that project has made available; ANSAXNET, the on-line discussion forum for things Anglo-Saxon; the various projects in process in hypertext; Labyrinth, the World-Wide Web resource for Old English; SEENET (the electronic analogue to EETS); the electronic *Beowulf*; and databases. His survey prompts the question whether these resources mark a revolution in studies within Old English or whether they merely allow us to do more of what we were doing before and more quickly. His answer, in part an account of how using the Old English Corpus made possible a previously unthinkable project, is a cautious 'yes' and a provocation to further discussion.

Chapters 7 and 8 engage in conversation with each other and with a number of other essays in the volume. In their own ways, they are heirs to a Nietzschean perspective on history which opened this introduction.

In Lees's essay, this takes the form of an explicit argument for political engagement; in Pasternack's essay, it forms the underpinning of the post-modern approaches she addresses and, I would argue, lies behind her choice of Jameson's Marxian critique for her reading of *Beowulf*.

Noting that feminism as a set of practices is both a politics and a hermeneutics, Clare Lees explores the ways in which feminist approaches to Old English texts draw attention to the presuppositions of the discipline. As Lees charts ways in which feminist scholars have engaged Old English texts in the past and are at present pursuing their work, she addresses a critical methodological issue: how do feminists negotiate between the methods and techniques of conventional studies and the strategies of feminist theory and praxis? Her question, crucial for feminist scholarship, is equally of concern for the discipline as a whole, since it addresses the ways in which political desire and objective technique may be made to work productively together.

Lees's analysis of feminist scholarship on Old English texts addresses questions of method, the history of the discipline, and the ideological implications of the framing of research questions. Her discussion of feminist engagements with the ways in which origins have been constructed in the discipline reveals the gendered nature of the nineteenth-century (as well as the current) project of Anglo-Saxon studies. Similarly, her examination of history and methodology in the discipline addresses both the nature of the evidence available for study and the implications of questions addressing this evidence. In addressing the gendered vision of labor in Anglo-Saxon England, Lees suggests that reading women also requires reading men, and the representation of masculine warrior culture in the surviving texts points to the constructed and gendered aesthetics of the canon of OE writings. Indeed, to look at the representation of women is to question the function and representation of gender in these works. These concerns are woven together in her illustrative reading of *Elene*, where she suggests ways in which readers of Old English literature can use various strategies of feminist criticism to produce readings which show the operations of gender and agency in OE narrative.

In her survey of the application (and the applicability) of post-modern theories to the reading of OE texts, Carol Braun Pasternack shows how a number of these approaches — semiotics and textuality, Lacanian psychoanalysis, deconstruction, the archeology of culture — have provoked new forms of historical analyses, not only of the OE texts themselves, but also of the culture which produced them and the cultures which receive them. Pasternack focuses on two areas of study in these 'foundational moments' of post-structuralist thought, the subject and the text. While the latter seems familiar, the former is perhaps less so. The 'subject' in post-structuralist thought is a precise formulation for what we rather loosely think of as the 'self'. It is important to note the grammatical nexus in which the word 'subject' operates. Indeed, Lacanian psycho-analysis receives Freud through the linguistic theory of Saussure. And this approach to self-formation makes possible a particular way of historicizing the 'subject' by analyzing the linguistic systems of a culture, for it shifts focus from the individual as constructed by humanism to a subject in and of language, in and of systems of power. 'Text' in post-structuralist thought may also feel slightly unfamiliar. In part, this may be because deconstruction reads the whole of reality as a 'text' subject to analysis. But it may also be because in semiotic theory the tidy boundaries of a discrete text slip away in the face of intertextuality and in the reconstruction of the relationship between text and reader. Semiotic and deconstructive approaches both draw on and challenge source study.

In her illustrative reading of *Beowulf*, Pasternack addresses the vision of the heroic past, using post-structural analysis to probe the slippages and contradictions in that construct. Her argument engages the question of oral and written in the text, story-telling, and manuscript: it presses for a close analysis of the language (and an acceptance of the contradictions individual words seem to embrace), and urges a form of historicism in which past and present are constructed to reflect on each other. Such an analysis both uses and challenges traditional scholarly approaches.

The approaches presented in this volume are offered not as prescriptions for method, but rather as overviews of ways of reading and invitations to explore further work. While they focus individually on particular forms of reading (for heuristic purposes distinguishing themselves from other current approaches), it should be obvious that each approach necessarily draws on a number of others. Among the great pleasures, and challenges, of working in Old English is the number of skills it requires. If the 'philologers' of the past needed knowledge of languages, and history, and manuscripts, practitioners in the present must know them too – and more. Our fin-de-siècle looks back on a century of prodigious change and on intellectual movements which present us with stunning changes in looking at the world. Our challenge in looking forward is to think of the ways in which these new perspectives help us to ask new questions in Old English.

Notes

1 W. R. Keylor, *Academy and Community: The Foundation of the French Historical Profession* (Cambridge, MA, 1975), pp. 41–2. In French *science* means both 'science' and 'knowledge'; similarly, *Wissen(schaft)* in German.
2 F. Nietzsche, 'On the Uses and Disadvantages of History for Life', in *Untimely Meditations*, trans. R. J. Hollingdale with an introduction by J. P. Stern (Cambridge, 1983), p. 67.
3 H. Sweet, ed., *King Alfred's West-Saxon Version of Gregory's 'Pastoral Care'*, 2 vols., EETS 45 and 50 (London, 1871–2; repr. 1934), II, p. v.
4 Sweet, *Pastoral Care*, p. ix.
5 Early English Text Society, Advertisement, November 1910, p. 2. For all its prodigious work in editing and publishing, the Society hardly perceived itself to be participating in a Golden Age of interest in early texts: 'But the Society's experience has shown the very small number of those inheritors of the speech of Cynewulf, Chaucer, and Shakespeare, who care two guineas a year for the records of that speech. "Let the dead past bury its dead" is still the cry of Great Britain and her Colonies, and of America, in the matter of language. . . . Until all Early English MSS. are printed, no proper History of our Language or Social Life is possible.'
6 Sweet, *Pastoral Care*, p. ix.
7 The English translation, *Introduction to the Study of History*, trans. G. G. Berry, with a preface by F. York Powell (London and New York, 1898), offers a perspective on the manual which might occasion wry reflection today: 'There are several points on which one is unable to find oneself in agreement with MM. Langlois and Seignobos, but these occur mainly where they are dealing with theory [!]', p. ix. The *Introduction* saw eleven American reprints through 1932. It ought to be pointed out that Seignobos himself made a careful distinction between method in the natural sciences and in history. Langlois, however, seemed not to have such reservations. On the latter point see Keylor, *Academy and Community*, pp. 78–9. For the development of positivist history in the United States see P. Novick, *That Noble Dream: The 'Objectivity question' and the American Historical Profession* (Cambridge, 1988), esp. pp. 21–46.
8 H. Aarsleff, *The Study of Language in England, 1780–1860* (Minneapolis and London, 1983).
9 E. R. Curtius, *European Literature and the Latin Middle Ages*, trans. W. R. Trask (Princeton, 1953), p. 15.

10 See, for example, L. Patterson, *Negotiating the Past* (Madison, 1987).

11 A third mode, oral-formulaic criticism (later, oral-traditional criticism) took up a very interesting position on the margins of the quarrel between formalist and exegetical (also known as 'historical') criticism, where it produced its own method of reading OE verse. Although its method, viewed from a fairly abstract level, shared with exegetical criticism a disregard for the individual and a totalizing (if different) historical narrative, oral-formulaic criticism took theoretical pot-shots from both sides. For an account of the development of this approach see chapter 5 below.

12 S. B. Greenfield, *The Interpretation of Old English Poems* (London and Boston, 1972), p. 28.

13 For an illustrative survey of the protean appearances of 'historicism' see G. G. Iggers, 'Historicism' in *Dictionary of the History of Ideas: Studies of Selected Pivotal Ideas*, ed. P. P. Wiener, 5 vols. (New York, 1973), II, pp. 456–64. Nicholas Howe, in chapter 4 below, surveys the various appropriations of history in the reading of OE texts and argues for a vital historicism in Old English.

14 Primary among these is B. F. Huppé, *Doctrine and Poetry: Augustine's Influence on Old English Poetry* (Albany, 1959); see also M. E. Goldsmith, *The Mode and Meaning of Beowulf* (London, 1970), esp. pp. 55–9. For a later, nuanced approach see R. E. Kaske, with A. Groos and M. W. Twomey, *Medieval Christian Literary Imagery: A Guide to Interpretation* (Toronto, 1988). For general lines of the early controversy over patristic exegesis see D. Bethurum, ed., *Critical Approaches to Medieval Literature* (New York, 1960); for an overview of the historical implications see L. Patterson, *Negotiating the Past*; for the interpretation of OE poetry particularly, see R. M. Liuzza, 'The Return of the Repressed: Old and New Theories in Old English Literary Criticism' in *Old English Shorter Poems: Basic Reading*, ed. K. O'Brien O'Keeffe, Basic Readings in Anglo-Saxon England 3 (New York, 1994), pp. 103–47.

15 See A. D. Schrift, *Nietzsche's French Legacy: A Genealogy of Poststructuralism* (New York and London, 1995).

16 See, for example, J. M. Foley, *Traditional Oral Epic: The 'Odyssey', 'Beowulf', and the Serbo-Croatian Return Song* (Berkeley, CA, 1990) for comparative work in Homeric, Old English, and South Slavic texts, and A. Orchard (chapter 5 below) for comparative work in Anglo-Latin, Old English, and African-American sermon styles.

17 See below, chapter 1, n. 13.

18 See K. O'Brien O'Keeffe, 'Source, Method, Theory, Practice: On Reading Two Old English Verse Texts', *Bulletin of the John Rylands University Library of Manchester* 76 (1994), 51–73 (also reprinted separately by the Manchester Centre for Anglo-Saxon Studies).

19 A. Frantzen, *Desire for Origins: New Language, Old English, and Teaching the Tradition* (New Brunswick, NJ, 1990), pp. 83–95 and 238–9.

20 At mid-century, Karl Popper offered a highly polemical definition and attempted refutation of historicism. In this he looks back to a Marxian theory of history and its various avatars in the totalitarian regimes before and after the Second World War. In so doing, Popper wished to undercut the attempt to interpret history through a master narrative. See Popper, *The Poverty of Historicism* (London, 1986; first published 1957) and for a response see, among others, H. White, 'Historicism, History, and the Figurative Imagination' in his *Tropics of Discourse: Essays in Cultural Criticism* (Baltimore and London, 1978), pp. 101–20 at 118, n. 1.

The comparative approach

MICHAEL LAPIDGE

•

The comparative approach is instinctive to human intelligence. From
our very infancy we learn by comparing like with like, and by distinguishing the like from the nearly like and the other. Students of cog-
nitive psychology describe the process as 'discrimination learning' (a
term coined by Marvin Levine), and the term 'analogy' is used by psy-
chologists to denote a partial similarity between different situations
which elicits further inference, and hence understanding. Similar terminology is used by students of comparative literature, who seek to
make discriminations (as in the title of a celebrated book by René
Wellek, the doyen of American comparatists) between works of literature in different languages having partial similarities; by the same
token, comparatists describe resemblances in style, structure, mood, or
idea between works which have no other connection as 'analogies'. By
studying analogies and learning to make discriminations between par-
tially similar works in different languages, comparatists may be said to
replicate an important aspect of human learning. Because of its
instinctive nature, the comparative approach is accessible to any
student of literature who is versed in at least two languages, and in the
case of Old English has been practised by critics of very various ability,
since the time when Old English literature first emerged as a subject of
interest in its own right. In what follows, I shall attempt to trace the
course of comparative analysis from the early nineteenth century
onwards, in order to illustrate the presuppositions under which
comparative analysis has been attempted, and also to indicate areas
where this most accessible of critical methods may yet yield interesting
results.

Although during the seventeenth and eighteenth centuries there was an ever-growing awareness of the nature and extent of Old English literature, the awareness was motivated by theological rather than literary concerns. Only with the beginning of the nineteenth century – and coinciding in effect with the publication in 1815 of *Beowulf*, the one undisputed literary masterpiece surviving from the Anglo-Saxon period – does the literature become a subject of interest in its own right. The first students of Old English literature brought to their study the training in classical literature which comprised the curriculum of a gentleman's education in those days; inevitably, their perceptions of Old English literature were shaped by this training, and characteristically they appraised the newly discovered vernacular literature by comparing it to the more familiar Greek and Latin classics. Thus Grímur Jónsson Thorkelin (1752–1829), the first editor of *Beowulf*, found frequent occasion in the (Latin) preface of his edition to compare *Beowulf* to Vergil's *Aeneid*. A few years later, John Josias Conybeare (1779–1824), sometime Professor of Anglo-Saxon at Oxford, made numerous comparisons between *Beowulf* and the *Iliad* and *Odyssey* in his posthumous *Illustrations of Anglo-Saxon Poetry* (1826). Typically, he viewed *The Battle of Maldon* in Homeric terms:

The whole [*sc. The Battle of Maldon*] approximates much more nearly than could have been expected, in the general features of its composition, to the war scenes of Homer. If names like Byrhtnoth and Godric could be substituted for Patroclus and Menelaus, it might be almost literally translated into a cento of lines from the great father and fountain of poetry; and, as it is, it reads very like a version from one of the military narratives of the Iliad, excepting its want of the characteristic similes.

In the same vein Thomas Wright (1810–77), in the brief history of Old English literature which prefaces his *Biographia Britannica Literaria* (1842), compared the description of Beowulf's funeral mound overlooking the sea (*Beo* 3155–8) to the description of the tomb of Themistocles overlooking the Piraeus, as described by the obscure comic poet Plato and preserved by Plutarch in his Life of Themistocles; he went on to legitimate such comparisons by noting that 'the Romances of the Anglo-Saxons hold historically the same place in literature which belongs to the Iliad and Odyssey'. By the second half of the nineteenth century, however, the corpus of Old English verse was much better known, so that scholars were able to emphasize its unique qualities rather than its partial similarities to classical literature; the reaction is encapsulated in a remark by Bernhard ten Brink in his influential *Geschichte der englischen Literatur* (1877), who insisted that *Beowulf* ought to be seen as a literary work in its own right and not compared with works such as the *Iliad* or *Chanson de Roland*.[1]

Meanwhile, during the first half of the nineteenth century in Germany, Old English literature was being viewed from a wholly different perspective. As German national consciousness grew, German scholars viewed the early northern literatures – whether in Old Norse, Old English, or Old High German – as manifestations of the one Teutonic spirit. This viewpoint underlies, for example, two monumental works of early nineteenth-century German scholarship: *Die deutsche Heldensage* by Wilhelm Grimm (1829) and *Deutsche Mythologie* by his brother Jacob (1835; 2nd edn., 1844, etc.). Many of the German scholars who, in their wake, studied and edited Old English literature came to that study with sound training in Old Norse and the other early Germanic dialects: Ludwig Ettmüller (1802–77), for example, whose *Engla and Seaxna Scopas and Boceras* (1850) is an important monument of Anglo-Saxon scholarship, was also an early editor of Old Norse eddic verse. Inevitably, the tendency to read Old English in the context of Old Norse brought important analogies between the two literatures into sharp focus. But they were viewed solely as analogues until an important discovery in 1873 revealed that their relationship might be more intimate than had been suspected. In that year the Icelandic scholar Guðbrandr Vigfusson (1828–89), then resident in Oxford, happened to read *Beowulf*; and he noted at once the structural similarities between Beowulf's fights with the Grendelkin and Grettir's fights with Glámr and the monster at Sandhaugar in the *Grettissaga*, similarities which were underlined by the occurrences of the (somehow related) *hapax legomena* which are used in the two works to describe the blade which the hero uses to kill the monster (*hœftmece* in *Beowulf*, *heptisax* in *Grettissaga*).[2] Vigfusson's discovery was communicated in the first instance to colleagues at Oxford, and one such colleague, Frederick Metcalfe (1815–85), on the basis of this and other partial similarities between Old English and Old Norse, undertook an extensive comparative study of the two literatures in his *The Englishman and the Scandinavian* (1880). Interestingly, Metcalfe's comparison led him to an opinion of the superiority of Old Norse verse:

But the generality of the Anglo-Saxon poems . . . have the sober and sombre touch about them so characteristic of the people. A perpetual Lent seems to brood over their spirit. There is hardly a spark about them of dithyrambic fire. They excite our curiosity as to what the lost specimens are like, but we cannot avoid the conclusion that the Anglo-Saxon poet, as he was inferior in position to the Old Northern scald, so was he in poetic fervour, in vigour of genius, in culture of imagination, no match for his Northern brother.

Comparison of Old English and Old Norse literature has also proved a fruitful avenue of approach in more recent times.[3]

By the late nineteenth century, the corpus of Old English literature was known more or less in its full extent; the achievements of nineteenth-century German scholarship had begun to be assimilated by English and American scholars. At this point, one of the great masterpieces of the comparative method was written by a genial scholar who had an unrivalled knowledge of European literature in all languages, ranging from classical antiquity to the present but embracing the Middle Ages in particular, namely William Paton Ker (1855–1923). Ker's *Epic and Romance* (1897) is permeated with unselfconscious reference to Homer ('the creed of Maldon is that of Achilles') or to Latin literature ('the characters in *Beowulf* are . . . not much more clearly individual than the persons of a comedy of Terence'), as well as to the Norse family sagas, the poetic Edda, and finally to the corpus of French epic verse. The breadth of Ker's reference makes exhilarating reading today, a century after its first publication. A similar exhilaration may be derived from Ker's *The Dark Ages* (1904), still, I think, the best introduction to European literature in all languages of the early medieval period. Here one finds an even wider span of comparison than in *Epic and Romance*, so that the difference between Old English and Old Norse verse is characterized as that between Miltonic verse and the couplets of Waller; or the speeches of Satan in *Genesis B* are said to be reminiscent of those in Vergil and Ovid; or, concerning Cynewulf: 'It would not be misleading to compare Cynewulf with [Giambattista] Marini [*rectius* Marino], if it were not that Marini's faults have been exaggerated by the critics.' One wonders how many present-day Anglo-Saxonists will appreciate the point of such a comparison.

What underpinned comparisons of the sort articulated by Ker – between Old English on one hand, and Greek or Latin or Old Norse on the other – was the then-prevalent perception that the languages and literatures of Europe were members of a single continuous literary tradition, and hence that comparative criticism of any members of that tradition was, in the words of Matthew Arnold in his *Essays in Criticism* (1865), 'a criticism which regards Europe as being, for intellectual and spiritual purposes, one great confederation, bound to a joint action and working to a common result; and whose members have, for their proper outfit, a knowledge of Greek, Roman, and Eastern antiquity, and of one another'. A similar perception was expressed some years later by T. S. Eliot, in *The Sacred Wood* (1920), for whom 'the whole of the literature of Europe from Homer ... has a simultaneous existence and composes a simultaneous order'. But the educational tradition which enabled such visions — grounded on the study of the Bible and of Greek and Latin classics — was to disintegrate in the years following the Great War, with the result that few scholars today know the Bible thoroughly, and fewer still know the classics of Greek and Latin literature, or read them with enjoyment except in translation. Comparative criticism in modern times is qualified by ignorance of the educational tradition alluded to by Arnold and Eliot, and has instead been challenged by different tastes and concerns. The result is that the belle-lettristic approach to comparative criticism so elegantly expounded by W. P. Ker has given way to approaches circumscribed by other theoretical considerations.

One such approach was generated by the field-work of late nineteenth- and early twentieth-century anthropologists, such as Franz Boas, Margaret Mead, Bronislaw Malinowski, and E. E. Evans-Pritchard (to name but a few). As a result of their work, it became possible to view the achievements of western civilization in the wider perspective of other peoples and civilizations, 'primitive' or otherwise. The viewpoint afforded by such perspectives has been described as 'cultural relativism'. Cultural relativism inevitably has implications for the practitioners of the comparative method, for the field of comparison is widened to include non-western literatures and cultures.[4] The implications were spelled out in a classic article by the Marxist critic, Viktor Zhirmunsky:

The comparative study of these common trends of literary evolution leads to a comprehension of some of the general laws of literary development and of the social preconditions, and at the same time to an understanding of the historical and national peculiarity of each individual literature.[5]

The theoretical position envisaged by Zhirmunsky — that it is valid to compare the social preconditions which determine the literary development of societies — had, in the case of Old English literature, been adumbrated already by W. P. Ker, who noted in *Epic and Romance* that 'the circumstances of an heroic age may be found in numberless times and places, in the history of the world'. A decade or so later, H. M. Chadwick (1870–1947), in *The Heroic Age* (1912), was to elucidate fully the implications of Ker's statement, by analyzing the common characteristics of Teutonic and Greek heroic poetry, society, government, and religion in the 'heroic age', and ultimately the causes and antecedent conditions of the heroic age:

So far as our records go back, we find among the Teutonic peoples, as among the Gauls and the early Greeks, a numerous class who prefer the military life to the labour involved in agriculture. . . . It is the existence of this military element which in various epochs of European history and under similar cultural conditions has produced the phenomena comprised under the term 'Heroic Age'. (p. 461)

In *The Heroic Age* Chadwick concerned himself principally with Homeric and 'Teutonic' literatures, but on occasion adverted to Welsh poetry and even to a Serbian epic on the Battle of Kossovo (thus anticipating Milman Parry's researches on Serbian epic by a number of years). However, in *The Growth of Literature* (3 vols., 1932–40), written jointly with his wife, Nora Kershaw Chadwick (1891–1972), the scheme was vastly expanded. Coverage was extended so as to include not merely epic/narrative verse, but also various other genres, classified by the Chadwicks in a fivefold scheme: narrative poems (Type A); poems dealing with situation or emotion, consisting mainly of speeches (B); poems of didactic interest (C); celebration poetry (D); and personal poetry (E). In addition, the scope of literatures under review was expanded in vol. I beyond Greek and Teutonic so as to include Irish as well as Welsh (Nora Chadwick was a Celticist by training), together with occasional reference to Slavonic and Hittite. Subsequently, in vols. II and III, the scope was extended still further, so that vol. II treated Russian oral literature, Yugoslav oral poetry, early Indian (Sanskrit) literature, and early Hebrew literature, and vol. III treated the oral literature of the Tatars, of Polynesia, of the Sea Dyaks of North Borneo, and of some African peoples as well (Galla, Bantu, Yoruba, and Tuareg).

Throughout the three volumes the focus is increasingly on oral literature, with the Chadwicks' interest increasingly turning to anthropology.
They thus take us to the threshold of the revolution in Old English
studies effected by awareness of the work of Milman Parry on Serbian
oral epic, and in particular to the impact of oral-formulaic theories of
composition (a subject treated elsewhere in this volume, chapter 5). The
important point is that the Chadwicks vastly expanded the bases of
comparative criticism from the European classical tradition to world literature. *The Growth of Literature* in many ways represents the apogee
of the comparative method. It provides a powerful demonstration of
Zhirmunsky's tenet concerning comprehension of 'the general laws of
literary development and of the social preconditions' of literature.[6]
More tellingly, it may be seen as a vindication of the arguments of the
influential French comparatist, René Etiemble, concerning the existence, in all literatures, of what he called 'literary invariables' (*invariants littéraires*), that is to say 'the conditions without which there is no
artistic creation at any time or place'.[7] But in spite of (or perhaps
because of) its vast scope and coverage, *The Growth of Literature* has
had few successors: the most recent book to emulate its scope and
comparative method was probably C. M. Bowra, *Heroic Poetry* (1952).
Although students of Old English literature have in recent decades had
occasion to study the techniques of oral literature, *The Growth of
Literature* is seldom if ever quoted or read.

One reason for the neglect may be that at the time *The Growth of
Literature* was published (1932–40), a new critical movement had
emerged which called into question the basic assumptions and procedures of the comparative method, namely 'New Criticism' or, as it was
(and is) called in Cambridge where in effect it originated, 'practical criticism'. First championed in the 1920s by critics such as I. A. Richards and
William Empson, 'New Criticism' was concerned to elucidate the
uniqueness of a literary work, without regard to the historical context or
social conditions which produced it. As 'New Criticism' came to be
practised by students of Old English literature – most notably in the
1960s, say, by Stanley B. Greenfield – interest in the comparative work
done by the Chadwicks inevitably waned. In face of the challenge posed
by 'New Criticism', students of comparative literature were obliged to
rethink the theoretical bases on which their discipline rested.[8]
'Comparative literature' was accordingly redefined so as to embrace,

rather than to oppose, the methods of literary analysis espoused by 'New Critics'. This wider conception of the discipline can be seen in a manifesto issued in 1970 by René Wellek:

[Comparative literature] will study all literature from an international perspective, with a consciousness of the unity of all literary creation and experience. In this conception . . . comparative literature is identical with the study of literature independent of linguistic, ethnic, and political boundaries. It cannot be confined to a single method: description, characterization, interpretation, narration, explanation, evaluation, are used in its discourse just as much as comparison.[9]

In attempting to define the parameters of their discipline, comparatists were forced to address the central concept of 'influence': the question of whether inquiry should be limited to demonstrable historical links between works in different languages, or should concern itself instead with 'typological affinities' or 'analogies', that is to say, 'resemblances in style, structure, mood or idea between works which have no other connection'.[10] The distinction is crucial to the study of Old English literature, given that much scholarly endeavour in the field is currently being devoted to the identification of 'sources', that is to say, demonstrable historical links between works in different languages (typically, but not exclusively, between Latin source and Old English reflex). This approach to Old English literature is treated elsewhere in this book (chapter 3). In what follows, therefore, I shall concern myself with criticism which has attempted to identify resemblances between literary works which have no other connection. As we shall see, the distinction between 'source' and 'analogy/analogue' is often a very fine one.

A standard handbook on comparative literature signals three fields which are especially suitable for comparative analysis: literary movements and trends; motifs, types and themes; and genres and forms.[11] With respect to the first of these categories, comparatists typically have in mind literary and stylistic movements which spanned a number of European literatures, for example mannerism (euphuism in England, gongorism in Spain, marinism in Italy), expressionism, impressionism, surrealism, and so on. It is not wholly apposite to think of Old English literature in terms of literary movements. One might argue that the 'hermeneutic' style (that is, the ostentatious parade of unusual, often arcane and apparently learned vocabulary, such as archaisms, neologisms, and grecisms), which is prevalent in tenth-century Anglo-Latin literature, also had a reflex in the vernacular, in, say, the Old English poem 'Aldhelm' or 'The Rhyming Poem'.[12] But two isolated poems scarcely constitute a literary movement.

The comparatists' second category, that of motifs, types, and themes, has proved an exceptionally fertile field for students of Old English literature, so much so that it is simply impossible to list here even the most distinguished contributions. Suffice it to say that Anglo-Saxonists have applied comparative analysis to a wide range of themes, including those of kinship, comitatus, and exile, community and drinking, feasting and sleep, the hall, treasure, weapons (especially shields and swords, and including spiritual warfare), beasts of battle, kingship, lordship, patronage, witchcraft, fate (*wyrd*), transience (*ubi sunt*), consolation, stability and chaos, *sapientia* and *fortitudo*, and others. Much valuable scholarly energy has been devoted to tracing legends attested in other Germanic literatures (for example, those of Weland or Siegmund). Specifically Christian themes, too, have been (and continue to be) explored: those of the deadly sins, the Fall, the Crucifixion and the Cross, the harrowing of Hell, the Ascension, the final Judgment, the penitent damned, visions of heaven and hell, demons, legends of Lucifer, Cain, Joseph, and others. Attention has also been devoted to the identification of literary 'types' or *topoi* which occur in many literatures in addition to Old English: the hero on the beach, the traveler recognizes his goal, the poet contemplates the heavens, and so on.[13] No doubt the study of motifs, types, and themes will continue to be a fruitful avenue of research for those Anglo-Saxonist comparatists who read outside the confines of Old English literature. And as an incentive to further work in this field, there would be considerable merit in compiling a bibliography of results achieved so far in this domain.

It is particularly in the study of literary genres (or genology, as comparatists call it) that the comparative method has yielded — and can still be made to yield — significant results. I should like to illustrate this assertion by considering (briefly) four genres of Old English: gnomic, enigmatic, epic, and lyric verse. I begin with gnomic verse. In *The Growth of Literature*, the Chadwicks devoted a chapter to gnomic poetry (I, 377–403), in which they distinguished two types of gnomic verse (statements of action and conduct pertaining to universals; and statements of observation in which no choice or judgment is involved); they then applied this twofold distinction to Old English verse, in particular

Maxims I and *II*, and compared the English gnomes to those in Old Norse (*Hávamál, Sigrdrífumál*) and to some selected examples of Welsh and Irish gnomic poetry. But their treatment did not go much beyond mere classification,[14] and it was left to others to elaborate the comparative resources of the Celtic material: notably K. H. Jackson (a pupil of the Chadwicks), in *Early Welsh Gnomic Poems* (1935), and P. L. Henry, in *The Early English and Celtic Lyric* (1966), which contains extensive treatment of Irish parallels. New impetus to the study of gnomic verse came in 1976 with the publication of T. A. Shippey's *Poems of Wisdom and Learning in Old English*; in this work Shippey attempted to identify a genre of Old English 'wisdom poetry', and then provided a useful anthology of such poetry (including, notably, *Precepts, Vainglory, The Fortunes of Men, Maxims I* and *II, The Rune Poem*, the second *Dialogue of Solomon and Saturn*, and others). Consensus about what constituted the genre of 'wisdom poetry' enabled subsequent scholars to compare this genre with wisdom poetry in other cultures and languages. Amongst a growing body of comparative analysis, two recent monographs deserve mention: Elaine Tuttle Hansen, *The Solomon Complex* (1988), which contains valuable discussion of wisdom literature from ancient Sumeria, Babylon, Egypt, and Israel, and C. Larrington, *A Store of Common Sense* (1993), which provides analysis of Old Icelandic poems such as *Hávamál* and *Hugsvinnsmál* alongside the corpus of Old English wisdom poetry.[15] One of the merits of the book is its discussion of the Latin *Disticha Catonis* as the source of the *Hugsvinnsmál*. Given that the *Disticha Catonis* formed part of the Anglo-Saxon curriculum by the late tenth century, if not earlier – they are quoted by Byrhtferth and Ælfric Bata – it is possible that comparative analysis of the *Disticha* and Old English wisdom poetry would yield interesting results and help to illuminate the distinction between native and learned gnomic tradition. In any case, this is one genre where comparative study has successfully helped to throw the distinctive features of Old English wisdom poetry into clear relief.

Riddles, or 'enigmatic' verse, are a genre well represented in Old English, but less so in Old Norse (excepting a collection in *Hervarar Saga*), scarcely in Greek, and not at all in Welsh and Irish. The evidence, thus baldly stated, might suggest that the Old English riddles are a vernacular reflex of Latin learned tradition, for, in contrast with Greek and the other vernaculars, Latin riddles (or *enigmata*) are well attested from late antiquity onwards. For these reasons, riddles are treated with exceptional brevity by the Chadwicks in *The Growth of Literature* (I, 412–14). Nevertheless, given the well-attested Latin tradition, riddles offer unusual scope for comparative treatment; furthermore, in spite of the Chadwicks' reticence, the work of anthropologists on popular riddles can helpfully illuminate the Old English riddles, which by contrast are seen to represent learned, literary production. The learned tradition properly begins with the late Latin poet Symphosius, who composed one hundred three-line riddles as an *extempore* party-piece; but it was Aldhelm who took over from Symphosius the outward form of the Latin riddle and transformed it into a serious vehicle for meditation on the mysteries (hence Aldhelm's title for his riddles: *enigmata*) of the universe. Aldhelm's collection of one hundred *enigmata* (he took the number over from Symphosius) had an immediate impact in Southumbria, and several later poets, including Tatwine, Eusebius, and Boniface, composed Latin riddle-collections. The Old English riddles of the Exeter Book are in some sense a reflex of this Latin tradition: some of them are direct translations from Latin antecedents (the 'Lorica' and 'Creatura' riddles), and the number of riddles in the collection (ninety-odd) seems to have been modelled on the Latin collections of Symphosius, Aldhelm, and Tatwine-Eusebius. The most recent editor of the Old English riddles, Craig Williamson (*The Old English Riddles of the Exeter Book*, 1977), drew extensively on the Latin tradition for his commentary, but this is an area of Anglo-Latin studies which is not yet thoroughly understood (a number of Latin riddles are as yet unpublished), and one which may yield results to comparative analysis.[16]

In the case of epic (by which one means, in effect, a long narrative poem concerning martial exploits), there has been a massive amount of comparative analysis, particularly of *Beowulf*. Because the poem contains various folkloric motifs, parallels have been adduced from as far afield as Burma and Brazil. Closer to home, Indo-European parallels have been noted in Iranian, Indian (Sanskrit), and Irish literature.[17] There is also, as we have seen, a long tradition of comparing *Beowulf* to the poems of Homer and to Vergil's *Aeneid*. This tradition is probably best represented by Ker's *Epic and Romance* and Chadwick's *The Heroic Age*, both of which contain extensive treatments of the *Iliad* and its relevance to *Beowulf*; but there has also been a number of valuable contributions to this comparative study in more recent times.[18] In these discussions, the *Iliad* is treated as an 'analogue' to *Beowulf*, that is, a work having resemblances in style, structure, etc., but having no other connection with the Old English poem. And yet there may be a genuine connection. The most convincing case for such a connection was made by Ingeborg Schröbler in 1939;[19] and it may be that the case will gain confirmation from evidence, recently brought to light, concerning the literary activities of two Greeks who taught at Canterbury in the late seventh century, namely Theodore of Tarsus and Hadrian, sometime abbot of Nisida. It is not inconceivable that either or both of these men could have known the Homeric poems (or parts of them) by heart, in which case we would have a plausible context for knowledge of Homer in England. While much more work is needed in this domain, the possibility should at least remain open.

Another classical text which has been linked with *Beowulf* since that poem's first publication in 1815 is Vergil's *Aeneid*. Of course the theme, scale, and structure of the *Aeneid* are utterly different from *Beowulf*'s; on the other hand, there is good evidence that Vergil was studied diligently in Anglo-Saxon schools, and may accordingly have been well known to the (literate) author of *Beowulf*. There has accordingly been considerable scholarly energy devoted to identifying reminiscences of the Roman poet in *Beowulf*.[20] Valuable as this work has been, it falls in the domain of source-study, whereas the comparatist's brief is to look beyond the minute detail of source-analysis to wider questions of form and style. Yet there are intriguing parallels between the two works, as an example may illustrate. It is one of the most curious features of the narrative of *Beowulf* that the principal action is not narrated solely from the perspective of an omniscient narrator, but is interwoven with the personal perceptions of the characters themselves. Thus, in the first dramatic confrontation between Beowulf and Grendel, once the monster has entered Heorot, his movement through the hall and towards Beowulf is described from the narrator's vantage point ('on fagne flor feond treddode' [725] – 'he gefeng hraðe . . . slæpendne rinc' [740a–1a]– 'forð near ætstop, nam þa mid handa . . . he onfeng hraþe' [745b–8b]) until the very moment when Grendel seizes Beowulf. The vantage point then shifts abruptly, and Grendel's own perception of what is happening replaces the objective description of the previous narrative:

> Sona þæt onfunde   fyrena hyrde
> þæt he ne mette   middangeardes,
> eorþan sceata   on elran men
> mundgripe maran;   he on mode wearð
> forht on ferhðe;   no þy ær fram meahte.
> Hyge wæs him hinfus . . . .   (750–5)

[Immediately the author of crimes *perceived* that he had not encountered a stronger hand-grip in any man in any corner of the earth; *in his mind* he became terrified in spirit; he couldn't escape quickly enough. *His thought* was to be gone . . . (italics mine)]

This shift in narrative perspective serves to underline Grendel's terror. It is a stroke of psychological realism which may not seem unnatural to modern readers nurtured on Stendahl, Flaubert, and their twentieth-century successors. But our familiarity with techniques of the modern novel should not blunt our awareness of how extraordinary a moment this is in the context of early medieval literature; indeed it is not easy to think of a parallel in western literature earlier than *Beowulf* (whatever dating one accepts for the poem). For that reason it is worth drawing attention to a similarly extraordinary moment in Vergil's *Aeneid*, namely the final confrontation between Aeneas and Turnus, champion of the Rutulians, whose homeland Aeneas's conquest threatens to destroy. Aeneas, fiercely armed and brandishing his gigantic spear, advances menacingly on Turnus; for his part, Turnus seizes a huge stone with the intention of casting it at Aeneas. But at the very point of casting it, Turnus's knees buckle and he freezes in terror, and – in one of the most moving passages in the poem – Vergil's description shifts abruptly from that of objective narration to the mental perceptions of Turnus:

> ac velut in somnis, oculos ubi languida pressit
> nocte quies, nequiquam avidos extendere cursus
> velle videmur et in mediis conatibus aegri
> succidimus – non lingua valet, non corpore notae
> sufficiunt vires nec vox aut verba sequuntur:
> sic Turno, quacumque viam virtute petivit,
> successum dea dira negat. tum pectore sensus
> vertuntur varii; Rutulos aspectat et urbem
> cunctaturque metu letumque instare tremescit,
> nec quo se eripiat, nec qua vi tendat in hostem . . . . (XII.908–17)

[And, just as in dreams, when at night listless calm presses upon our eyes, we dream that we seek in vain to escape by frantic running and collapse exhausted in the midst of our efforts — we cannot speak, the body's normal strength is insufficient and neither voice nor words come forth — so it was with Turnus, for with whatever effort he sought to find an escape, the cruel goddess [Juno] frustrated his attempt. Various images then pass through his mind; he looks at the Rutulians and their city; he falters in fear and trembles at the prospect of death; he sees no way of escape and no way to attack the enemy . . . .]

It is surely striking that the narrative device used by Vergil to describe a moment of intense terror should subsequently have been used in a similar situation by the *Beowulf*-poet, whether or not there is any other point of contact between the two works. A search by comparatists to identify similar passages of 'psychological realism' in classical and early medieval literature would help to illuminate the work of both these great poets.

Finally, lyric verse, or verse which serves as the vehicle for outpouring of personal emotion and reflection, characteristically (in the case of Old English) on the transience of earthly life: poems such as *The Wanderer*, *The Seafarer*, *The Husband's Message*, *The Wife's Lament*, and others, referred to generally by Anglo-Saxonists as 'elegies'. Because the Old English elegies fall between two of the Chadwicks' categories — poems consisting mainly of speeches (B) and personal poetry (E) — they are treated only cursorily in *The Growth of Literature*. But lyric poetry is found in nearly all literatures, and offers enormous scope for the comparative method. The Old English elegies have been compared to classical elegiac verse, especially that of Ovid, and to the large corpus of personal laments in Welsh and Irish;[21] but, given the universality of lyric verse, an even broader approach would seem justifiable. Let me indicate the sort of comparison which I have in mind by putting a passage of *The Wife's Lament* alongside a poem by Tennyson. In the Old English poem, the woman narrator describes the desolation of the landscape in which she finds herself:

> Heht me mon wunian   on wuda bearwe,
> under actreo   in þam eorðscræfe.
> Eald is þes eorðsele,   eal ic eom oflongad,
> sindon dena dimme,   duna uphea,
> bitre burgtunas,   brerum beweaxne,
> wic wynna leas.   (27–32)

[I was commanded to live in a grove of trees, under an oak-tree, in the cave. This cave is old, I am wholly consumed with longing, the valleys are gloomy, the hills steep, painful (to see) are the town-enclosures, overgrown with briers, a dwelling-place bereft of joys.]

Those critics who have attempted to visualize the relative positioning of the oak-tree and cave have been frustrated, for the simple reason that the poet is describing a mental landscape, not a physical one; in its loneliness and desolation it is a visible embodiment of the narrator's invisible grief. The description serves, in the words of T. S. Eliot, as an 'objective correlative' of the woman's emotions.[22] The success which the Old English poet achieved may be seen clearly from comparison with a similar description by a much more recent poet. In one of his earliest poems, 'Mariana' (1830), Tennyson evoked a woman's desperate loneliness and sense of desertion by describing a landscape reminiscent (in its effect) of that in *The Wife's Lament*:

> About a stone-cast from the wall
>   A sluice with blacken'd waters slept,
> And o'er it many, round and small,
>   The cluster'd marish-mosses crept.
> Hard by a poplar shook alway,
>   All silver-green with gnarled bark:
> For leagues no other tree did mark
>   The level waste, the rounding gray.
> She only said, 'My life is dreary,
>   He cometh not,' she said;
> She said, 'I am aweary, aweary,
>   I would that I were dead!'[23]

Tennyson's gnarled poplar serves the same function as the oak-tree in the Old English poem: both are stark and solitary reminders of the absent lover. By the same token, the creeping mosses evoke the painfully slow passage of time spent alone, as do the overgrown briers in *The Wife's Lament*. Although separated by as much as a millennium, therefore, the two lyric poets were able to exploit a similar technique in their evocation of a woman's desperate loneliness. Comparison in this case serves to emphasize the remarkable concision and economy of the Old English poet's diction.

Here as elsewhere, the purpose of the comparative approach is to accentuate, through counterpoint, the distinctive and individual features of a particular work of literature. Its application requires no lengthy apprenticeship in the vocabularies of the latest theoretical movements; it is immediate and direct, and may be practised by any reader possessed of wide literary culture and sensitivity. In this sense, it is not so much 'method' as response. It has been practised since Old English literature first came to light in the early nineteenth century, and in various guises is flourishing today; indeed the comparative approach could even be said to embrace various post-modern critical stances: semiotics, deconstruction, or psychoanalysis, to name only three. Though it has a long and distinguished past, therefore, the comparative approach may also be said to have a bright future in Anglo-Saxon studies.

Notes

1 For Conybeare, see *Illustrations of Anglo-Saxon Poetry*, ed. W. D. Conybeare (London, 1826), p. lxxxviii; in a note, Conybeare specifies that 'It may be more particularly compared with the battle in which Patroclus fell' [*sc. Iliad* P and R = books 16–17]. For Wright, see *Biographia Britannica Literaria*, 2 vols. (London, 1842–6), I, 11–12. For ten Brink, see *Geschichte*, I, 35: 'Hier lag nun das Epos von Beowulf zum ersten Male als ein greifbares Ganzes vor, ein Ganzes freilich, das man nicht mit der Ilias oder mit dem französischen Rolandslied vergleichen darf.'

2 G. Vigfusson, *Sturlunga Saga*, 2 vols. (Oxford, 1878), I, p. xlix, n. 1; on the discovery, see A. Liberman, 'Beowulf – Grettir' in *Germanic Dialects: Linguistic and Philological Investigations*, ed. B. Brogyanyi and T. Krömmelbein (Amsterdam, 1986), pp. 353–401. The links between *Beowulf* and *Grettissaga* have now been treated exhaustively by A. Orchard, *Pride and Prodigies: Studies in the Monsters of the Beowulf-Manuscript* (Cambridge, 1995), pp. 140–68.

3 F. Metcalfe, *The Englishman and the Scandinavian, or, A Companion of Anglo-Saxon and Old Norse Literature* (Oxford, 1880), p. 152. More recent comparative studies of Old English and Old Norse include: J. Opland, 'A *Beowulf*-Analogue in *Njálssaga*', *Scandinavian Studies* 45 (1973), 54–8; C. J. Clover, 'The Germanic Context of the Unferth Episode', *Speculum* 55 (1980), 444–68; H. Damico, '*Sörlaþáttr* and the Hama Episode in *Beowulf*', *Scandinavian Studies* 55 (1983), 222–35, *Beowulf's Wealhtheow and the Valkyrie Tradition* (Madison, WI, 1984), and '*Þrymskviða* and Beowulf's Second Fight: The Dressing of the Hero in Parody', *Scandinavian Studies* 58 (1986), 407–28; and R. Frank, 'Did Anglo-Saxon Audiences have a Skaldic Tooth?', *Scandinavian Studies* 59 (1987), 338–55.

4 The implications of cultural relativism for comparative criticism are brilliantly elucidated by D. W. Fokkema, 'Cultural Relativism Reconsidered: Comparative Literature and Intercultural Relations' in *Douze cas d'interaction*

culturelle dans l'Europe ancienne et l'Orient proche ou lointain (Paris, 1984), pp. 239–58.

5 V. M. Zhirmunsky, 'On the Study of Comparative Literature', *Oxford Slavonic Papers* 13 (1967), 1–13 at 2; see also S. S. Prawer, *Comparative Literary Studies: An Introduction* (London, 1973), pp. 54–5.

6 It was apparently C. L. Wrenn who, in a presidential address to the Modern Humanities Research Association in 1968, associated Zhirmunsky's theoretical position with *The Growth of Literature*: see Prawer, *Comparative Literary Studies*, pp. 55–6. Prawer quotes Wrenn as if the address in question, entitled 'The Idea of Comparative Literature', had been published; but although the proceedings of the conference *were* published (*The Future of the Modern Humanities*, ed. J. C. Laidlaw [Leeds, 1969]), Wrenn's address was not among them. It may be interesting to note that after the death of H. M. Chadwick, Nora Chadwick went on to collaborate with Viktor Zhirmunsky; this collaboration resulted in their joint publication, *Oral Epics of Central Asia* (Cambridge, 1969).

7 R. Etiemble, *Hygiène des lettres, III. Savoir et goût* (Paris, 1958), pp. 166–7: 'la littérature comparée paraît féconde en ceci au moins qu'elle permet de découvrir ce que j'appellerai les *invariants littéraires*: les conditions sans lesquelles en tout temps, en tous lieux, il n'y a pas de forme belle'. See also A. Marino, 'Etiemble, les "invariants" et la littérature comparée' in *Le mythe d'Etiemble: hommages, études et recherches* (Paris, 1979), pp. 157–67, esp. 158–62.

8 See D. W. Fokkema, 'Comparative Literature and the New Paradigm', *Canadian Review of Comparative Literature* 9 (1982), 1–18; see also R. Wellek, *Concepts of Criticism* (New Haven, CT, 1963), pp. 282–95.

9 R. Wellek, *Discriminations: Further Concepts of Criticism* (New Haven, CT, 1970), p. 19.

10 A. O. Aldridge, *Comparative Literature: Matter and Method* (Urbana, IL, 1969), p. 3; see also discussion by Zhirmunsky, 'On the Study', p. 7; Prawer, *Comparative Literary Studies*, pp. 51–73; and cf. Wellek, *Discriminations*, pp. 15–17.

11 See F. Jost, *Introduction to Comparative Literature* (Indianapolis, IN, 1974), pp. 83–7, 174–87, and 129–33 respectively.

12 See M. Lapidge, 'The Hermeneutic Style in Tenth-Century Anglo-Latin Literature', *Anglo-Saxon England* 4 (1975), 67–111 (on 'Aldhelm', see p. 83); J. W. Earl, 'Hisperic Style in the Old English "Rhyming Poem"', *PMLA* 102 (1987), 187–96; and, in general, R. Derolez, 'Anglo-Saxon Literature: "Attic" or "Asiatic"? Old English Poetry and its Latin Background', in *English Studies Today*, ed. G. H. Bonnard (Bern, 1961), pp. 93–105, repr. in *Essential Articles for the Study of Old English Poetry*, ed. J. B. Bessinger and S. J. Kahrl (Hamden, CT, 1968), pp. 46–62.

13 For orientation, see S. B. Greenfield and F. C. Robinson, *A Bibliography of Publications on Old English Literature to the end of 1972* (Toronto and Manchester, 1980) [hereafter GR], nos. 612–94 ('General Works: Studies of

Themes and Topics') and 915–1254 ('Old English Poetry: Studies of Themes and Topics'). Many more studies of themes and topics will be found in the annual bibliographies of *Anglo-Saxon England*, from 1972 onwards, but several recent essays deserve mention as illustration of present-day comparative criticism: R. Frank, '*The Battle of Maldon*: Anachronism or *nouvelle vague*' in *People and Places in Northern Europe 500–1600: Essays in Honour of Peter Hayes Sawyer*, ed. I. Wood and N. Lund (Woodbridge, 1991), pp. 95– 106; P. Szarmach, 'The (Sub-)Genre of *The Battle of Maldon*' in *The Battle of Maldon: Fact and Fiction*, ed. J. Cooper (London, 1993), pp. 43–62; and J. Harris, 'Love and Death in the Männerbund: An Essay with Special Reference to the *Bjarkamál* and *The Battle of Maldon*' in *Heroic Poetry in the Anglo-Saxon Period: Studies in Honor of Jess B. Bessinger*, ed. H. Damico and J. Leyerle (Kalamazoo, MI, 1993), pp. 77–114.

14 Cf. P. L. Henry, *The Early English and Celtic Lyric* (London, 1966), p. 92: 'The chief merit of the Chadwick treatment is that its criteria facilitate comparison; its chief demerit that the criteria can be applied without a really close analysis of the material.'

15 E. T. Hansen, *The Solomon Complex: Reading Wisdom in Old English Poetry* (Toronto, 1988), esp. pp. 12–40; C. Larrington, *A Store of Common Sense: Gnomic Theme and Style in Old Iceland and Old English Wisdom Poetry* (Oxford, 1993). See also N. F. Barley, 'A Structural Approach to the Proverb and Maxim, with Special Reference to the Anglo-Saxon Corpus', *Proverbium* 20 (1972), 737–50; T. A. Shippey, 'Maxims in Old English Narrative: Literary Art or Traditional Wisdom?' in *Oral Tradition, Literary Tradition: A Symposium*, ed. H. Bekker-Nielsen *et al.* (Odense, 1977), pp. 28–46. There is also an earlier study by B. C. Williams, *Gnomic Poetry in Anglo-Saxon* (New York, 1914).

16 For anthropological approaches, see R. A. Georges and A. Dundes, 'Toward a Structural Definition of the Riddle', *Journal of American Folklore* 76 (1963), 111–18; E. K. Maranda, 'Theory and Practice of Riddle Analysis', *Journal of American Folklore* 84 (1971), 51–61; and I. Hamnett, 'Ambiguity, Classification and Change: The Function of Riddles', *Man* 2 (1967), 379–92. For the learned (Latin) tradition in Anglo-Saxon England, see my brief sketch in *Aldhelm: The Poetic Works*, trans. M. Lapidge and J. Rosier (Cambridge, 1985), pp. 61–9 and 242–7.

17 Iranian: GR 1964; Indian: GR 2147, 2167, 2295; Irish: GR 1876, 1926, 1967, 1970, 2031, 2035, 2223, 2226, 2231, 2250, 2303, 2308, 2325, 2331, 2355; and see also M. Puhvel, *Beowulf and Celtic Tradition* (Waterloo, 1979), and D. N. Dumville, '*Beowulf* and the Celtic World: The Uses of Evidence', *Traditio* 37 (1981), 109–60.

18 H. V. Routh, *God Man and Epic Poetry: A Study in Comparative Literature*, 2 vols. (Cambridge, 1927), II, pp. 1–24; J. de Vries, *Heroic Song and Heroic Legend*, trans. B. J. Timmer (London, 1963); A. C. Watts, *The Lyre and the Harp: A Comparative Reconsideration of Oral Tradition in Homer and Old English Epic Poetry* (New Haven, CT, 1969); W. Whallon, *Formula,*

Character, and Context: Studies in Homeric, Old English, and Old Testament Poetry (Cambridge, MA, 1969). As the last two titles suggest, much recent discussion of Homer in the context of Old English literature pertains to the (allegedly) 'oral' formulas in the Homeric poems.

19 '*Beowulf* und Homer', *Beiträge zur Geschichte der deutschen Sprache und Literatur* 63 (1939), 305–46; see also J. W. Duff, 'Homer and *Beowulf*: A Literary Parallel', *Saga Book of the Viking Society for Northern Research* 4 (1905–6), 382–406. There are also studies on this subject by A. S. Cook, but these are characteristically reckless and unreliable: 'Greek Parallels to Certain Features of the *Beowulf*', *PQ* 5 (1926), 226–34; and '*Beowulf* 1039 and the Greek ἀρχι-', *Speculum* 3 (1928), 75–81.

20 F. Klaeber, 'Aeneis und Beowulf', *Archiv* 126 (1911), 40–8, 339–59; A. Brandl, 'Hercules und Beowulf', *Sitzungsberichte der preussischen Akademie der Wissenschaften, phil.-hist. Klasse* (1928), no. XIV, 161–7; *idem*, '*Beowulf*-Epos und Aeneis in systematischer Vergleichung', *Archiv* 171 (1937), 161–73; R. Imelmann, *Forschungen zur altenglischen Poesie* (Berlin, 1920), pp. 188–203, 235–7, and 467–9; T. B. Haber, *A Comparative Study of the 'Beowulf' and the 'Aeneid'* (Princeton, 1931), esp. pp. 45–67 (broad similarities), 68–87 (parallels in phraseology), and 88–133 (parallels in motif and sentiment). None of these discussions mentions the Turnus passage treated here.

21 See H. Reuschel, 'Ovid und die angelsächsischen Elegien', *Beiträge zur Geschichte der deutschen Sprache und Literatur* 62 (1938), 132–42; K. H. Jackson, *Studies in Early Celtic Nature Poetry* (Cambridge, 1935), pp. 110–26; and Henry, *The Early English and Celtic Lyric*.

22 *The Sacred Wood* (London, 1920), p. 100: 'The only way of expressing emotion in the form of art is by finding an "objective correlative"; in other words, a set of objects, a situation, a chain of events which shall be the formula of that *particular* emotion; such that when the external facts, which must terminate in sensory experience, are given, the emotion is immediately invoked.' Cf. E. G. Stanley, 'Old English Diction and the Interpretation of *The Wanderer, The Seafarer* and *The Penitent's Prayer*', *Anglia* 73 (1955), 413–66 at 434: 'The finest Old English figurative diction is that in which a state of mind or moral concept evokes in the poem the description of a natural phenomenon, associated by the Anglo-Saxons with that mood or moral concept.'

23 *Tennyson: Poems and Plays*, ed. T. H. Warren, rev. F. Page (Oxford, 1953), p. 7; cf. the acute discussion by C. Ricks, *Tennyson* (New York, 1972), pp. 45–51. It is not impossible that 'Mariana' was inspired by knowledge of *The Wife's Lament*, which Tennyson could have known through the agency of his close friend John Mitchell Kemble. Although the Exeter Book was not published integrally until 1842 (by Benjamin Thorpe), *The Wife's Lament* had been included in Conybeare's *Illustrations* (1826), pp. 244–9. Note also that Tennyson translated *The Battle of Brunanburh* (ed. Warren, pp. 496–8) into modern English verse.

2

Source study

D. G. SCRAGG

•

Nowadays originality in art is considered a desirable quality, but in earlier centuries it was less significant. From ancient times artists consciously borrowed one another's ideas, a practice endorsed by critics from Aristotle onwards. The study of a writer's sources has for two centuries been a widely accepted means of understanding the workings of his or her mind, for in selecting, reorganizing and modifying ideas from earlier writers, authors display their own particular cast of thought. Most of the identifiable sources used by Anglo-Saxon writers are in Latin, and the change of language in itself may be revealing. At the very simplest level of translation, the choice of particular words or phrases to express those in the original reveals much about the meaning of Old English lexical items (for which, it must always be remembered, we have no native informants), about individual Anglo-Saxons' understanding of the meaning of Latin terms, about the range of synonyms and collocations available in English, and about ways that Anglo-Saxon authors found of conveying concepts foreign to England and the English. As we move further from literal translation to the incorporation of the ideas of a written source into the thought processes of a native writer, we gain ever more valuable, if often less tangible, evidence of the intellectual and more widely cultural climate of Anglo-Saxon England, and at the same time increase our understanding of the intricate structure of the literature and its web of imagery. In the words of Edward B. Irving, Jr., writing about the poem *Andreas*: 'Careful consultation of [the fairly close Latin source] lets us see what forms the poet's imagination imposes on his given material and gives us the clearest idea of the kind of poet he is.'[1]

The term 'source' (or in earlier literature 'source-book') has been used variously by different critics. Most now use it to denote a work drawn upon, directly or indirectly, by a later author. Occasionally the term is used to include a wide range of influences that are seen in a text, including myths and legends, such as the references to Germanic legend in *Beowulf*, but it is preferable to confine 'source' to written material (or material that may be thought to have reached the author in written form, even if no manuscript copy survives), and to consider themes which an author may have drawn from oral tradition under a different heading. The precise relationship of the source and the text which draws upon it also needs definition. Terms such as 'primary source' and 'proximate source' are ambiguous, and it is more useful to call the text which an author had before him or her the *immediate* source. This does not imply, of course, that the actual manuscript copy of the immediate source used by an author need survive. By immediate source is generally meant a surviving text which has, to all intents and purposes, the same form as that which an author used. Sources which the author of the immediate source was using, or those at an even greater distance, should be called *antecedent* sources. For example, Old English homilists regularly drew material from Gregory the Great's *Homilies on the Gospels*, which thus constitute their immediate source. But Gregory frequently quotes the Old Testament, which is then an antecedent source for the Anglo-Saxon writers. Another term frequently used loosely is *analogue*. Analogues are two or more texts which draw either immediately or at greater distance upon the same source, although none is in the same line of transmission from that source as another. The significance of analogues for source study is that they prove the existence of written sources even when those sources do not themselves survive. A good illustration of a pair of analogues is provided by *Christ III* (*The Ascension*) and Vercelli homily VIII. Both draw material from a sermon attributed to Caesarius of Arles, but they have in common details which are not found in any copy of Caesarius which has yet been noted. Yet neither is dependent upon the other. The details are drawn from a lost common source − perhaps, since similar details occur in other Old English homilies, a specifically English one.[2]

Identification of a writer's sources is not always a simple matter. By definition, a source must exist before it is borrowed. Hence chronology is important in the determination of a writer's sources, and in the medieval period, when many works are preserved anonymously, it may be difficult to show which of two authors using the same idea is the source and which the borrower. Also, for a source to be borrowed, it has to be possible for the borrower to have known the source. Even when questions of chronology and transmission have both been addressed, the source critic needs to be sure that there is more than coincidence in two writers expressing the same idea in similar words. King Alfred, Abbot Ælfric, Archbishop Wulfstan, and an anonymous homilist all refer to the concept of the three orders of society, those who till the land, those who defend it, and those who pray. Since we know three of the authors in this case, chronology dictates that Ælfric and Wulfstan may have drawn the idea from King Alfred but not the other way round. But other evidence, such as the wider context of the passage in question, is needed to show that it was Wulfstan that drew on Ælfric for this division, and the anonymous homilist, working in a scissors-and-paste fashion largely with Wulfstan materials, who drew on Wulfstan. (It is worth noting here that written sources in the period were not always in Latin. This is one of many examples of homilists drawing upon earlier vernacular writings.) The relationship of the Alfred and Ælfric references is even more difficult to determine. Context suggests that Ælfric did not use King Alfred directly here (even though he may have known what the king had written). Each may have drawn this idea independently from a common source (i.e. they may be analogues), or it might have needed no written source but have been a commonplace of the intellectual thought of the day.[3]

Source study began as an adjunct of the nineteenth-century development of modern textual criticism which is sometimes improperly called 'scientific'. In the attempt to establish an authoritative text, an author's sources were seen as objective evidence against which to set the more subjective conjectural emendation. The movement first affected Old English studies in investigations into the patristic background of religious poems and the Latin antecedents of a range of prose writings from homilies and saints' lives to romantic tales from the orient. One of the earliest is Jacob Grimm's edition of the poems *Andreas* and *Elene*, in the introduction to which Latin and Greek sources are proposed. The extent of Grimm's investigations is all the more remarkable, from a historical perspective, when it is realized that the edition appeared in 1840, only a few years after the sole manuscript witness, the Vercelli Book, first came to the notice of Anglo-Saxonists. In the latter part of the nineteenth century and for most of the twentieth, in Old English studies as in those of classical and modern writers, the tracing of sources has been seen as so important to the establishment of the text that no edition could be considered authoritative without a section on the author's sources.

Editors and critics have used sources for a variety of investigative purposes. In King Alfred's translation of Boethius' *De consolatione Philosophiae*, prose was separated from verse on the grounds that the verse followed the Metra of Boethius' Latin even before the distinguishing features of Old English poetic form were recognized. Distinctive choice and use of sources have sometimes been used to support arguments over authorship, for example in Bruno Assmann's attribution of the prose *Judith* to Ælfric.[4] But for literary critics, as against textual ones, by far the most important uses of source studies are in the analysis of an author's style, as suggested by the quotation from Irving above, and in the area of intellectual history: tracing the dissemination of European thought, showing the distinctive contribution to it of Anglo-Saxon authors, and determining the education and reading available to the Anglo-Saxons.[5] In establishing the uses and purposes of source study as an approach to reading Old English texts, it will be necessary to examine each of these in turn.

Comparison of Old English religious poetry with its sources shows stories adapted to a new cultural context to give them greater intelligibility. It is perhaps a necessary concomitant of the formulaic nature of Old English poetry that characters taken over from Latin narratives become stock types in heroic situations. Abraham is a war-lord with his warrior band, Cain an exile, dangerously exposed, the saints loyal thegns, and even the Cross is at once a follower of Christ and a protecting lord for those who embrace its service. But making foreign stories accessible is not necessarily a mechanical act, as some examples from the poem *Judith* will show. The story is adapted from the apocryphal book of Judith in the Old Testament, but, as we find with many of the poems in the Old English canon, the poet treats the source with considerable freedom, simplifying and rearranging the action, and extending some sections, notably Holofernes' feast for his retainers, Judith's prayer, and the final battle. If the last is dismissed as no more than poetic convention (though it is noteworthy that there is no battle description in the source), the first two are potentially more interesting ways of seeing 'the kind of poet' (in Irving's words) that we are dealing with. Both are part of the poet's characterization, that of Holofernes drawn from the tradition of heroic verse and that of Judith from the example of the lives of virgin saints.

Although the poem survives in an incomplete state, there is sufficient to show how the poet organized the biblical material, for example by reducing the many named characters of the Book of Judith to two, Judith herself and her principal opponent, Holofernes, leader of the Assyrians who were besieging the Hebrew city of Bethulia in which she dwelt. The reduction has a polarizing effect, focusing attention on the archetypal battle which the imagery of the Old English story represents. For the beginning of the story we are dependent on the biblical account, which has Judith, a beautiful widow, volunteering to save her city by visiting Holofernes. On reaching the Assyrian camp, she is taken before the captain, lying on his bed which is covered by a beautiful canopy of gold studded with jewels. He is captivated by her beauty and invites her to a private banquet. It is here that the Old English fragment begins and the divergencies between the two accounts emerge. Whereas the biblical feast is attended by Judith in all her finery, who flirts with Holofernes and causes him to drink more wine than he had ever drunk at any time in one day since he was born, in the poem the cosy tête-à-tête has become a great Germanic drinking party, given by a heroic war-lord to all of his faithful retainers, and Judith is not present. Throughout the poem, she is presented in the role of the virgin martyr, resisting the wicked tyrant. She is the handmaid of the Lord, her faith constantly being emphasized, and her chastity is threatened but not endangered because of God's protection. The struggle is manifestly between conflicting forces, as we see from verbal parallels drawn between Holofernes and God (e.g. each is called 'þearlmod ðeoden gumena', lines 66 and 91). An equally significant change in presentation to that of Judith affects Holofernes, who is undermined by being characterized as the evil lord of Germanic society. At the feast, the imagery shows that the generosity of the Anglo-Saxonized leader has become dangerously excessive. The poet uses variation to suggest the large quantity of wine being consumed – huge vessels, cups, beakers, and brimming flagons – and describes Holofernes himself as behaving riotously. The feast culminates with the retainers lying in a drunken stupor as if they were dead, and the simile is prophetic.

It is knowledge of the source which allows us to understand fully the structure of the poem. Holofernes' excessive drinking, mentioned in just one verse (Jud. 12:20), is a single narrative thread in the biblical account, a device necessary to the mechanics of the story in preventing him from carrying out his intention of raping Judith and depriving him of his senses so that Judith can kill him. But for the Old English poet not only Holofernes but all his retainers are tainted with the sin of gluttony, and the audience is prepared by their conduct for the Assyrians' defeat. The parody of the generous lord entertaining his followers is, however, only one part of the poet's characterization of the Assyrian leader. Further narrative skill is displayed in the use made of the ornate canopy over Holofernes' bed. In the poem, this is chronologically displaced, shifted forward from its place in Judith's introduction to Holofernes to beyond the feast, by which time the audience has become aware of Holofernes' overbearing, and distinctly unheroic, character. It is also transformed from a symbol of its owner's magnificence to another instance of his failure as a Germanic chieftain, because through it he can see but not be seen, and his use of it is thus the ultimate condemnation of him in heroic terms, a leader spying on his men but inaccessible to them. The final irony is that when the Bethulians have been galvanized by Judith's showing them Holofernes' head on her return to the city, they descend upon the Assyrians who turn to him for help. But in the poem – and only in the poem – the retainers are more afraid of disturbing their lord, still thought to be abed with Judith, than of the approaching Bethulians, and the poet paints a picture of them ludicrously coughing outside his tent as loudly as they dare, until finally the curtain is drawn to reveal both the army and its leader without a head. The Assyrians flee, lacking loyalty to a lord who has not taken the trouble to attract any. The source is most valuable to critics here. It shows that though the poet is literally translating the source *canopeum* by *fleohnet*, his (or her) mind took fire from the Vulgate word and moulded it to his own use.

It is rare in Old English studies for the precise source of an Anglo-Saxon text to be identified. Even in the case of *Judith*, the variety of Bible versions available before the Vulgate text became fixed and the existence of biblical commentaries on which the Old English poet may have drawn makes it difficult to be precise about which exactly were the source or sources used,[6] although in the case of the golden canopy we can be almost certain that the chronological displacement and the dramatization of its use after the beheading are the poet's own invention. As with the Bible, so with most of the Latin sources of Old English literature: in an age when texts, both Latin and English, were copied by hand, changes were constantly made in the course of transmission, and the likelihood of a source surviving in exactly the form known to an Anglo-Saxon author is slim. Of some 250 manuscripts, for example, containing all or part of the *Historiae adversum paganos* of Orosius surviving from the Middle Ages, only one (itself fragmentary) is known to have any association with Anglo-Saxon England, and its text is less close to the Old English translation of the work contemporary with King Alfred than other surviving versions. So how have source critics established what books the Anglo-Saxons used? In the answer to that question we may learn much about what source studies have revealed about the dissemination of texts and manuscripts.

The best scholars have always recognized that of far greater moment than the sources themselves is the use that an author, named or otherwise, made of the inherited material. Among the most influential studies is the doctoral work by Max Förster on Ælfric's reading for the Catholic Homilies, published at the end of the nineteenth century, in which he showed how Ælfric blended sources and what he added of his own.[7] The starting point for Förster's work is the list of authorities that Ælfric himself names in his prefaces, from which he traced Ælfric's degree of dependence, both in terms of his own freedom of expression and in terms of the declining scale of importance of the various patristic writers named. Gregory the Great is the chief source, then Bede, followed by Augustine, but there are other major influences, including Smaragdus and Haymo of Auxerre. Scholars now recognize that Förster underestimated the significance of the last two,[8] the problem being that both are themselves heavily dependent on Gregory, Bede, and Augustine, and it is difficult to tell when Ælfric used the patristic writers as immediate sources and when they were his antecedent sources. But there is a further problem which has been faced only in the later twentieth century. Ælfric wrote in the comparative obscurity of the monastery at Cerne Abbas in Dorset. Is it possible that he could have had available to him there a library rich enough to furnish him with all the authorities on which he drew, and which he could quote extensively and apparently verbatim? The answer came in the work of Father Cyril Smetana, who showed forty years ago that rather than using the patristic writers direct, Ælfric's immediate source was a popular Latin homiliary composed for Charlemagne by Paul the Deacon.[9] Paul's homiliary survives in many versions, adapted and expanded from the original, and the precise form available to Ælfric has yet to be located. What is not clear, and cannot be until Ælfric's version is ascertained, is how far he himself added to Paul's synthesis from his own reading. It also used to be thought that Ælfric was responsible for the extensive abbreviation of the source material used in his Lives of Saints, but it is now known that the abbreviation had already been made in his immediate source, a legendary which probably originated in northern France or Flanders in the late ninth or early tenth century and which was available in England by Ælfric's day. This collection of lives has become known as the Cotton-Corpus legendary, a title derived from the earliest manuscript in which it survives, now divided between two locations, London, British Library, Cotton Nero E. i and Cambridge, Corpus Christi College 9. Again, since this manuscript was actually written late in the eleventh century, it cannot be that used by Ælfric himself but is a copy similar to the one he had.[10]

Such advances in scholarship are not confined to the work of Ælfric and are continuing in the present day. The St Père homiliary (again the name derives from the earliest surviving manuscript, the late-tenth-century Chartres, Bibliothèque Municipale, 25, all but destroyed in the Second World War) is another continental collection of Latin homiletic pieces, which was made probably about the same time as the Cotton-Corpus legendary and which also arrived in England during the tenth century. It has been shown recently that either individual pieces in this collection or a selection of paragraphs from different pieces in the collection were the immediate sources for eight Anglo-Saxon anonymous homilies. Furthermore, close study of the way in which the sources were translated, the selection of the same Old English words always to represent particular Latin ones, and, most particularly, the use of distinctive phraseology in linking passages between sections drawn from extant sources suggest that four of the anonymous homilies are by the same writer. We are back in the position of Assmann and his study of Ælfric's *Judith* of a century ago in once again being able to ascribe texts to a single author on the basis of source study, although in this case the name of the author is not known.[11]

Comparison of Old English works with their sources has the further usefulness of directing attention to the intellectual interest of Anglo-Saxon authors and the audience for whom they wrote. King Alfred and his helpers were responsible for translating from Latin into English a range of the works which they felt were 'most necessary for all men to know'. Yet their translations, although often close, are rarely continuous word-for-word glosses. The Old English translation of Bede's *Historia ecclesiastica* abbreviates the original very considerably in a way that highlights the different interests and concerns of early eighth-century England, when Bede wrote, and those of the late ninth century, when the translation was made, for example by excluding references to people and places.[12] Similarly the vernacular version of Orosius, which is also anonymous, is by an author who 'had no hesitation in making radical but unacknowledged alterations to his primary source, expanding freely but also cutting, rewriting some sections, but generally retaining the order and arrangement of his original' in order to effect a transformation 'from an exercise in polemic using historical material to a survey of world history from a Christian standpoint'.[13] Alfred's own translation of the *Regula pastoralis* of Pope Gregory the Great leaves out little of the original, but there are very many points at which the king departs from a literal translation in order to make a moral point more clearly or to explain something which might have meant more to a sixth-century Roman audience than it could to his own. His translation is also in many ways a very personal document, as detailed examination of his departures from the source shows. When, for example, he is translating Gregory's explanation of the symbolism of the priest's robe being made of gold and purple, he adds his own interpretation of the second: 'purpura, ðæt is cynelic hrægl, forðæm hit tacnað kynelicne anwald' ('purple, which is a royal vestment, since it is a sign of royal authority'). This is not simply an attempt to gloss a Latin term which his audience might not understand, for the word *purpura* had already been used earlier in the chapter without such a gloss. Detailed examination of the whole context and comparison of it with the source shows that it is the concept of royal authority which is uppermost in Alfred's mind at that point.[14]

When an Anglo-Saxon author specifies the authorities he is using, the source critic's task is somewhat simplified. But even here it is necessary to be wary. It is rare in Old English to find an author who is dependent upon a single source. Alfred himself in his subsequent 'translations', of Boethius's *De consolatione Philosophiae* and Augustine's *Soliloquia*, became more adventurous in combining material from different sources, and the study of the way in which he did so shows us much about his reading, his intentions, and his expected audience. What is usually regarded as his final work, on the *Soliloquia*, begins with a remarkable image of the writer's collection of sources being like a builder obtaining timber from the forest. (The image, not in the source, is all the more memorable as the king envisages members of his audience immersing themselves in his sources with a thoroughness not available to Alfred himself, as a worldly ruler oppressed with the manifold affairs of state, a subject he reverts to regularly.)

Ic lære ælcne ðara þe maga si and manigne wæn hæbbe, þæt he menige to þam ilcan wuda þar ic ðas stuðansceaftas cearf, fetige hym þar ma, and gefeðrige hys wænas mid fegrum gerdum, þat he mage windan manigne smicerne wah, and manig ænlic hus settan, and fegerne tun timbrian, and þær murge and softe mid mæge on-eardian ægðer ge wintras ge sumeras, swa swa ic nu ne gyt ne dyde.[15]

[I advise everyone who has the strength and sufficient wagons to go to the same wood where I cut building posts, to obtain more for himself there, and load his wagons with the beautiful poles, so that he can construct many fair walls and establish many splendid buildings and build a beautiful town, and there dwell happily and comfortably, winter and summer alike, as I was never able to do.]

He goes on to list Augustine, Gregory, and Jerome and 'many other holy fathers' as the sources he drew upon in creating his work, regarding it not as a translation as such but as a beautiful and original new town, whose workmanship we can best appreciate by considering the building materials as well as the tools that he used.

Later prose writers excelled Alfred in the blending of material from known sources to brilliant effect. John Pope, writing in the tradition of source scholars such as Förster, has an eloquent passage on the use Ælfric made of his sources which shows just how important it is for us to give careful consideration to this matter and to have access to the sources in order to compare them with the Anglo-Saxon text if we are to comprehend fully the vernacular author's achievement:

[Ælfric] sometimes treats his authorities with such freedom that, quite apart from personal comments and topical applications, his work approaches original composition, not merely in style, as we tend to expect, but even in substance. His disclaimers of originality and his occasional references to authorities are by no means sufficient to guide us to a just estimate of his accomplishment. Under their influence we are quite as likely to exaggerate as to underestimate his indebtedness to the Latin expositors. Those who study the sources of the homilies discover how little in them beyond the Biblical passages is closely translated, how often Ælfric omits, condenses, expands, rearranges, synthesizes two or more interpretations, rejects one in favour of another, imports examples or parallel texts, reminds us of something he has dealt with more extensively elsewhere. The very intensity of his effort to be faithful to his role as interpreter has made him take full responsibility for what he says. The thought is scrupulously traditional yet fully digested and feelingly his own.[16]

What Pope indicates of Ælfric is true of other writers of the period: we need a knowledge of the sources to gain an appreciation of an author's achievement. But unlike Ælfric, other writers are not always exact about their debt to others. Many, in both prose and verse, acknowledge their use of 'holy books', without specifying any further. Others acknowledge authorities that they have not used, either because they feel that these will give their work greater orthodoxy, or because they are not aware that they are falsifying. Still others are silent about their sources. Such attitudes provide great difficulties for source scholars.

In poetry, precise identification of a source may often be even more problematic than in prose because a poet needs to alter material to satisfy the constraints of the metre, and may adapt the source to fit a different pattern of imagery and, ultimately, meaning. But the result is to make the study of poetic sources just as significant and urgent as is the study of the sources of prose. And just as the exact source used by a prose writer is unlikely to survive, so that used by a poet is rarely extant. Cynewulf's poems are based on Latin sources, yet none has been found which corresponds exactly with the text that Cynewulf presents us with. Until more evidence is discovered, the critic must decide which of the discrepancies are the result of a failure to locate the precise source and which are the product of conscious adaptation. Poets, like the prose writers discussed above, sometimes blend ideas from more than one source, or absorb into a main source ideas from the intellectual climate of their day, and the critic needs to be alive to such alterations. Even in that part of the anonymous religious verse which has extant Latin sources that are followed more or less closely, there are departures, some of which indicate how far the modern reader is from his or her medieval counterpart. The poem *Exodus* is based upon the Old Testament, but a full understanding of one of its most impressive metaphors, the cloud pillar which protects the Israelites, involves recognition of the origins of the image not only in various parts of the Book of Exodus but in other parts of the Old Testament too.[17] In contemplating this point, we see that the poet, and presumably the audience for whom the poem was intended, had a different degree of exposure to the Bible (perhaps through its use in the liturgy) than most readers of Old English today. It is source scholars who have alerted us to the mode of thinking of the poet and to the cultural milieu in which the poem was composed.

How, then, should an editor or critic new to the task go about sourcing a text? The first imperative, as the best source scholars have frequently pointed out, is wide reading. Many of the most important advances in the field have come about by serendipity. But it is possible to offer more pointed advice on the direction reading should take. The source hunter needs a detailed knowledge of the Bible, and this means not just the Vulgate version but also, and perhaps more usefully, the Old Latin Bible, since it is this version which is often quoted by Latin writers, and such quotations may be retained by Anglo-Saxon authors, giving notice of their dependence on a written source. Once a biblical quotation has been identified, standard continental commentaries should be consulted, such as those by Haymo and Hrabanus Maurus. Obviously Latin writers frequently named by native authors, such as Jerome, Augustine, Gregory, Isidore, and Bede, need to be thoroughly absorbed too. If the task of reading through all of the voluminous works of these writers seems prohibitive, an alternative strategy, at least for the beginner, is to look for the recurrence of a theme from one item to another, even in pieces by different authors, since a theme in one piece that occurs in another may point to two authors drawing on the same source. Such a case is the Caesarian Doomsday speech in *Christ III* and Vercelli homily VIII, discussed at the beginning of this essay. Sometimes the source for a theme in a poem which has been the subject of close scrutiny for many years may have been identified long before it is noticed in an anonymous homily.[18] If the Old English work to be sourced is a homily, it may be possible to associate it with a particular festival, either by its rubric or by the incorporation of a pericope, and Latin pieces for the same occasion in homiliaries known to have been drawn on frequently are an obvious starting point. Continental homiliaries such as the St Père collection (discussed above) have been very productive of new source material in recent years.

Until recently, scholarly attention to the Latin background of Anglo-Saxon England has been relatively neglected, so that even good modern editions of the major Latin sources of Anglo-Saxon authors were lacking. For example, anyone wishing to read the supposed source of one of the seventy or so verse or prose saints' lives of the period is normally forced to rely on the *Acta sanctorum* edition, based usually on manuscript versions of the lives made long after the Norman Conquest. In this case, however, a list of earlier manuscripts can be found in the *Bibliotheca hagiographica latina* compiled by the Bollandists a century ago but with more recent supplements, through which it is possible to investigate variant readings and thereby to determine the version closest to the Anglo-Saxon text. For the Latin patristic and Carolingian background to Old English literature, the reader still has very often to rely on the nineteenth-century *Patrologia latina*, which its editor, Jacques-Paul Migne, drew largely from earlier printed texts, some dating from as early as the sixteenth century. Gradually, more reliable modern editions of these texts are becoming available, with a detailed apparatus of variant readings, in Corpus Christianorum, Series Latina, which will eventually include all Christian texts and authors to the eighth century, and Corpus Christianorum, Continuatio Mediaevalis, which continues the series with later works. But as long as *Patrologia latina* remains the standard scholarly work of reference for major authors, like cannot be compared with like: what an Anglo-Saxon author wrote cannot be examined in conjunction with a work close to the one we think he knew. Because very many manuscripts of seminal Latin texts survive, some uncatalogued, the source hunter needs some signposts to help him or her find the form or forms of a text known in Anglo-Saxon England.

New developments, both technological and scholarly, are in the making to help the source scholar. Although there is no better way of developing a facility in source studies than by familiarizing oneself with the reading matter available to the Anglo-Saxons themselves, the electronic age is providing tools which offer some short-cuts, and others are being added year by year. A concordance to the 220 volumes of *Patrologia latina* is available now on CD-ROM, published by Chadwyck-Healey. More useful to the source hunter is the CETEDOC Library of

Christian Latin Texts on CD-ROM, published by the Belgian firm of Brepols, which contains all the volumes of the Corpus Christianorum series, the complete works of major authors not yet in Corpus Christianorum (or whose volumes in that series are not yet comprehensive) such as Augustine and Gregory, and the Vulgate. There is one serious drawback with CETEDOC in that only the text is on the database and not the apparatus, which is precisely what the source critic needs in order to check which version of a Latin text is closest to the work of the Anglo-Saxon author. But it nevertheless offers enormous scope for concordance work. Regular updates will add further Corpus Christianorum volumes as they are published. Another CD-ROM at present being published by Brepols contains an archive of Celtic-Latin literature, which will be very useful since many recent investigators have stressed the influence of Hiberno-Latin writings on Anglo-Saxon authors.

A new scholarly advance which, if not solely aimed at assisting the student of sources, will certainly do so, offers an increase in knowledge of what surviving books have any direct association with Anglo-Saxon England. This is the projected inventory by Helmut Gneuss provisionally entitled *A Handlist of Anglo-Saxon Manuscripts*, which aims to describe the contents of all manuscripts written or owned in England before 1100. This will be especially important for the Latin material since Neil Ker's *Catalogue of Manuscripts Containing Anglo-Saxon* has been available for many years. Gneuss has produced an interim report on his work in the form of a preliminary list of the manuscripts with a very brief guide to their contents.[19] The finished inventory will offer a full set of bibliographical references for the manuscripts, enabling information on what is known of their history to be reached quickly and easily. The work is an essential foundation study which will make it possible to see what books were certainly known to the Anglo-Saxons, while its indexes will help trace the extent of the Anglo-Saxons' reading of particular texts and authors as revealed by surviving manuscripts.

A second major advance relating to the study of peculiarly insular traditions of standard Latin works is an international collaborative project known as *Sources of Anglo-Saxon Literary Culture* (abbreviated as *SASLC*). For many years the only survey of knowledge of Latin authors in Anglo-Saxon England has been the single volume *Books Known to the English, 597–1066* by Jack Ogilvy,[20] which lists Latin authors alphabetically and shows the influence that each exerted on surviving writings, both Latin and English, of the Anglo-Saxon period. Ogilvy's training was in Latin and his knowledge of vernacular materials, especially manuscripts, was patchy and unreliable. The book has many omissions and a not inconsiderable number of errors. Consequently in 1983 a group of scholars at the eighteenth International Congress on Medieval Studies at the Medieval Institute of Western Michigan University decided to inaugurate a scheme to widen its scope. The succeeding project, *SASLC*, organized in the United States, based at three universities and supported by the US National Endowment for the Humanities, aims at a scrupulous search for evidence of knowledge of all classical, patristic, and Carolingian texts in Anglo-Saxon England. The approach remains similar to that of Ogilvy in that the Latin authors are listed alphabetically and their influence traced in English and Anglo-Latin writers, but the scope of the inquiry is much wider, taking in oral as well as written material and evidence from booklists as well as from surviving manuscripts. Entries are by individual scholars but follow a standard formula, each offering a brief account of the evidence for knowledge of an individual work in England, supported by detailed bibliographical lists. The completed work is expected to be published in hard copy in four volumes and also, perhaps, electronically. At an early stage, a trial version was published to invite scholarly reaction and constructive criticism,[21] and this makes clear that *SASLC* as it is published will become one of the most significant works of scholarship of its generation.

Alongside *SASLC*, and in many ways related to it, is another large-scale international project, *Fontes Anglo-Saxonici: A Register of Written Sources Used by Authors in Anglo-Saxon England*. Work on compiling the register began at the same time as *SASLC*, but in the initial stages at least it has proceeded more slowly, partly because it is more ambitious and long-term, as is explained below, partly because it is based in Britain and government funding has been more difficult to obtain. The growth of the organization and its development has been charted in an annual progress report published in the *Old English Newsletter* since volume 19 (1986). The two projects are complementary, the one being the obverse of the other: where *SASLC* works forward from Latin authors to Anglo-Saxon England, *Fontes Anglo-Saxonici* works backwards from texts written in England to their sources in English, Latin, or Greek. From the outset, the objective of *Fontes Anglo-*

Saxonici has been completeness: to identify all written sources which were incorporated, quoted, translated, or adapted anywhere in English or Latin texts which were written, or were likely to have been written, in Anglo-Saxon England, including those by foreign authors. Although the corpus of English texts to be sourced is clear from the language in which they are written, the first difficulty faced by the originators of the project was that there exists no agreed corpus of Anglo-Latin texts. During the five-year period 1988–93 Alicia Corrêa, working under the direction of Michael Lapidge, the Director for Anglo-Latin of *Fontes Anglo-Saxonici*, produced a bibliography of almost 2000 entries which consisted of only the metrical poetry, letters, and liturgy in Anglo-Latin. This gives some idea of the scale of the Anglo-Latin side of the project and the huge task which lies ahead.

The slow beginnings of *Fontes Anglo-Saxonici* are also due to the fact that it was recognized from the outset that the project was so large that careful attention must be given to establishing procedures which would endure, procedures which have to be followed scrupulously by the many scholars contributing to it. One of the avowed aims of the project is to encourage the universal use of a single terminology, and the definitions of immediate and antecedent source and analogue used above derive directly from it. Sources are also defined, within the project, as 'certain', 'probable', or 'possible', revealing the editors' further concern for exactness in the entries. The register consists of a database on which each Old English and Anglo-Latin text is entered separately and segmentally, each segment being defined by the use by its author of a single source continuously. Whenever the author departs from his source significantly or turns to a different one, a new segment begins. In this way it can be seen very precisely not only what materials were drawn on and how their use is distributed, but which parts of an Anglo-Saxon work have no identifiable sources. Scanning the database can thus provide a reader with a complete list of the sources used by a writer in the period, whether one or many, how thoroughly the sources are blended with one another, and what gaps remain in the evidence, either because the author used no source or because one has yet to be discovered. Additionally, the database offers a list of the sources drawn upon by all the authors whose texts are entered (the 'books known to the English'), and it will show which authors drew upon an individual source, where they used it, and how often. Each text also has a complete bibliography of source studies associated with it, indicating clearly the growth of understanding of the sources for that particular text, and acknowledging the debt of the contributor to earlier authorities. Work on the database has proceeded steadily since 1988, and a list of the texts sourced has been published each year as part of the annual bibliography in *Anglo-Saxon England* since volume 18. Brepols have agreed to produce a CD-ROM of the database, and as has been the case with other CD-ROMs, it is anticipated that an interim version containing, in this case, all the vernacular homilies and prose saints' lives together with the Latin poetry will be produced before the end of the century, with a final CD-ROM being published some years later.

Both *SASLC* and *Fontes Anglo-Saxonici* rely heavily on the efforts of the community of scholars, since in both cases entries are provided by individuals. Consequently, one of the major developments arising from the establishment of the two projects has been the generation of a considerable amount of new work on sources. But the focusing of so much scholarly endeavour on a particular area has not been without some critics, however central to the discipline as a whole that area may be thought by others to be. Raising the profile of source studies has prompted questions about the basis of its contribution generally, the objections being related to the critical concern that studying the text as transmitted is obfuscated by editorial search for an 'original' or authorial text which is bolstered by the citing of sources.[22] Perhaps the most telling answer to those voicing such objections is that source material generated by the new projects is more and more feeding into other areas. The *Dictionary of Old English*, for example, cites Latin sources as a help towards definition. This brings us right back to the beginnings of the modern study of the Anglo-Saxon period. Source study, after all, has stood the test of time. In the sixteenth century it was only by comparison of Anglo-Saxon texts with their Latin antecedents that antiquarians began to understand Old English. By the end of the nineteenth century, identification of Latin sources offered scholars an opportunity to study the cultural context of Anglo-Saxon literature, and gave rise to the twentieth-century search for the range of literature known to the Anglo-Saxons, and the precise form that the books they had available took. As we move into the twenty-first century, the technological revolution has put detailed analytical study of the sources within our reach. With the work of such projects as *SASLC* and *Fontes Anglo-Saxonici*, precise knowledge of the relationship of Anglo-Saxon authors and the books they quarried will become clear, allowing for significant progress to be made in charting the history of ideas in northern medieval Europe, and in seeing just what impact the Anglo-Saxons themselves made to that intellectual development. It has to be stressed too that many postmodernist critics accept the importance of charting the conceptual universe within which the Anglo-Saxons flourished. Such vital information as that which distinguishes transgressive texts from those which support the dominant ideology, for example, can best be gained from an insight into the materials that Anglo-Saxon authors worked with. For postmodernists working in areas such as these, source studies is not a dusty and out-moded discipline but one at the forefront of critical studies generally.

Notes

1 E. B. Irving, Jr., 'A Reading of *Andreas*: The Poem as Poem', *ASE* 12 (1983), 215–37.

2 See E. B. Irving, Jr., 'Latin Prose Sources for Old English Verse', *JEGP* 56 (1957), 588–95, and *The Vercelli Homilies and Related Texts*, ed. D. G. Scragg, EETS os 300 (Oxford, 1992), pp. 139ff.

3 Alfred inserted his comments on the three orders into his translation of Boethius, chapter 17; see *King Alfred's Old English Version of Boethius De Consolatione Philosophiae*, ed. W. J. Sedgefield (Oxford, 1899). The Ælfric passage is in his Letter to Sigeweard; see *The Old English Version of the Heptateuch*, ed. S. J. Crawford, EETS os 160 (London, 1922), pp. 71–2. Wulfstan adapted it; see *Die 'Institutes of Polity, Civil and Ecclesiastical'*, ed. K. Jost (Bern, 1959), pp. 55ff. The homily, which some scholars believe is a compilation by Wulfstan himself, is no. 50 in *Wulfstan: Sammlung der ihm zugeschriebenen Homilien*, ed. A. Napier (Berlin, 1883).

4 B. Assmann, 'Abt Ælfrics angelsächsische Homilie über das Buch Judith', *Anglia* 10 (1888), 76–104.

5 Sometimes an author's style and his training are confused, as in an uncharacteristically rash statement by Kenneth Sisam that Cynewulf was trained 'to admire the orderly progress of a Latin sentence, and to prefer its clarity to the tangled profusion of the native style' ('Cynewulf and his Poetry', *Studies in the History of Old English Literature* [Oxford, 1953], p. 17). It should be noted, in fairness, that the comment was first published in 1933.

6 The Old English verse paraphrases of Genesis and Exodus in the Junius manuscript are not based entirely on versions of the Vulgate Bible but occasionally draw on Old Latin (i.e. pre-Jerome) versions as well. For instances

in *Genesis*, see *Genesis A*, ed. A. N. Doane (Madison, 1978); for those in *Exodus* see *Exodus*, ed. P. J. Lucas (London, 1977), notes to lines 389–96 and 555a. For the possible use of biblical commentary in the composition of *Judith*, see B. F. Huppé, *The Web of Words* (Albany, NY, 1970). The relevant commentary is conveniently summarized in A. W. Astell, 'Holofernes's Head: *Tacen* and Teaching in the Old English *Judith*', *ASE* 18 (1989), 117–33. Further details of the Anglo-Saxon poet's rearrangement of the biblical narrative can be found in the useful summary by Albert S. Cook in his *Judith: An Old English Epic Fragment* (Boston, MA, 1904), pp. xxxiv–xxxvi.

7 *Über die Quellen von Ælfrics Homiliae Catholicae*, I: *Legenden* (Berlin, 1892), and 'Über die Quellen von Ælfrics exegetischen Homiliae Catholicae', *Anglia* 16 (1894), 1–61.

8 On Haymo, see *The Homilies of Ælfric: A Supplementary Collection*, ed. J. C. Pope, EETS os 259–60 (London, 1967–8), esp. pp. 155–61. On Smaragdus, see J. Hill, 'Ælfric and Smaragdus', *ASE* 21 (1992), 203–37.

9 See C. L. Smetana, 'Ælfric and the Early Medieval Homiliary', *Traditio* 15 (1959), 163–204.

10 See P. H. Zettel, 'Saints' Lives in Old English: Latin Manuscripts and Vernacular Accounts', *Peritia* 1 (1982), 17–37.

11 See J. E. Cross, *Cambridge Pembroke College MS. 25: A Carolingian Sermonary Used by Anglo-Saxon Preachers*, King's College London Medieval Studies 1 (London, 1987), and D. G. Scragg, 'An Old English Homilist of Archbishop Dunstan's Day' in *Words, Texts and Manuscripts: Studies Presented to Helmut Gneuss*, ed. M. Korhammer (Cambridge, 1992), pp. 181–92.

12 For more detailed examples, see D. Whitelock, 'The Old English Bede', *PBA* 48 (1962), 57–90.

13 Quoted from Janet Bately's introduction to her edition, *The Old English Orosius*, EETS ss 6 (London, 1980), p. xciii.

14 *King Alfred's West-Saxon Version of Gregory's Pastoral Care*, ed. H. Sweet, 2 vols., EETS os 45, 50 (London, 1871) I, p. 85, ll. 9–10. For the fuller context and Alfred's changes to it in detail, see my 'An Introduction to *Fontes Anglo-Saxonici*', *OEN* 26.3 (1993), Appendix B, 1–8 at 4–5. For a different view of the quoted passage, see R. W. Clement, 'The Production of the *Pastoral Care*: King Alfred and his Helpers', *Studies in Earlier English Prose*, ed. P. E. Szarmach (Albany, NY, 1986), pp. 129–52 at 136.

15 *King Alfred's Version of St. Augustine's Soliloquies*, ed. T. A. Carnicelli (Harvard, 1969), p. 47, ll. 6–12.

16 *Homilies of Ælfric*, p. 150.

17 See the references in *Exodus*, ed. Lucas, notes to ll. 71ff.

18 Such an index is now available for homilies in R. DiNapoli, *An Index of Theme and Image to the Homilies of the Anglo-Saxon Church* (Hockwold cum Wilton, Norfolk, 1995).

19 H. Gneuss, 'A Preliminary List of Manuscripts Written or Owned in England

up to 1100', *ASE* 9 (1981), 1–60. See also N. R. Ker, *Catalogue of Manuscripts Containing Anglo-Saxon* (Oxford, 1957; suppl. 1990).

20 J. D. A Ogilvy, *Books Known to the English, 597–1066* (Cambridge, MA, 1967), to which was added *Addenda et Corrigenda* in *Mediaevalia* 7 (1981 [1984]), 281–325 (reprinted as *Old English Newsletter Subsidia* 11 [1985]), taking the bibliography to 1981.

21 *Sources of Anglo-Saxon Literary Culture: A Trial Version*, ed. F. M. Biggs, T. D. Hill, and P. E. Szarmach with the assistance of K. Hammond (Binghamton, NY, 1990).

22 See especially R. Waterhouse, '"Wæter æddre asprang": How Cuthbert's Miracle Pours Cold Water on Source Study', *Parergon* 5 (1987), 1–27, and A. J. Frantzen, *The Desire for Origins: New Language, Old English, and Teaching the Tradition* (New Brunswick, NJ and London, 1990).

3

Language matters

DANIEL DONOGHUE

•

Language-based approaches to the study of Old English go back to the earliest days of Anglo-Saxon studies, when in the sixteenth century scholars like John Joscelyn and Laurence Nowell took the *Grammar* and *Glossary* that Ælfric compiled to teach novices Latin through Old English and used it in reverse to teach themselves Old English through Latin. As collaborators with Archbishop Matthew Parker, Joscelyn and Nowell were leading figures in a project to glean evidence supporting the antiquity of Reformation doctrine from Anglo-Saxon manuscripts. Their efforts led, among other things, to the publication in 1566 or 1567 of *A Testimonie of Antiquitie, shewing the auncient fayth in the Church of England touching the sacrament of the body and bloude of the Lord here publikely preached, and also receaued in the Saxons tyme, aboue 600 yeares agoe*. It contains the first printed texts in Old English, most notably and controversially Ælfric's *Sermon on the Sacrifice on Easter Day*, which was presented (after selective editing) as evidence against the doctrine of transubstantiation. But a less conspicuous part of this ambitious programme was the compilation of the first modern dictionaries and grammars of Old English.[1] In the years since the Reformation the ideological motivations for pursuing Anglo-Saxon studies have changed considerably, but every period has continued to produce studies on Old English language. Today, if the number of recent publications on lexicography, grammar, syntax, and metrics is any indication, the field is undergoing something of a renascence. Beginning students have their choice of a number of outstanding textbooks, handbooks, dictionaries, and computerized tutorials. And specialized scholarship has a greater variety of research tools available than ever before.

But the state of language studies is not one of unrelieved optimism. Fewer students are coming to the study of Old English with a knowledge of Latin or any other useful language. And the specialists may seem to have little consensus about the ultimate goals of language study and the means to achieve them. They confront basic questions about what it seeks to do, the kinds of language skills and methodology required, and the changing relationships among different approaches. Among these, the apparent divide between philologists and linguists has been around so long that it has become something of a tradition itself, with each group publishing in different journals, attending different conferences, and receiving training and holding positions in different university departments. Each side is thought to view the other with some suspicion. Philologists, as the customary thinking goes, direct their work to textual editing and to compiling reference works such as grammars and dictionaries. They like to amass empirical data and keep their theory on a low, descriptive level. While they often toil in the fields of charters and glosses, their greatest satisfaction comes from elucidating passages of *Beowulf* and other well-known Old English poems. Linguists, on the other hand, move quickly from a sampling of data to higher-level theory in the hope of establishing rules with sweeping explanatory power. For syntax, they prefer simple prose, as in the *Chronicle*, as the closest approximation to the spoken language; otherwise they prefer texts with identifiable dates and dialects. Their conclusions do not necessarily elucidate passages of Old English, but rather contribute to an understanding of the way language works, with perhaps universal grammar as an ultimate goal. For example, a linguist might assume an early date for the Cynewulf and Cyneheard episode in the *Chronicle* entry for 755 in order to make a point about archaic word order, while a philologist might find the textual evidence for dating to be the most interesting question.[2] A shorthand way of summarizing the differences is that while a philologist studies language, a linguist studies Language.

While most Anglo-Saxonists might recognize the shortcomings in this division of labor, this summary overstates the case, at least in light of the course of language studies today. I can illustrate the point by reviewing some publications over the past ten years. In 1985 Bruce Mitchell published his authoritative *Old English Syntax*, the fruit of forty years of sustained research. In the same year B. Elan Dresher published *Old English and the Theory of Phonology*, his doctoral dissertation from the

University of Massachusetts. The point of the comparison is not that one came from a mature scholar and the other from a relative newcomer, but that each deliberately limited the frame of reference to either philology (Mitchell) or linguistics (Dresher). By contrast the year 1992 saw the publication of three books that blur the traditional division: R. D. Fulk's *A History of Old English Meter*, Richard M. Hogg's *A Grammar of Old English*, and Richard M. Hogg, ed., *The Cambridge History of the English Language. Volume 1: The Beginnings to 1066.* Each shows the fusion of the two methodologies in different ways. Fulk, who was trained as a linguist, reassesses the philological tests used for dating Old English poetry from a perspective that is informed in both theoretical and historical linguistics. Aside from the specific merits of his study, one of the remarkable results is the rehabilitation of early philologists like Sarrazin and Kaluza. In the introduction to his *Grammar*, Hogg admits he does not find the philology/linguistics debate helpful and sees instead a 'symbiotic relationship' between the empiricism of one and the theoretical orientation of the other. Perhaps most tellingly, the seven contributors to the *Cambridge History* are drawn (without comment or fanfare) from the ranks of both philologists and linguists.[3]

One can also point to the recent florescence of metrical studies as a very tangible demonstration of the way theory and empiricism have informed one another in a way that has brought about a number of interesting convergences, which can be measured in, for example, the repeated questioning of Sievers's five types and of Kuhn's two well-known laws, and in the attention paid to resolution. What has brought about this apparent and sudden meeting of minds? It is impossible to say with any certainty, but the following may have some role. First, the split has not been as clean as I have presented it here. For many years there has been a good amount of cross-pollenation, especially between historical linguists and philologists. Secondly, there have recently been more fruitful exchanges between theoretical and historical linguists, which has had the salutary effect of making theory more comprehensible to non-linguists. Thirdly, the theoretically inclined now ignore data at their peril because so much is readily available through the *Microfiche Concordance*, electronic media, Mitchell's *Old English Syntax*, and other research tools. It is no longer justifiable to generate rules governing syntax, for example, on the basis of a sampling of one text like the *Anglo-Saxon Chronicle* or *Beowulf* (a method that has been a source of exasperation for philologists). Finally, both groups may be driven toward each other for institutional reasons. Linguistics departments have borne the brunt of downsizing in many universities in recent years. Many have shrunk in size and others have been eliminated altogether. And for a variety of reasons philologists have come to feel more marginalized within English departments, making them more likely to turn elsewhere for collegiality.[4]

The discussion so far assumes an equivalence between philology and linguistics as approaches that are exclusively language based, but philology can also have a much broader, interdisciplinary meaning. Linguists quite often have distinguished it from their own field by speaking of it as a kind of cultural study based on an examination of literary texts (as opposed to the spoken language). Ferdinand de Saussure for example writes, 'Next appeared philology. . . . Language is not its sole object. The early philologists sought especially to correct, interpret and comment upon written texts. Their studies also led to an interest in literary history, customs, institutions, etc.' He goes on to criticize philology (which he associates with the study of classical languages) for being deficient in one respect: 'it follows the written language too slavishly and neglects the living language.' Roman Jakobson also associates philology with textual study when he more enigmatically but suggestively defines it as 'the art of reading slowly'.[5]

The second edition of the *Oxford English Dictionary* (1989) gives more citations for *philology* (not found in the 1909 entry) by linguists such as Leonard Bloomfield, Otto Jespersen, and B. L. Whorf, who contrast philology's broad approach with the more specialized focus of linguistics. But the *OED* also points to a regional difference between the United States and England in attributing the broader sense. The definitions of *philology*, senses 1 and 3 are:

1 Love of learning and literature; the study of literature, in a wide sense, including grammar, literary criticism and interpretation, the relation of literature and written records to history, etc.; literary or classical scholarship; polite learning. Now *rare* in general sense **except in the U.S.**

3 *spec.* (in mod. use) The study of the structure and development of language; the science of language; linguistics. *Now usu. restricted to the study of the development of specific languages or language families, esp.*

research into phonological and morphological history based on written documents. (Really one branch of sense 1.) ***This sense has never been current in the U.S.*** Linguistics *is now the more usual term for the study of the structure of language, and, with qualifying adjective or adjective phrase, is replacing* philology *even in the restricted sense.*

While the definitions here make a number of fine distinctions, they point to a significant difference between Great Britain, where 'philology' and 'historical (or comparative) linguistics' are interchangeable, and the US, where they are not. The passages in bold type are new to the second edition and indicate that the word has undergone a significant shift in meaning along with its regional distribution from the beginning to the end of this century. Despite the authoritative tone inevitable in lexicography, the newly added qualifications point to uncertainty about the use of the word today. If *linguistics* is 'now the more usual term' and 'is replacing' *philology* in the restricted sense (although the wording is ambiguous, I take the final sentence to apply to the use of the word everywhere) then either the *'rare'* sense 1 is becoming more common or *philology* is being used less and less in any sense. The tentative distinctions in the newer passages are particularly unsettling in the context of the *OED*, which as a lexicographical project must deal with linguistics and philology — however defined — every day.

If the *OED* is uncertain about the word's meaning, what hope do the rest of us have? Perhaps not coincidentally, the year 1990 saw the publication of three extensive discussions of the history of philology, its role today, and its future. All three, the 'New Philology' issue of *Speculum*, the 'What is Philology?' issue of *Comparative Literature Studies*, and Allen J. Frantzen's *Desire for Origins*, assess the change (or the reluctance to change) in the way philology is practiced and received in the current climate of the academic world.[6] These are not the only recent assessments of medieval philology, which, like other academic disciplines, has given itself over to much stock-taking and self-analysis, but they are serious and extensive discussions. While nearly everyone sees a future role for philology, many urge it to move away from its positivist and textual orientation to a more interdisciplinary and theoretically informed approach. There is also a call for a return to the manuscripts as sites that encode more than the mere text and to attend to marks of punctuation and spacing, which may stand as graphic traces of oral delivery, and to semantically insignificant words such as discourse particles.

Perhaps the most provocative of the reassessments of philology are those that interrogate basic assumptions about it as a means of knowing the past. Jonathan Culler urges us to begin questioning the assumption that philology itself is 'basic or foundational' or that it is

> a kind of first knowledge that serves as the precondition of any further literary criticism or historical and interpretive work. . . . That questioning could take the form of identifying various ways in which philological activity and especially the reconstruction of cultures performed by philology turns out to be itself based on concepts or schemes that philology . . . ought to help us put into question. The critique of the notion of the foundational character of philology would take the form, in other words, of showing how philological projects rely uncritically on literary and cultural conceptions that come from the domains of thought that are supposedly secondary.[7]

Philology is not a neutral tool for disclosing past cultures, but is itself culturally constructed in the questions it asks and its selection of texts. But, Culler continues, philology also has a self-critiquing potential in its traditional attention to structures of language and rhetorical strategies, which enables it (when turned upon itself) to disclose its own constructedness. Thus philology is not foundational in the sense that its cultural and aesthetic assumptions stand as timeless truths, but rather in its potential to examine the structure of language prior to the meaning it produces. The philologist should have a double perspective, with one line of sight on the interpretation of past cultures and the other on the critical methodology that makes interpretation possible. With a double perspective, philology has the potential to renew itself.

'Renewal', in the sense of *renovatio*, is likewise a key term in Stephen Nichols's introductory essay in the *Speculum* issue devoted to 'New Philology', and indeed he uses the term to characterize New Philology's return to the manuscript culture of the Middle Ages. This movement toward renewal is very much in the spirit of Culler's interrogation of foundational assumptions: it proclaims not a complete break with the past or a rejection of earlier philology, but rather a redirecting of attention, the asking of new questions, and a return (in this case) to a certain kind of manuscript study. R. Howard Bloch's essay in the same volume begins with a more skeptical questioning of a movement that proclaims itself the 'New Philology':

Use of the labels 'new' and 'old', applied to the dialectical development of a discipline, is a gesture sufficiently charged ideologically as to have little meaning in the absolute terms — before and after, bad and good — that it affixes. On the contrary, to the extent that calling oneself 'new' is a value-laden gesture which implies that something else is 'old' and therefore less worthy, it constitutes a rhetorical strategy of autolegitimation — with little recognition, of course, that the process itself of declaring oneself 'new' is indeed very old, or at least as old, where the present case is concerned, as Vico's *Nuova Scienza*, which some see as the beginning of philological science.[8]

In the rest of his essay, Bloch distances himself from the rhetorical agenda of the 'New Philology' by using it only with quotation marks, and his prescriptions for recovering the 'original spirit of philology' again involve a mixture of older philological concerns (the attention to structures of language, interdisciplinarity, and the semantic richness of medieval poetry) and newer (linguistics, Lacan, reception theory).

Another consequence of 'the rhetorical strategy of autolegitimation' in calling oneself 'new' (though Bloch does not mention it) is that it reduces the 'old' to a static, monolithic sameness: the 'other' against which the new defines itself, as if the methodology and the motivation for medieval or Anglo-Saxon studies were the same in the early nineteenth century as in the late twentieth century. The recent increased attention to the subject, culminating in the 1990 publications, performs a valuable service of self-assessment, but it would be misleading to assume that since the nineteenth century there had not been moments of *renovatio* which had had the cumulative effect of redefining philology. Perhaps I can best illustrate what I mean by discussing a 1984 study that anticipates in its details many of the new directions urged on philology. Christine Fell's short article 'A *friwif locbore* Revisited' examines one of Æthelbirht's laws, which reads in its entirety, 'Gif friwif locbore leswæs hwæt gedeþ, xxx scll' gebete': ('If a freewoman, with long hair, commits any misconduct, she is to pay 30 shillings compensation').[9] In her examination of *friwif, locbore,* and *leswæs*, Fell surveys previous critical interpretations, especially those of Liebermann, Thorpe, Attenborough, and Whitelock, and along the way speculates about the cultural assumptions implicit in the way they associate hair length and the free-born status of the woman in question. In formulating her own interpretation of the law, she draws on other Old English and medieval laws, wills, poetry, and Old Norse literature, and engages in semantic field study by using, among other tools, the *Microfiche Concordance* (which she corrects in two places). Finally she proposes a new translation: 'If a free woman in control of the keys does anything seriously dishonest she is to pay thirty shillings compensation.' The crucial element in her reassessment is the redefinition of *locbore*, dissociating it from a woman's hair and linking it instead with the role Anglo-Saxon women played as guardians of the keys for locked boxes. While the new interpretation has much to recommend it, Fell does not have any illusions about offering conclusive 'proof'. She sensibly realizes that another interpretation may some day displace hers.

In many respects Fell's article fits comfortably in the recent consensus for philology: it is ambitiously interdisciplinary, it explores the cultural assumptions that shape critical interpretation, and it is aware of the limitations of its claims. That it does not explicitly invoke theory or inspect the twelfth-century manuscript does not necessarily weaken the argument. Within the limited aims of *explication de texte* its method works, and, significantly, it is not a reading that Jacob Grimm or Felix Liebermann would have produced. The point here is not just that Fell's article anticipates some of the new directions of philology, but that many studies published in that last twenty years – to pick a round number – do the same. They have laid the foundation for the current movement toward *renovatio* in philology.

Sometimes 'renewal' takes the form of questioning old assumptions. Many studies of Old English syntax, for example, uncritically invoke hypotaxis and its association with clausal subordination (or embedded clauses), as opposed to parataxis and its association with nonsubordination. But to what extent were the terms hypotaxis and parataxis, which ultimately derive from classical grammars, consistent with the way the Anglo-Saxons used their own language?[10] The possibility of a poor fit with the structure of Old English does not have to involve classical grammars. Twentieth-century linguistic categories can be suspect as well. To what extent is a word class like *auxiliary* in OE consistent with its use in modern English? If one of the current ways of identifying an auxiliary is to use it in a tag question, such as 'You'll sing, won't you?' and if OE has no examples of tag questions, then in what way can we speak of auxiliaries in OE? ('Cedmon, sing me hwæthwugu, nilt þu?') Does the absence of tag questions mean that *sceal* is no different from *breac* as a finite verb? Should one nevertheless continue to round up the usual suspects (*sceal, mæg, mot, cann, wile,* etc.)? Or does the reliance on tag questions as an identifying feature need to be questioned?

The New Philology's appeal for a return to the manuscript culture holds considerable possibilities for language study, such as syntactic glosses, orthographic variants concealed by editorial emendation, and accent marks and punctuation. Other new directions include the use of computerized corpora, which holds great promise for the study of orthography, the lexicon, syntax, and sociolinguistics, and in discourse analysis of Old English. Computers can begin to redress the imbalance in the selection of texts studied, because the searches can be as extensive as the database itself. While its potential is great, the computer is still only a tool that can best be used by someone who knows its limitations. In discourse analysis, for example, the sheer size of a database may seem to compensate for the absence of native informants, but the texts still represent only a limited sampling of the language, and the artificiality of most Old English prose can never reproduce the subtleties and nuances of speech or the knowledge of native informants. The computer user must also bring to the task an extensive knowledge of the language in order to ask the right questions. Matti Rissanen, for example, has skilfully exploited the computer's potential in several sociolinguistically oriented studies of lexically insignificant words based on the *Helsinki Corpus of English Texts.* One study tracks the use of indefinite pronouns, particularly the distinction between the *hw-* indefinites (*hwa, hwæt,* and *hwilc*) and the alternatives *ænig* and *sum,* across 'varying types of texts and in different syntactic and functional environments'.[11] The *hw-* forms are found more often in 'stipulative/directive' texts (such as laws and the Benedictine Rule) which tend to be more generalized, universal, and timeless. The *ænig* and *sum* forms are more common in 'narrative/homiletic' texts, such as *Orosius* or the *Chronicle,* which are linked to specific events. The *hw-* forms are also more common in conditional clauses and at the head of clauses. Because of these contextual and syntactic constraints, Rissanen concludes, the once common *hw-* indefinite lost out to the more neutral but less constrained *ænig.* The attention to 'little words' like indefinites, and to the context in which they are used, is characteristic of sociolinguistic approaches, and might be extended to study, for example, contexts in Old English where gendered discourse plays a significant role.

One persistent criticism of old philology concerns the strong legacy of nineteenth-century logical positivism (usually taken to be neogrammarian) as the driving force behind its aspirations to be an exact science producing objective conclusions. Despite the occasional gesture toward objectivity in some recent studies, even the most empirical philologists are aware of the limitations of their claims. The contrary view, that the methodology of late twentieth-century philology naively continues the reconstructive project of nineteenth-century positivism, is a notion that needs questioning no less than the notion of philology as foundational. Every generation of philologists and historical linguists brings subtle and sometimes not-so-subtle changes to the methodology. Today, for example, the model for linguistic approaches has shifted from the exact sciences to the social sciences, influenced, no doubt, by the development of linguistics as a separate discipline.

Recent discussions of methodology are quite clear on this point. R. D. Fulk's introduction to *A History of Old English Meter* gives perhaps the fullest account of the kind of inductive logic that characterizes linguistic inquiry: 'constructing and testing hypotheses, rendering probable (that is, *validating*) what cannot be proved'.[12] The result is not a take-it-or-leave-it assertion of a self-evident truth about language, but a hypothesis that can be tested and modified in its details, critiqued for the data, or challenged with a better hypothesis. And if philologists speak of 'rules' and 'laws' in a way that seems absolute, they should be understood in the context of hypothesis formation and testing. As Fulk and others describe it, at some point in the process a methodological fiction is invoked which treats the hypothesis as fact in order to test its applicability, but this status is provisional. Perhaps at heart the reason philologists and linguists strive to formulate and test hypotheses is that their personal experience with language has convinced them that it is systematic. Despite the inevitable vagaries and idiosyncrasies in language, those who study it seek to understand the underlying system and reveal the regularities.

Fulk is not alone in distancing philology from positivism. In a similar fashion Thomas Cable aligns 'the incremental process of observation, hypothesis, testing, and revision' of his own approach to alliterative meter with Charles Sanders Peirce's theory of abduction.[13] In both Fulk's induction and Cable's abduction, the methodology of philology and historical linguistics has no association with logical positivism.

Both induction and abduction proceed by proposing hypotheses to explain some observed phenomenon, and the hypothesis is accepted until a competitor comes along with greater explanatory power. Neither procedure leads to absolute certainty but rather to relative probability, and both frankly admit the subjective element in hypothesis formation. Both abduction and induction also involve circularity and deduction at the moment the hypothesis is turned around to test its applicability to the original phenomena: 'let's assume it's true . . .'. The hypothesis will always be vulnerable to revision or to replacement by a rival hypothesis, perhaps in response to new data.

An interesting illustration of this process is the recent attention given to two formulations by Hans Kuhn in 1933 regarding the placement of metrically unstressed elements at the beginning of a verse clause. The following discussion considers the more prominent of the two, Kuhn's first Law, which he called the *Satzpartikelgesetz*, sometimes called the Law of Sentence Particles. Briefly, Kuhn divides words into three categories: (1) stressed words, such as nouns, adjectives, non-finite verb forms, (2) sentence particles (*Satzpartikeln*), which include 'substantive pronouns, many adverbs and finite verbs, conjunctions, to some extent also adjectival pronouns, occasionally infinitives and predicate nouns, and possibly also vocatives', and (3) proclitics (*Satzteilpartikeln*), which are unstressed words that form a phrase with another word, such as demonstratives, adjectival pronouns, and prepositions.[14] Put simply, the first Law says that all unstressed sentence particles fall in a metrical dip either before or immediately after the first stressed word of the clause; the implication is that any sentence particle found elsewhere receives metrical stress. Bliss took what was essentially a descriptive *Gesetz* by Kuhn and tightened it up to make it predictive, where it became an important element in his influential system of scansion.[15] An essential part of Bliss's reinterpretation of the law involved a more rigorous classification of sentence elements, especially the second group, the *Satzpartikeln*. Kuhn's original wording suggests a degree of flexibility or uncertainty in their classification such that almost every element is qualified (*viele . . . zum Teil auch . . . gelegentlich . . . vielleicht auch*), but Bliss assigned each element, most controversially in the case of the finite verb, exclusively to one category. With Kuhn's First Law regularized in this way, Bliss was able to use it as a mechanism for generating rules to classify Old English meter.

Recently the usefulness of Kuhn's first Law — or more precisely later applications of it — as a means for understanding meter and/or syntax has come under question. In an important study B. R. Hutcheson returns to Kuhn's original article for a close reading and concludes that the laws have nothing to contribute to an understanding of meter because from the start Kuhn accepts Sievers's system of scansion. 'What [Kuhn] has evidently done is to take Sievers's scansion and describe the placement of certain classes of words according to their occurrence under the preformulated scansion system.'[16] Kuhn's *Gesetzen* are descriptive, not prescriptive. If a verb lacks stress, for example, it lacks it because Sievers scanned it that way and not because of a prescriptive law that allocates stress. Hutcheson also points out the ambiguity of Kuhn's use of *Auftakt* (meaning at some times 'anacrusis' and at others 'upbeat of a clause') and his apparent inconsistency in classifying finite verbs. What emerges from Hutcheson's reanalysis is less a 'law' in the neogrammarian or the more recent theoretical sense than an observable tendency formulated with considerable imprecision.

Just what this observable tendency is and how to account for it is the topic of a number of other studies, some of which build on Hutcheson's reanalysis. Where Kuhn's formulation blends together meter and syntax, some recent alternatives follow the linguistic principle of maintaining a consistent distinction between fields of analysis (in this case syntax and meter). Russom, for example, has proposed a purely metrical substitute; Stockwell and Minkova have surveyed proposed syntactic models; Blockley and Cable even deny the significance of the pattern of unstressed syllables at the beginning of a clause.[17] They argue rather that what Kuhn observed and described is epiphenomenal and falls out from a combination of rather unremarkable and unrelated metrical and syntactic principles. Where else, they point out, could subject pronouns and clausal conjunctions be placed except at the beginning of a clause? A purely metrical or purely syntactic alternative to Kuhn's first Law would deserve serious attention because it would carry the appeal of simplicity and elegance. It would also avoid what Cable in another context has called the dangers of theorizing at 'an intermediate level of representation, where the facts in a commonsensical, positivistic way seem to be most obvious. One should have instead a double vision of [local effects] and also a simple explanatory generalization. The intermediate level will take care of itself.'[18] Kuhn's first Law thus has several disadvantages: it is, as Hutcheson demonstrates, ambiguously formulated; it conflates two levels of analysis (meter and syntax) which are usually kept apart; and it is, suspiciously, a commonsensical middle-level theory.

But in the push to find 'pure' substitutes are we throwing out the baby with the bathwater? I would argue that we are. Kuhn's essential insight in the *Satzpartikelgesetz* is that at the beginning of the verse clause meter and syntax are inextricably related. Meter alone, for example, cannot account for the order of sentence elements at the beginning of a clause, and syntax alone cannot predict whether an initial element will be stressed.

One way to assess the validity of Kuhn's insight is to construct a negative hypothesis. Let us assume that the *Satzpartikelgesetz* does no useful work. Then let us imagine constructions where metrical and syntactical constraints would be minimal, in clauses of two or more half-lines. (If all clauses were one half-line long, there would be little need for this discussion.) In limiting the constraints I omit the following: (1) clauses that begin with a relative, a conjunction, or a word like *þa* or *swa* that may be a conjunction; (2) imperative constructions and clauses with subject pronouns, because each of these necessarily locates a dip at the beginning of a clause for reasons that may be purely syntactic; (3) clauses without a clause-initial dip; (4) half-lines that require specific placement, such as double alliteration and the light verses known as Sievers Type A3, because each of these, for metrical reasons, is associated with the on-verse; (5) clauses that begin in the middle of the long line (that is, in the off-verse); (6) two constructions involving auxiliaries, which elsewhere I call the bracketing pattern and verbal-auxiliary half-lines.[19] In this 'constraint-deprived' environment, the remaining half-lines would have only one alliterating element and could thus fit the metrical requirements of either the on- or off-verse. The clause would consist of a full verse line (at the least), and the first half-line would contain a metrical dip.

To eliminate all such clauses is to eliminate most of the clauses in *Beowulf*. But the remainder isolate conditions that might reveal what, in the absence of Kuhn's Law and with few metrical or syntactic constraints, determines element order and stress assignment in verse clauses. The crucial test is to see if there are clauses in which the second half-line *could* switch places with the first without violating metrical or syntactic principles. If they cannot switch places or if there are very few such clauses, then we have reason to doubt the usefulness of Kuhn's first Law. Perhaps it is epiphenomenal and indeed does no useful work. An important, common element in these reversible half-lines is that the first one contains a clause dip. If there are a large number of such reversible half-lines, then we must be able to explain their order, which is to explain why we do not find such dips in a non-initial half-line.

Three examples of reversible half-lines are in the first line of the following passages from *Beowulf*:

> Forgeaf þa Beowulfe   bearn Healfdenes
> segen gyldenne   sigores to leane;   (1020–1)
>
> Me ðis hildesceorp   Hroðgar sealde,
> snotra fengel   (2155–6a)

and

> Ful oft gebeotedon   beore druncne
> ofer ealowæge   oretmecgas.   (480–1)

These examples show the kind of clauses remaining after eliminating all conjunctions, double alliteration, and so on. They begin with an unstressed verb, oblique pronoun, or an adverb, and the meter of the first half-line is either Sievers's Type C (Bliss's small d) or Type B. For all of these the order of the first two half-lines could be reversed and yield an acceptable line, syntactically and metrically:

> * bearn Healfdenes   forgeaf þa Beowulfe
>
> * Hroðgar sealde   me ðis hildesceorp

and

> * beore druncne   ful oft gebeotedon.

Not only are the reversed half-lines regular in meter, but the syntax seems even smoother. The first two change to SVO constructions (e.g. 'Hrothgar gave me this armor'), and the third likewise puts the subject (or part of it) before the verb. While the reverse order of these examples yields smooth syntax, many such clauses would not show such improvement: after switching places some seem more contorted in element order and others are just as awkward or smooth as the original. Yet no matter how they impress us aesthetically, the reversed half-lines would

be allowable constructions in a minimally constrained environment –
without Kuhn's first Law.

By my count there are forty-eight such reversible half-lines in
Beowulf: forty-eight lines in which the half-lines may be reversed to put
the clause dip in a non-initial position.[20] That the reversed order is
avoided in *Beowulf* (and other poems) shows that a constraint probably
applies: the order of the half-lines seems too consistent to be attribut-
able to chance. If forty-eight seems small in comparison with the 1200 or
so clauses that are excluded, it would be misleading to assume that the
remainder all refute Kuhn's Law, or that they accord with purely syntactic and/or metrical principles. That is far from the case. The forty-
eight are simply specific constructions where with no other changes the
half-lines can be reversed. Of course the switching of the half-lines is
hypothetical, but it helps us visualize the consequences of Kuhn's first
Law. If it didn't exist, we would have to invent it or something like it.

A substitute for Kuhn's first Law would have to account not only for
reversible half-lines, but at least one other feature of verse, or more precisely, a non-occurrence. Syntax dictates that any clause beginning with
a relative or conjunction will necessarily have an initial clause dip
(because it begins with *ac, gif, þe, þæt*, etc.). But it does not explain why
a second clause dip never appears, especially in longer clauses, like

> þæt hie ær to fela micles
> in þæm winsele   wældeað fornam,
> Denigea leode.   (*Beowulf* 695a–7b)

In such longer clauses unstressed particles like *ær* are consistently
grouped with other particles at the beginning, even when they could be
placed in another dip, in this case before *in þæm winsele*. If no constraint prevents a second metrical dip, then we should expect at least a
small number of unstressed particles in a later half-line. What prevents a
poet from redistributing the wealth of particles? They could, in theory,
be tucked into the first dip in the front of any Type B or Type C half-line
later in the clause. Another example could be a clause such as

> Symle ic him on feðan   beforan wolde.   (*Beowulf* 2497)

Moving *him* from the first half-line to the beginning of the second (**him*
beforan wolde) is not only allowable in a world without Kuhn's first
Law, but gives good syntax. (Compare 'gesihð him biforan fealwe

wegas', *Wanderer* 46.) Naturally there are not a large number of such examples because of the peculiar conditions that would make this hypothetical displacement possible, but if a second dip were possible — if nothing like Kuhn's Law prevents it — we should expect to find one now and then. An adequate substitute will thus have to answer the questions 'Why only one dip?' and 'Why is it clause-initial?'

Some of the present dissatisfaction with Kuhn's Law arises from the perception of it as a middle-level theory that explains much of the data but is too open-ended, too baggy. For example it makes no predictions about where a 'displaced' particle will end up, whether its stress is different from that of other stressed elements, or whether it will participate in alliteration. It has nothing to say about initial half-lines made up entirely of particles, one of which must receive stress and alliterate. Among particles, it does not distinguish between those that are usually 'displaced' and those that never seem to be.

Where Kuhn's Law is too capacious and so close to the data that it permits patterns that never happen, the 'pure' theories' narrower focus fails to account for patterns that do happen. If Kuhn is too inclusive, the others theories are too exclusive. The explanatory strength of Kuhn's first Law is its very impurity, its mixing of syntax and meter in one descriptive formula: one metrical dip containing all unstressed particles at the beginning of the clause. A purely metrical theory works only within the unit of the half-line and thus cannot account for the placement of one half-line before another. A syntactic theory might account for a subject pronoun consistently at the beginning of a clause, but cannot indicate the conditions that make an auxiliary stressed or unstressed. At some point, every syntactic theory applied to poetry must introduce a consideration of metrical scansion. The question is whether it should be applied in a localized way after the syntactic rules or as an integral part of the metrical grammar, as Kuhn prefers.

To make the *Satzpartikelgesetz* a more adequate theory Kuhn's fundamental insight must be preserved: that at the beginning of clauses, meter and syntax are inextricably related. B. R. Hutcheson has made significant steps in this direction by reclassifying the sentence elements according to their participation in stress, making four well-defined categories: (1) stressed elements (always found in a position of metrical stress), (2) clitics, words, or prefixes that are usually unstressed, (3) stressable words, which are sometimes metrically stressed, sometimes not, and (4) non-stressable words, which are almost never stressed but are not proclitic.[21] The major difference between Kuhn's threefold and Hutcheson's fourfold categorization is that Hutcheson divides the *Satzpartikeln* into two groups, (3) and (4), only one of which is associated with metrical stress with any degree of regularity. In fact, given the similarity in the lack of stress attributed to elements from (2) clitics and (4) non-stressable words, they could be treated as one category. Thus the number of sentence elements about which Kuhn's first Law has anything crucial to say is limited to (3) stressable words: finite verbs, quantitative adjectives, many adverbs, and perhaps personal pronouns. In addition to reclassifying some sentence elements, Hutcheson's modification of Kuhn's first Law also directs greater attention to alliteration and divorces the law entirely from predictions about metrical stress.

Another profitable way to consider the importance of the phenomenon Kuhn described in his laws is to consider the reception of the verse text. Old English poems in manuscript are notoriously sparse in their punctuation in comparison with the punctuation available for other kinds of writing in Anglo-Saxon England.[22] But if an identifiable class of unstressed elements appeared consistently and exclusively at the beginning of a clause, Anglo-Saxon scribes and readers would be able to navigate through the syntax with lighter punctuation in a way that would be much more difficult to sustain with Latin verse or with Old English prose. To them a rhythmical run of unstressed syllables would unambiguously indicate a clause boundary even if (as in the case of *Forgeaf þā* [*Beowulf* 1020a]) it has elements that syntax does not require at the beginning. Today in reading our printed editions of Old English poems we are impatient to move past the metrically and semantically slight *swa*s, *ær*s and *com*s at the beginning of a clause to get to the weightier elements beyond. Modern punctuation encourages this kind of reading, but it comes at a cost. It would be wise for those revisiting Kuhn's *Satzpartikelgesetz* to consider not just metrical and syntactic theory but also a specialized kind of reception theory to which the manuscript context might point.

Voltaire once drily observed that the Holy Roman Empire was neither holy nor Roman nor an empire. Analogously, whatever emerges after the current reassessment of Kuhn's Law may be neither Kuhn's nor a law. If the *Satzpartikelgesetz* is too imprecisely formulated to stand as a hypothesis, Kuhn's essential insight about meter and syntax can helpfully shape the direction of the supplanting hypotheses. If so, the process may serve as a modest but instructive illustration of the growing inseparability of philology and linguistics, and the way new approaches can profitably revisit the old in what is ideally a continuous cycle of *renovatio*.

Notes

1 For a discussion of the way Ælfric's *Grammar* and *Glossary* were used, see R. E. Buckalew, 'Nowell, Lambarde, and Leland: The Significance of Laurence Nowell's Transcript of Ælfric's *Grammar and Glossary*', in *Anglo-Saxon Scholarship: The First Three Centuries*, ed. C. T. Berkhout and M. McC. Gatch (Boston, 1982), pp. 19–50. Though Parker's name usually appears as the primary author of *A Testimonie of Antiquitie* (London, 1566/7), Joscelyn is thought to have done much of the editorial work. See T. H. Leinbaugh, 'Ælfric's *Sermo de Sacrificio in Die Pascae*: Anglican Polemic in the Sixteenth and Seventeenth Centuries' in Berkhout and Gatch, pp. 51–68.

2 For an example of the former see E. C. Traugott, 'Syntax', in *The Cambridge History of the English Language. Volume I: The Beginnings to 1066*, ed. R. M. Hogg (Cambridge, 1990), pp. 168–289, at 278. And for an example of the latter see J. Bately, 'The Compilation of the Anglo-Saxon Chronicle, 60 BC to AD 890: Vocabulary as Evidence', *PBA* 64 (1980), 93–129, at 106–16.

3 Mitchell, *Old English Syntax*, 2 vols. (Oxford, 1985); Dresher, *Theory of Phonology* (New York and London, 1985). Fulk, *History* (Philadelphia, 1992); Hogg, *Grammar* (Oxford and Cambridge, MA, 1992), p. vii; Hogg, ed., *Cambridge History*.

4 For a concise survey of the recent book-length studies see the Introduction of B. R. Hutcheson, *Old English Poetic Metre* (Woodbridge, Suffolk, 1995), pp. 11–15. To these one should add important articles, such as C. B. McCully and R. Hogg, 'An Account of Old English Stress', *Journal of Linguistics* 26 (1990), 315–39, and D. Minkova and R. P. Stockwell, 'Syllable Weight, Prosody, and Meter in Old English', *Diachronica* 11 (1994), 35–64. For examples of linguistic theory made intelligible, see G. Russom, *Old English Meter and Linguistic Theory* (Cambridge, 1987), and S. Suzuki, 'Breaking, Ambisyllabicity, and the Sonority Hierarchy in Old English', *Diachronica* 11 (1994), 65–93. For the kinds of language resources available, see A. di Paolo Healey, 'Old English Language Studies: Present State and Future Prospects', *OEN* 20 (1987), 34–45.

5 De Saussure, *Course in General Linguistics*, ed. C. Bally and A. Sechehaye, trans. W. Baskin (New York, 1966), pp. 1–2. Jakobson quoted from C. Watkins, 'What is Philology?', *Comparative Literature Studies* 27 (1990), 25.

6 *Speculum* 65 (1990); *Comparative Literature Studies* 27 (1990); Frantzen,

Desire for Origins (New Brunswick and London, 1990). While all three studies are written primarily from the perspective of North American academics, the writers are from a variety of backgrounds and the issues they raise are of wider application. See also Jacek Fisiak, ed., *Historical Linguistics and Philology*, Trends in Linguistics 46 (Berlin and New York, 1990)

7 J. Culler, 'Anti-Foundational Philology', *Comparative Literature Studies* 27 (1990), 50. See also P. de Man, 'The Return to Philology' in *The Resistance to Theory*, Theory and History of Literature 33 (Minneapolis, 1986), p. 24.

8 R. H. Bloch, 'New Philology and Old French', *Speculum* 65 (1990), 38.

9 C. Fell, 'A *friwif locbore* Revisited', *ASE* 13 (1984), 157–65; translation by D. Whitelock quoted from Fell.

10 See D. Donoghue and B. Mitchell, 'Parataxis and Hypotaxis: A Review of Some Terms Used for Old English Syntax', *NM* 93 (1992), 163–83.

11 M. Rissanen, 'On the Happy Reunion of English Philology and Historical Linguistics' in *Historical Linguistics and Philology*, ed. J. Fisiak, Trends in Linguistics: Studies and Monographs 46 (Berlin, New York, 1990), pp. 353–69 at 354.

12 Fulk , *History*, p. 9.

13 T. Cable, *The English Alliterative Tradition* (Philadelphia, 1991), pp. 103–13.

14 'Zur Wortstellung und -Betonung im Altgermanischen', *Beiträge zur Geschichte der deutschen Sprache und Literatur* 57 (1933), 1–109 at 5; translation quoted from C. B. Kendall, *The Metrical Grammar of 'Beowulf'* (Cambridge, 1991), p. 17.

15 A. J. Bliss, *The Metre of Beowulf*, rev. edn. (Oxford, 1967). Kendall's *Metrical Grammar* similarly 'tightens up' the second of Kuhn's laws as the basis for his reanalysis of meter.

16 'Kuhn's Law, Finite Verb Stress, and the Critics', *SN* 64 (1992), 129–39. See Mitchell, *Old English Syntax* §3947 for an early expression of skepticism in view of its apparent circularity.

17 See the summary of approaches by R. P. Stockwell and D. Minkova, 'Kuhn's Laws and the Rise of Verb-Second Syntax' in *Old Germanic Languages in a Comparative Perspective*, ed. T. Swann (Berlin, 1993); M. Blockley and T. Cable, 'Kuhn's Laws, Old English Poetry, and the New Philology' in *Beowulf: Basic Readings*, ed. P. Baker (New York, 1995), pp. 261–79.

18 Cable, *The English Alliterative Tradition*, p. 39.

19 D. Donoghue, *Syntax and Style in Old English: The Test of the Auxiliary* (New Haven, 1987).

20 Reversible half-lines appear in the following lines: 111, 258, 312, 340, 480, 669, 758, 791, 883, 1020, 1035, 1076, 1114, 1228, 1363, 1386, 1443, 1457, 1484, 1531, 1543, 1795, 1804, 1840, 1841, 1907, 1920, 1944, 2101, 2107, 2111, 2152, 2155, 2363, 2367, 2401, 2435, 2602, 2705, 2785, 2873, 2903, 2936, 2946, 2986, 3031, 3077. Taken from E. Van Kirk Dobbie, ed., *Beowulf and Judith*, ASPR 4 (New York, 1953). A possible exception to the order of the half-lines is

> Beo wið Geatas glæd,   geofena gemyndig,
> nean ond feorran   þu nu hafast.   (1173–4)

In the second line, the clause dip is *þu*, which appears to be the second half-line of a clause. But even this counterexample, which has attracted considerable editorial comment, shows how easily non-clause-initial dips could be formed if a constraint did not prevent them.

21 'Kuhn's Law', p. 133.
22 See K. O'Brien O'Keeffe, *Visible Song: Transitional Literacy in Old English Verse*, Cambridge Studies in Anglo-Saxon England 4 (Cambridge, 1990); and M. B. Parkes, *Pause and Effect: An Introduction to the History of Punctuation in the West* (Berkeley, 1993).

4

Historicist approaches

NICHOLAS HOWE

•

> Of course it is a truism, of which much has been made, that we cannot see the past. But we can work hard and faithfully to *portray* it, to understand and explain it.
>
> Iris Murdoch

> It was deism that first taught us to accept the pain of historicity.
>
> Irving Howe[1]

As they interpret the remains of a past culture, all works on Old English language and literature are historical in method and intent. Even an austerely self-contained philological study has its place in this reconstruction because it helps us to decipher the textual culture that the Anglo-Saxons produced in their own time and place. Crafting an elegant taxonomy for the functions of Old English verbs and untangling the manuscript confusions that explain otherwise mystifying synonymies between Latin and Old English words in glossaries are forms of intellectual pleasure. But each also provides us with some entry into Anglo-Saxon England through the most compelling mass of evidence that survives from that culture, namely, its language. To cite only classic works, Bruce Mitchell's *Old English Syntax* (1985) or Herbert Dean Meritt's *Fact and Lore about Old English Words* (1954) and *Some of the Hardest Glosses in Old English* (1968) go a long way toward illuminating the intellectual practices of the Anglo-Saxons by studying their language.

Indeed, the claims of philology on historicism become most palpable when one recollects that modern scholars define the Anglo-Saxons, if only as a premise for argument, to be those people who lived in England from perhaps 600 CE onwards and who spoke or (less often) wrote a Germanic language known conventionally as Old English. Through philology or, more precisely, a philology influenced by historicist concerns, one can best register the ways in which a common language underlay whatever degree of social cohesion the Anglo-Saxons felt as a group.

From the start, the most truthful and necessary admission to make about historicism as a critical position is that there have been too many different types of historicism, too many conflicting appropriations of that term, to allow one to limit it to a single criterion or catch-phrase. The term has been used over the last century and more for very different descriptive purposes and also for sometimes contradictory critical positions. At a given moment, 'historicism' can be a neutral term to denote a study that interprets a text within the conventions of the society that produced it, or to identify a study that begins with a theoretical perspective and then verifies it through a detailed examination of cultural artifacts. These two types of studies are alike in shaping their claims by moving from general premises to particular details; in that sense, they share a mode of rhetorical presentation, if not of substantive argument. One historicist critic may define the general in terms of historical conventions (e.g. the religious values of a given time and place) and another may define it in terms of analytical categories (e.g. the sociological significance of religion as a human activity). To complicate matters, a third scholar at the very same moment might use 'historicism' as a dismissive label to attack a study that (in his or her mind) sacrifices the subtleties of a text to some over-arching and thus benighted theoretical perspective. Many scholars who find historicism abhorrent would argue that recovering the past is best accomplished through the careful amassing and coordinating of verifiable facts. For them, a period or culture must be represented (to use the inevitable cliché) 'in its own terms', that is, without distortions of anachronistic perspective or belief.

Historicism has come more recently to signal the belief that one must scrutinize the premises of one's own work and, more pointedly, that one must recognize the subtle and inescapable interactions between the historical moment at which one writes as a critic and the historical moment about which one writes. Context becomes a more complex and shiftable notion than mere historical background, more problematic than placing *Beowulf* beside the treasures unearthed at Sutton Hoo so that one can 'do' both the poetry and the archeology. To offer a context means also to engage the ways in which the contingencies of one's own historical moment impinge – sometimes for the better, sometimes for the worse, but inescapably so – on one's critical practice.

This belief that our representations of the past do not go untouched by our own condition may help to shape a more careful, because more skeptical and less universalizing, historicism. To say 'not untouched' here is to admit that the personal can and does shape historicist practice without conceding the extreme position that representations of the past are inescapably subjective and thus without truth value. This nihilist position is alluring in its stringency, but it forces its adherents to argue the theoretically pure though finally sterile claim that the past is unknowable and untouchable. By contrast, the pragmatism of Georges Duby suggests how it is that research gets done and books get written: 'The historian's work is therefore never more than an approximation, the free response of one individual to the scattered vestiges of the past.'[2] If one may cite a personal instance of authorial condition informing historical study, the uneasy fascination with cultural dislocation that runs through my *Migration and Mythmaking in Anglo-Saxon England* (1989) had much to do with my move from New York City to Oklahoma as it was being written.[3] Whether this means that the book's arguments about the ways Anglo-Saxons remembered and retold their ancestral migration stories reflect authorial predicament more accurately than historical reality is for others to judge.

Some scholars will find the claim that one's own time and place are central to historicist criticism too obvious to mention, while others will find it too solipsistic to accept. Such responses follow at least in part from where – intellectually as well as geographically – one practices the work of Old English scholarship. North Americans, to make a rough generalization, seem more likely to hold the first view, and Europeans the second. British scholars split more evenly among themselves, partly along generational lines. That there is a necessary self-consciousness to historicist work must be stressed, if only to define and defend it against those who believe the study of the past can yield objective or valuable findings only when freed from the contaminations of the present. The claim that the present touches on, and even invigorates, our sense of the past may seem less troubling when made by a scholar from a previous generation, one adept in the practice of a New Critical medievalism. As

Charles Muscatine wrote in 1957: 'Our own generation has necessarily its peculiar sensibility. To use such terms as "irony", "ambiguity", "tension", and "paradox" in describing Chaucer's poetry is to bring to the subject our typical mid-century feeling for an unresolved dialectic.'[4]

At the end of that same century, as it makes its turn into a new millennium, the desire to historicize our literary and cultural practice suggests our uncertainty that there is a workable connection between past and present. Our position is less Muscatine's 'unresolved dialectic' than a haunting anxiety that the past, even if it can be reimagined or recovered, will be mute when we press it to speak to our moment. But the consequence of not making that connection is great, and we must admit the sting in Walter Benjamin's observation: 'Every image of the past that is not recognized by the present as one of its own concerns threatens to disappear irretrievably.'[5] If we fail to make pre-Conquest England a subject of interest, even in a quietly modest way, we risk trivializing ourselves as antiquarians who collect lore about the past as magpies collect bright, shiny objects. Nor is it clear that tracing the traditions which shaped Anglo-Saxon scholarship can ensure our place in the larger discipline of literary and cultural studies. However valuable it is to unriddle our scholarly pedigree – and Allen J. Frantzen has shown vividly in his *Desire for Origins* (1990) that it is indeed a fascinating and complex tale – this form of historical inquiry cannot by itself transform us into engaged cultural critics. For it threatens to become a kind of meta-commentary which finally does not engage the original object of study (the Anglo-Saxons and their culture) or the appropriations of that study for political and literary purposes in later periods. At moments, this inquiry can seem a search for precursors, an attempt to learn how earlier scholars defined themselves as Anglo-Saxonists in more flourishing eras so that we might recover in our own dark time (as it may seem to us) the prestige our field once had in English departments. As readers of Old English poetry know, the trope of genealogy measures both nostalgia for the past and anxiety for the future.

Faced with these often contradictory theories and forms of historicism, it can be useful to consider how Anglo-Saxonists of two previous generations worked within the scope of historicist scholarship: Ritchie Girvan in *Beowulf and the Seventh Century* (1935) and Bernard F. Huppé in *Doctrine and Poetry: Augustine's Influence on Old English Poetry* (1959). As his title implies, Girvan argues we possess a sufficiently coherent knowledge of Anglo-Saxon England in the seventh century to recognize that the imagined depictions of social and religious life in *Beowulf* correspond to the cultural milieu of that period rather than to that of the earlier time when the poem takes place. It thus must follow that *Beowulf* comes from the seventh century and, more locally, from the kingdom of Northumbria. Girvan's strategy is to present a portrait of social conditions in seventh-century England as a theoretical model and then to find these same conditions depicted in *Beowulf*. Huppé's study, as its title announces, draws its exegetical-patristic framework from Augustine's writings in order to set Old English poetry within a larger category of medieval texts created to instill the Christian ideal of *caritas* or 'charity' in an audience.

Of the two, Huppé is more avowedly historicist. He argues that modern readers must place Old English poetry within the governing and inescapable theological beliefs of a larger Christian culture:

The Christian theory of poetry was clear and definite; it was subscribed to by all Christians. The practice of Latin Christian poetry was in accord with the theory. Caedmon's English poetry was also in accord with the theory. Since the body of OE poetry is Christian, it should be studied, whatever its subject, from the point of view of basic Christian theory and practice.[6]

In this study, the patristic tradition provides a normative — some might say an overly determined — context for reading Old English texts. If read from a certain distance, Girvan and Huppé seem to differ more in polemical stance than in historiographical vision: one idealizes social milieu, the other patristic background. And each does so to assert that the past can only be reconstructed within a large interpretive schema. Both believe that the text must be read within the accepted or, from another perspective, the hegemonic ideas and forms of its culture. In this way, they seem to differ fundamentally from formalist critics, such as J. R. R. Tolkien, who practiced a more ahistoricist reading of Old English texts.

The claims of Girvan and Huppé can appear disarmingly naive to later readers whose historicist practices have been shaped by such originary texts as Friedrich Nietszche's 'On the Uses and Disadvantages of History for Life' (1874) or Walter Benjamin's 'Theses on the Philosophy of History' (1940) as well as the works of New Historicist critics who revitalized the study of the English as well as the American Renaissance starting in the early 1980s.[7] Viewed through the filter of a stringent historicist theory and method, Girvan's and Huppé's books seem valuable today as object lessons about the great temptation facing those who practice any variety of historicism: the slippery, if convenient, elision of texts and contexts to confirm an argument. Or, more simply, the desire to remake the past so that it conforms to one's own reading of a text.

More pointedly, a contemporary historicist critic would argue that Girvan offers little independent or non-literary evidence for his reconstruction of seventh-century Anglo-Saxon England, and in fact creates his vision of that era largely from *Beowulf*. In this circular exercise, Girvan draws from *Beowulf* to create a seventh-century context that he will then use to date that text. Willing to conflate context and text, environment and poem, Girvan can easily make *Beowulf* read as a work of the seventh century. What seem at first glance to be two critical acts are in his practice one and the same, and thus become mutually confirming. A revisionist critic might further identify the confusions of Girvan's historicism by noting that others who use this same method of conflating poetic text and historical context do so to argue very different dates for the poem.[8] This critic would therefore question the assumption (often unacknowledged) that underlies attempts to date the poem from its internal representations of social milieu: that we can derive an accurately datable sense of historical context for the poem from sources that are independent of the poem and thus sufficiently reliable or objective to allow us in turn to draw on them to date and place the poem. Put another way, our context for *Beowulf* has been as fluid (and often, as self-serving) as our text of *Beowulf*. Yet just as we have grown uneasy about emending the text of *Beowulf* or other medieval works to suit our readings, so we should grow cautious about reconstructing self-confirming contexts for them. The critical skepticism that characterizes current historicist practice should make us suspicious of any attempt to conflate text and context to date or otherwise interpret *Beowulf*.

Huppé's method in *Doctrine and Poetry* invites a similar, though not quite identical, critique. His book is based, a revisionist critic might argue, on a master-narrative about medieval culture that is at once modern and fabricated: the assumption that all of its texts have the same didactic intention and can be opened with the same key of patristic exegesis. To an unconverted reader, this historicism distorts the relations between text and context by creating a single context for all texts and thus, at least potentially, reducing them all to a single text. (And, of course, the vernacular, Germanic text will suit this *a priori* Latin, Christian context with an easy exemplarity!) The historicism of patristic-exegetical critics distances, and often betrays, the past by ignoring its competing strands of belief, practice, expression, of all that circulates within and makes for a messy, living culture.

Reducing *Beowulf and the Seventh Century* and *Doctrine and Poetry: Augustine's Influence on Old English Poetry* to their barest claims ignores much in each that is valuable. Doing so may even repeat the error ascribed to them, that of reshaping the records of the past to justify an interpretive position. Still, their uneasy and troubling notions of historicism demand scrutiny because each has in its own way given that critical approach a suspect, if not a bad, name in Old English studies. Those who would today practice a historicist criticism in Old English studies must guard against the danger of being too certain that they know what the Anglo-Saxons thought and felt about their lives and their world. They must guard against the overly generalized and all-encompassing forms of reading used by critics such as Girvan and Huppé. At the same time they must have sufficient regard for historical study to reject the facile if tempting theoretical position that categorizes any attempt to speak with some certainty about the past as an act of cultural imperialism.

Perhaps the most salutary means of finding one's way through these critical arguments as they have shaped Anglo-Saxon studies is to return to the article that all later critical studies in the field have had to confront: J. R. R. Tolkien's '*Beowulf*: The Monsters and the Critics' (1936). At first reading, this essay seems opposed to any historical or historicist approach, and that may finally be its position. But there is much in it that can be read as articulating a covert historicism. In sentence after memorable sentence, Tolkien rode a necessary, though finally not sufficient, thesis that *Beowulf* had for too long been read merely as a historical source and not as a poem of great brilliance. In a much-quoted statement, he pronounced: '*Beowulf* has been used as a quarry of fact and fancy far more assiduously than it has been studied as a work of art.'[9] Written in the early days of the then-new New Criticism, with its vision of the literary work as atemporal artifact (what some American critics would call a 'verbal icon' or 'well-wrought urn'), Tolkien's argument promised to rescue *Beowulf* from historical drudges and dotty antiquarians.

Tolkien's essay has cast a long shadow over the criticism of *Beowulf* and thus, because of that poem's central place in the canon, over that of other Old English texts. Even the formidable Dorothy Whitelock, whose life-work stands as a monument to the historical study of literary texts, was compelled to shape her *Audience of Beowulf* (1951) around Tolkien's terms. She expressed the hope that *Beowulf* could tell us about the time and place of its composition but added that 'this does not mean I wish to use the poem merely as a quarry for social history. I propose to use the poem of *Beowulf* to elucidate the poem of *Beowulf*', that is, to treat it as a literary work.[10] Her use of the word 'poem' three times in two sentences seems a tacit homage to Tolkien, as does her nervous allusion to his dismissive term 'quarry'. Whitelock's response to Tolkien was not unique; other historicist readers of Old English texts offered similar concessions, though few did so as forthrightly. In retrospect, one clearly sees that Tolkien's essay did reshape the criticism of Old English texts, though arguably most deeply in the work a long generation later of such American critics as Stanley B. Greenfield and Edward B. Irving, Jr.

By unashamedly insisting on the literary quality of *Beowulf*, Tolkien opened the way for more sophisticated readings of other Old English texts. After him, historical critics who cited *Beowulf* or other Old English poems as evidence for the social organization or religious practices of Anglo-Saxon England risked being thought naive. If *Beowulf* were a masterpiece, only a churl would loot it for evidence. Looking back from a longer distance, those of us who attempt a historicist practice must finally be grateful to Tolkien. He freed the criticism of *Beowulf* from such side issues as the veracity of the poem's historical reportage or the theological orthodoxy of its doctrine. He made it possible to consider more intriguing questions such as the historical sense found in Old English texts (their own historicity) or the ways in which these texts participated in the larger work of cultural formation. The most successful explorations of *Beowulf*'s own historicity, for example, have been accomplished by subtle, even elegant readers of the poetry who argued from Tolkien's position. To cite two memorable examples, Robert W. Hanning's '*Beowulf* as Heroic History' and Roberta Frank's 'The *Beowulf* Poet's Sense of History' balance scrupulous attention to the text with an ironic awareness of historical contingency.

One might well argue that critics such as Hanning and Frank are successful because they respond to Tolkien's more nuanced claims, those we are likely to forget as we savor (or wince at) his depiction of historical critics as creatures out of 'Jabberwocky'. Tolkien had his own deep bias in arguing that the *Beowulf* poet possessed what he called an 'instinctive historical sense'. From this quasi-biological claim, Tolkien could conclude that

in *Beowulf* we have, then, an historical poem about the pagan past, or an attempt at one – literal historical fidelity founded on modern research was, of course, not attempted. It is a poem by a learned man writing of old times, who looking back on the heroism and sorrow feels in them something permanent and something symbolical.

While Tolkien invests the *Beowulf* poet with an instinctive historical sense, he does not do so on the basis of a carefully historicized study of the poem (such as Frank offers in 'The *Beowulf* Poet's Sense of History'), but rather through an essentialist claim about the author's assumed identity: 'The author has used an instinctive historical sense – a part indeed of the *ancient English temper* (and not unconnected with its reputed melancholy), of which *Beowulf* is a supreme expression; but he has used it with a poetical and not an historical object' (emphasis added).[11]

Tolkien's essentialist claim about the English sense of history may be historicized as much within his gloomy sense of England in the mid-1930s as within his critical reading of *Beowulf*. Nevertheless, this claim freed him from the need to offer any detailed historicist study of the text or context of *Beowulf*. That this historical instinct is an aspect of the national poetic character – especially as it resonates along a thousand years of native poetry from *Beowulf* through Spenser and Shakespeare down to Tolkien's own student W. H. Auden – seems too evident to deny. If that is so, then Tolkien can be said to have proved his point about *Beowulf*. Yet there is, finally, a certain tension in Tolkien's position. He wanted to read *Beowulf* as historical in spirit, as finding its theme in the distance between a fifth-century Germania and a later Anglo-Saxon England, but he also asserted that this distance could not be registered by historians. And in some sense he was right. It required historians or historicist critics of a less positivistic variety than Tolkien attacked to read this distance in *Beowulf* as something more than a moodily elegiac evocation of a lost time and place, of a pagan golden age. For Tolkien, the text's historicity was not to be taken as a quarry for cultural facts or antiquarian bric-a-brac, but as a sustained meditation on the past's richly subtle senses of its own past. Or, as Roberta Frank notes: 'Philosophically, in order to have a sense of history at all, the *Beowulf* poet had to hold certain premises about man and his role on earth. . . . Above all, he had to believe that pagan Germanic legend had intellectual value and interest for Christians.'[12]

Locating this sense of the past within the past, this meta-historicism, within the textual fabric of *Beowulf* and other Old English works is perhaps the most valuable advance recent critics have made from Tolkien's position of 1936. One of the most influential works to engage this issue, Fred C. Robinson's *Beowulf and the Appositive Style* (1985), begins its critical genealogy by acknowledging Tolkien's essay:

> there is considerable common ground among critics of the poem, especially those who, like me, start from a general acceptance of the landmark essay by J. R. R. Tolkien, '*Beowulf*: The Monsters and the Critics'. Central to this Tolkienian view of the poem is the contrast between the time and milieu of the poet and the time and milieu of the characters in his poem.[13]

Robinson's historicist move, the one that takes criticism beyond Tolkien, that explodes the implicit theoretical claims of '*Beowulf*: The Monsters and the Critics', is to explore this contrast and temporal distance not through the 'facts' of historians but more specifically through the enriching ambiguities of the poem's language. (For all that Tolkien seemed to urge this sort of literary-linguistic analysis, he did little of it in his essay.) The poetic work of setting two related but distinct cultural moments into a telling relation is accomplished (as Robinson argues) not so much through the poet's use of milieu (as in Girvan) or the imposed doctrinal formulations of the church (as in Huppé) but rather in the very language of the poem. Through the shifting senses of words, through the historically evocative synonymies or appositions of such key terms as *metod, dryhten, mægen*, and the like, the poet registers the temporal and thus cultural distance between pagan Germania and Christian England. Robinson's move is formalist in method, as it follows from the verbal texture of the poem, but it is historicist in intent, as it addresses the senses of the past carried by that verbal texture. *Beowulf and the Appositive Style* demonstrates Dominick LaCapra's necessary observation that the methods of historicism and formalism 'arose together historically, feed off one another, and may be combined in the work of the same figure'.[14] Put another way, the philologically trained critic committed to historicist issues can make of formalism not an end in itself but a set of interpretive tactics, a range of questions by which to engage the linguistic codes of cultural texts.

To return to the opening claim of this essay: the facts that may well help us best historicize Old English texts come first from the language in which these same texts are written and then from the physical manuscript contexts in which they survive. Beyond the standard philological reason for making this argument, that one must know the language well to read its texts well, there is a historicist reason for urging a linguistically informed criticism. As one reads the texts and culture of Anglo-Saxon England, one often despairs at its lack of thick documentary evidence such as survives from later periods of English history. In the relative absence of such archival materials, Anglo-Saxonists must turn to the language itself and perform a kind of linguistic ethnography or archaeology, a reading of the culture through its words and its grammar. In a direct sense, historicist criticism of Old English texts is most likely to be illuminating when it grounds itself in a sense of the language and yet also ventures beyond the self-imposed proscriptions of traditional philology.

The proof-text for most critical questions about Old English texts, as must now be evident, has been and remains *Beowulf*. The emphasis on *Beowulf,* in the critical tradition as well as in this essay, follows from various factors: it is the longest poetic text in Old English by a good measure; it has been well edited for a longer time than most other Old English texts; and, most crucially, it redeems Anglo-Saxon England from the taint of Dark Age barbarism by giving it a place in the literary tradition which begins with *Gilgamesh. Beowulf* has been the inescapable text for Anglo-Saxonists committed to varieties of historicist criticism for yet another reason. In its being the poem poses a pressing historical question: it is a work written in English for an English audience yet it depicts a culture far removed in time and place. Or, to put the matter more starkly, *Beowulf* tempts historicist critics precisely because it never uses a phrase like *Engla land*.

Beowulf poses its own riddle by not making all the overt claims about national identity that historical epics are usually said to make. What kind of poem is this that deeply engrains a sense of the past within its past, that honors the attempt to record the past through the performances of a scop or the recitals of a hero but never unambiguously locates the value of that past for an English audience? Such questions, as they define the distinguishing, culturally contingent aspects of *Beowulf,* have made it deeply attractive to those engaged in historicist studies of pre-Conquest England. But it is good to remember that *Beowulf* is not alone in its allure. Indeed, as one contemplates the ways in which various forms of historicism can inform our reading of Anglo-Saxon culture, it is texts other than *Beowulf* that can seem most immediately engaging.

For the sake of difference, I will start with a work of prose – if a running, interlinear gloss can be characterized as prose – that many of us first met early in our dealings with Old English and thus may be tempted to think ourselves done with: Ælfric's *Colloquy.* As Stanley B. Greenfield and Daniel G. Calder observe in their *New Critical History of Old English Literature*: 'The *Colloquy* is, perhaps, the most famous prose text from the Anglo-Saxon period; most students become acquainted with it early in their study of the language.'[15] Ælfric's work or, more often, excerpts from it appear in Old English textbooks; it is frequently evoked to add a touch of local color to descriptions of Anglo-Saxon life; and correspondingly it is rarely quoted in scholarly studies. It remains today the elementary text it was written to be: a transparent piece of social mimesis for young readers. Yet the ways in which we present and read the *Colloquy* as an independent Old English text are deeply misleading; by failing to print the Latin text it glosses we distance the work from its didactic and thus its social contexts. It may be even more misleading to print the Old English and Latin texts together, as does G. N. Garmonsway, with the Old English set in larger print as the main text and the Latin set in smaller print as the gloss. This reversal of emphasis and function between text and gloss reflects our desire to make the *Colloquy* into an Old English rather than a Latin composition. This choice allows us to teach the *Colloquy* as an Old English text about students as we teach Old English to our students. At bottom, it can be a self-referential academic joke.

That we should dehistoricize the *Colloquy* by printing it simply as an Old English text seems all the more remarkable when we consider how frequently the work is offered as trustworthy and vivid evidence for the Anglo-Saxon period. Consider this sentence from Garmonsway's edition that I and many others swallowed as undergraduates: 'To-day the work is chiefly of interest for the picture it presents of the life and activities of the middle and lower classes of Anglo-Saxon society, concerning which Old English literature is, in the main, silent.' Or this sentence from Kevin Crossley-Holland's widely used *The Anglo-Saxon World*: 'As we read its simple prose, we meet the ordinary unsung people of Anglo-Saxon England . . .'.[16] Given recent critical concerns with class, gender, and (most elusive for Anglo-Saxonists) race, the *Colloquy* promises to be a work of central, even unique value. And so it can be, but only if we reject the usual and rather naive view of it as transparent social representation.

We should not be so hasty to seize on the *Colloquy*'s depictions of plowmen, shepherds, hunters, fishermen, salters, bakers, merchants, and the like as accurate portraiture, as an eleventh-century anticipation of Henry Mayhew's sociological reportage in *London Labour and the London Poor* (1861–2). We must first resituate the *Colloquy* within its Latin text and, more crucially, its context of Latin didacticism. In doing so, we become more alert to the fact that its speakers are young boys of undesignated and presumably diverse social backgrounds playing at various occupational roles so that they may learn a language necessary for sacred purposes. That language will in turn grant them entry into a clerical class and thus distance them from being plowmen, shepherds, hunters, fishermen, salters, bakers, merchants, and the like. The *Colloquy* does not represent people fixed in, or even representative of, class and occupation, but rather records and yet also participates in the making of an elite class as it is defined by language and learning. A historicized reading of the *Colloquy* yields a text about the ways in which young boys were trained to enter the least fixed (or perhaps, most permeable) of the three social orders in Anglo-Saxon England: those who work, who pray, who fight. For it was only in the clerical order, the one that prayed, that membership was not irrevocably fixed by the literal circumstances of birth.[17]

This kind of historicist reading would also register the ways in which the *Colloquy* presents the site where class and power were negotiated and demarcated linguistically in Anglo-Saxon England: the monastic classroom where boys began to leave their vernacular Old English behind to master the sacred language of Latin. As the first student in the *Colloquy* says to the teacher, after explaining how he and his fellows spend many hours each day singing and reading texts: 'sed tamen uellem interim discere sermocinari latina lingua' ('ac þeahhwæþere ic wolde betwenan leornian sprecan on leden gereorde', 'nevertheless I wish in the meantime to learn to speak the Latin language', lines 15–16). That the teacher asks his students if they had been beaten that day for dilatory conduct or the like seems, in this context, more ominous than the usual donnish humor. Indeed the reference to the beating of students – 'Uultis flagellari in discendo?' ('Wille beswungen on leornunge?', 'Do you want to be beaten in your studies?', line 7) – reminds us of the discipline (in all senses of the term) within the Anglo-Saxon schoolroom. It is thus not at all too extreme to suggest that Ælfric purposely had his students play at being hunters, shepherds, and the like to induce them to learn to speak Latin, that is, to persuade them that by sweating out conjugations and glossary lists they might thereby renounce lives of ordinary physical labor and enter lives of spiritual discipline. Quite tellingly, Ælfric has his boys complain vividly about their fictional roles. The plowman, for example, works in the fields all day, then must feed and water his oxen, and finally carry out their dung. No wonder he says to the teacher: 'Etiam, magnus labor est, quia non sum liber' ('Geleof, micel gedeorf hit ys, forþam ic neom freoh', 'Sir, it is great labor because I am not free', line 35). Ælfric portrayed plowmen, hunters, and the like in order to lead his students to renounce that world and not (as we might want to believe) to give his boyish readers some pedagogical play or us some historical color for our background studies of Anglo-Saxon England.

The *Colloquy* is a more compelling text about the means by which members of an elite group acquired social and spiritual power than any Old English poem could be, precisely because it depicts the basis of power in a multilingual site. It is therefore not at all surprising that someone did gloss Ælfric's Latin with Old English, for that allowed easier access to the language of power and thus increased the text's force as a social instrument or, to use another term, as a *translatio* both linguistic and social. We should also notice that the worldly occupations played by students in the *Colloquy* are typically reserved for males, and serve as yet another reminder that the work was meant for an audience of young boys learning to enter a male clerical order, learning 'sicut decet monachum' ('swa swa dafnað munuce', 'as befits a monk', line 296).

As texts within a culture shift between languages they take on different functions. Ælfric's *Colloquy* reminds us of this when we place it in its context of Latin as the language of power, spirituality, learning. Perhaps we can dimly sense the effectiveness of Ælfric's work in nego-

tiating the cultural shift from vernacular idiom to learned language
when we note that modern editors include the *Colloquy* in textbooks for
much the same reason, except that the vernacular at stake is Modern
English and the scholarly language is Old English. As for the interlinear
gloss, students pencil that into their printed editions the night before so
that they can translate fluently from Old to Modern English in class.
And perhaps the discipline in these classrooms is less coercive because
more voluntarily accepted.

The ways in which modern scholars have leached the Latin context
and function out of Ælfric's *Colloquy* can be read as object lessons
about ignoring the multilingual valences of Anglo-Saxon texts. This
reconsideration seems especially necessary if we are to ask newer and
more historicized questions, such as 'How did the Anglo-Saxons construct their sense of place, both literal and cultural, from the map of the
world?' We might thus ask which Latin texts were turned into Old
English, not so much to serve the needs of a Latin Christianity trans-
planted into Anglo-Saxon England as to provide a sense of the cultural
other or elsewhere that enabled Anglo-Saxon readers to look beyond
their own cultural region.

Perhaps that culture's most diverse and complex representation of a
world beyond its own insular bounds may be found in the cultural atlas
we normally designate as London, BL, Cotton Vitellius A.xv. This manuscript contains three Old English prose texts – a fragmentary *Life of St.*
Christopher, Wonders of the East, the *Letter of Alexander to Aristotle* –
and two Old English poems, *Beowulf* and *Judith.* Interpretations of the
design and purpose of this manuscript have turned notoriously on the
presence of *Beowulf.* Kenneth Sisam concluded his influential essay, for
example, by saying of the manuscript: 'And if a cataloguer of those days
had to describe it briefly, he might well have called it "Liber de diversis
monstris, anglice".'[18] Yet would anyone have felt the need to see this
manuscript as a book of monsters if it did not contain *Beowulf*? The
looming presence of *Beowulf* in the manuscript forces us, as Sisam con-
cedes, to ignore *Judith* because it portrays no literal monsters, or else to
retrofit Holofernes into a spiritual monster of lust, drunkenness, or
(from a more recent perspective) imperialism. And all of which is worth
doing only because one wants an immediate manuscript context for
Beowulf and its monsters. But if we go back to Sisam's mock-rubric for
the manuscript, we can take the *anglice* which modifies *liber* as an

ironic and salutary reminder that not one of its texts is set in England. The *Life of St. Christopher, Wonders of the East,* and *Letter of Alexander to Aristotle* provide tantalizing evidence for the cultural work that the Anglo-Saxons did to locate themselves within Christian geography. Just as these prose works are translations from Latin to be read in the vernacular, so they are translations of the culturally alien or distant 'other' to be placed within the setting of the familiar world, that is, within the confines of the native vernacular. That they are, for us, inventions or fictions does not deprive them of historical value as texts for reading the ethnography of cultural and geographical belief in Anglo-Saxon England.

Treating the prose *Wonders of the East* and *Letter of Alexander* not as codicological glosses for *Beowulf* but instead as valuable ethnographic representations does challenge our usual disciplinary hierarchy of text and context. Rather than simply honor the vernacular poetic masterpiece as the object of critical desire, this challenge treats as worthy of study these sometimes sensationalistic, often tedious Old English versions of minor Latin works that lack even the saving merit of having been included among those texts most necessary for all men to know, as identified by King Alfred in his Preface to the Old English translation of Gregory's *Regula pastoralis.* There are signs, in some recent examples of our critical practice, that these Old English prose texts might be receptive to varieties of historicist criticism, especially one informed by Edward Said's *Orientalism* (1978). These readings would be most illuminating, I think, if they recognized that Anglo-Saxon Orientalism had less to do with colonizing the other than with registering the unnerving recognition of a world beyond — and in many ways different from — the provinces of Germania. Such readings would also serve a larger purpose in the discipline of correcting the bias toward nineteenth- and twentieth-century texts that marks most post-colonial theory. In this way, historicist studies of earlier peoples and periods can challenge the tendency of literary and cultural theory to construct master narratives that position themselves above contingencies of time and place.

The prose depictions of elsewhere and its monsters in Cotton Vitellius A.xv may have provided contemporary readers with the same *frisson* as do depictions of extra-terrestrial life and its aliens in our science fiction. Both genres unsettle readers by positing that there are places and beings out there unlike what we know here at home precisely because they metamorphose what we know here at home. As they represent monsters both human and animal, these works revise their readers' sense of what defines us here at home. If we consider the various works of Cotton Vitellius A.xv in this light, then we may see that by depicting regions in continental Europe, the Middle East, and Asia, they establish a vivid, expansive, and sometimes cautionary sense of place for an audience at home in Anglo-Saxon England. They form a *compilatio* in the sense that Martin Irvine uses the term: 'the selection of materials from the cultural library so that the resulting collection forms an *interpretive* arrangement of texts and discourse'.[19] For its time, this *compilatio* offered a 'modern' sense of place: that Anglo-Saxon England had become a cultural region where no monsters were immediately present, or one where monsters were distanced through their portrayal as ethnographic constructs. But this 'modern' reading of Cotton Vitellius A.xv is possible only if we take seriously those neglected works of Old English prose in the manuscript, the ones that have seemed embarrassing and disreputable to Anglo-Saxonists unless they could be redeemed as the proximate context for the unique text of *Beowulf*.

Reading Ælfric's *Colloquy* with a renewed sensitivity to the ways it depicts the creation of a clerical class makes it valuable for establishing a larger sense of social dynamics in Anglo-Saxon England. Reversing the order of priority in Cotton Vitellius A.xv, so that the revered poem becomes the context for the Old English texts of the *Wonders of the East* and the *Letter of Alexander to Aristotle*, has the welcome effect of forcing us to reconsider some of our assumptions about Old English canonicity. Could it be that the Anglo-Saxons thought these prose texts comparable to *Beowulf* as entertainment, or even preferred them? I am far from convinced by this last possibility, but it is invigorating to see that if we make what has been for *us* context (the prose in the manuscript) into the text of critical study, then we can glimpse a set of cultural questions and aesthetic preferences quite different from those we have traditionally attributed to the Anglo-Saxons. Put another way, this critical approach reflects the concern of historicist critics to trace connections between the various levels and sectors within cultural groups. At the very least, asking these questions about Cotton Vitellius A.xv reminds us that the value we place on *Beowulf* in our reconstructed histories of Anglo-Saxon England may say as much (if not more) about our vision of the culture than about that culture's vision of itself.

Reading Old English texts in a more critical and a more historicized way can also counter those who would appropriate them for a very different context in contemporary American politics. To illustrate this point, I reverse what Steven Justice has wickedly called 'the New Historicist two-step': the practice of opening one's essay with a telling anecdote and then moving to a canonical text.[20] My closing anecdote comes from the context of personal experience. In 1993, I received a manila envelope which had as its return address a post office box in Parma, Ohio. Inside was a flier that asked 'Are you a person who's not afraid to consider heretical ideas which scare the pants off those who think only "approved" thoughts?' and a copy of the forty-eight-page 'National Vanguard Books Catalog No. 15'. The language of the flier and catalog reminded me for a moment of 1930s leftist rhetoric. My hope that this mailing might have come from a relic Trotskyite cell outside of Cleveland was dashed when I opened the catalog to find Nora Chadwick's *The Celts*, Dorothy Whitelock's *The Beginnings of English Society*, J. M. Wallace-Hadrill's *The Long-Haired Kings*, R. W. V. Elliott's *Runes* as well as translations of *Beowulf, Njal's Saga, The Mabinogion*, and the like.

My scholarly vanity aroused, I turned the pages in hopes of finding my own *Migration and Mythmaking in Anglo-Saxon England*. I did not find it, I am relieved to say, because what I did find was books denying the Holocaust such as *Did Six Million Really Die?* and *The Hoax of the Twentieth Century*, as well as histories of Nazi Germany such as *Kunst in Deutschland*, 1933–1945 (in three volumes) and *Campaign in Russia: Waffen-SS on the Eastern Front*. The catalog also lists translations of Hitler's *Mein Kampf*: one (the blurb reads) 'accurate, but marred by anti-Hitler introductions and derogatory footnotes' and the other with 'no hostile comments, but the translation is not as faithful to the original text'.

This catalog, with its rancid and hateful politics, staked a claim that goes far beyond the usual academic position-taking: that the texts and contexts of Anglo-Saxon England are essential, even originary, to a racist, anti-semitic, and fascist politics in the United States. There to support this claim were Bede's *History*, Old English poems, Icelandic sagas, as well as books — by Chadwick, Whitelock, Wallace-Hadrill, Elliott and others — that are fundamental to serious scholarship. The blurb 'advertising' the Penguin translation of *Beowulf* fairly represents the politics of this catalogue:

Prose translation of the great 8th-century Anglo-Saxon epic poem. Although ostensibly Christian in its outlook, *Beowulf* is essentially a pagan tale, reflecting the manly values and attitudes of our pre-Christian ancestors, rather than the Levantine [for which, read 'Jewish'] values and attitudes which replaced them. A gripping tale of courage and cowardice, loyalty and betrayal.

In this text one finds an answer to the challenge posed by the more politically charged advocates of New Historicism: What does our critical practice do to change the world in which we live? How is our scholarship of value to the society that supports it? If, as Jeffrey N. Cox and Larry J. Reynolds claim somewhat hyperbolically, 'the great project of historicist criticism is liberation', then rebutting the racialist appropriation of Anglo-Saxon texts does have larger social value.[21] The historicized study of a culture sometimes dismissed as the province of 'dead, white European males' could counter the racist-historical claims of those who print catalogs with *Beowulf* featured next to stickers reading 'Earth's Most Endangered Species: The White Race'.

I do not mean to imply that only those who call themselves 'new' or 'historicist' readers of Old English texts would be repelled by the National Vanguard Book Catalog. That would be as absurd as claiming that Anglo-Saxonists by their very nature must have some sneaking affinity with its politics. To the extent that Anglo-Saxonists of all critical schools are repelled by its attempt to recruit early medieval culture to its politics, and to the extent that we argue against it in all available forums, we are in perhaps the most vital way practicing a truly historicized criticism. For it thus becomes a criticism that relates the texts and contexts of our discipline to issues of our political and literary culture that go far beyond the culture wars of the academy. And yet, we must remember, that valuable work depends finally on our ability to read the language, texts, and all else that remains of the Anglo-Saxon English.

Notes

1 Iris Murdoch, *The Green Knight* (New York, 1995), p. 274; Irving Howe, *A Critic's Notebook*, ed. N. Howe (New York, 1994), p. 185. I read an earlier and much briefer version of this chapter at a session of the 1994 Modern Language Association organized by Helen Damico. I owe many thanks to Georgina Kleege, Carole Fink, Thomas A. Bredehoft, Timothy J. Lundgren, Stacy Klein, Mary Ramsey, and, most profoundly, Katherine O'Brien

O'Keeffe for carefully reading earlier drafts of this essay. I should acknowledge here the influence of Lee Patterson's argument that some New Historicist critics have demonized or colonized the Middle Ages in order to dramatize their claims for the Renaissance. As they trivialize and darken the Middle Ages with over-simple formulations, these New Historicists are, as Patterson shrewdly notes, anything but new and instead are doomed to repeat the founding myth of Renaissance Humanism. Patterson's portrayal of a Middle Ages marginalized by a Renaissance New Historicism can have the effect (unintended, I think) of marginalizing the culture of pre-Conquest England. Or so it can seem to one who searches for some notice of the period in Patterson's persuasive claims for the medieval. See 'On the Margin: Postmodernism, Ironic History, and Medieval Studies', *Speculum* 65 (1990), 87–108.

2 G. Duby, *History Continues*, trans. A. Goldhammer (Chicago, 1994), p. 47.

3 N. Howe, *Migration and Mythmaking in Anglo-Saxon England* (New Haven, 1989); and also, 'Oklahoma Stories', *Southwest Review* 80 (Spring/Summer 1995), 207–29.

4 *Chaucer and the French Tradition* (Berkeley, 1966; repr. of 1957 edn.), pp. 9–10.

5 W. Benjamin, *Illuminations*, ed. H. Arendt (New York, 1969), p. 255.

6 B. F. Huppé, *Doctrine and Poetry: Augustine's Influence on Old English Poetry* (New York, 1959), p. 239.

7 For these essays, see F. Nietzsche, *Untimely Meditations*, trans. R. J. Hollingdale (Cambridge, 1983), pp. 59–123; and Benjamin, *Illuminations*, pp. 253–64. As should be evident, I do not use 'historicism' in the narrow, somewhat misleading sense (that of nineteenth-century German positivist historians) which Benjamin attaches to it for his own polemical purposes. For introductions to New Historicism as well as anthologies of New Historicist practice, see the following representative examples among many possibilities: J. J. McGann, ed., *Historical Studies and Literary Criticism* (Madison, 1985); B. Thomas, *The New Historicism and Other Old-Fashioned Topics* (Princeton, 1991); J. N. Cox and L. J. Reynolds, eds., *New Historical Literary Study: Essays on Reproducing Texts, Representing History* (Princeton, 1993), especially Cox and Reynolds, 'The Historicist Enterprise', pp. 3–38, and K. O'Brien O'Keeffe, 'Texts and Works: Some Historical Questions on the Editing of Old English Verse', pp. 54–68; and M. J. M. Ezell and K. O'Brien O'Keeffe, eds., *Cultural Artifacts and the Production of Meaning: The Page, the Image, and the Body* (Ann Arbor, 1994).

8 For attempts to date *Beowulf* from its representations of social milieu and cultural practice, see D. Whitelock, *The Audience of Beowulf* (Oxford, 1951); K. S. Kiernan, *Beowulf and the Beowulf Manuscript* (New Brunswick, NJ, 1981); C. Chase, ed., *The Dating of Beowulf* (Toronto, 1981); and the critical survey by R. M. Liuzza, 'On the Dating of *Beowulf*' in *Beowulf: Basic Readings*, ed. P. S. Baker (New York, 1994), pp. 281–302.

9 J. R. R. Tolkien, 'Beowulf: The Monsters and the Critics', PBA 22 (1936), 245–95, at 245–6. For a provocative challenge to Tolkien's essay from a feminist-historicist position, see C. A. Lees 'Men and Beowulf', in Lees, ed., Medieval Masculinities: Regarding Men in the Middle Ages (Minneapolis, 1994), pp. 129–48. For historicist studies of Old English texts before Tolkien, see J. W. Bright's politically suggestive essay, 'The Relation of the Cædmonian Exodus to the Liturgy', MLN 27 (1912), 97–103; and the sociologically informed work of L. L. Schücking, most accessibly his 'The Ideal of Kingship in Beowulf', in An Anthology of Beowulf Criticism, ed. L. E. Nicholson (Notre Dame, IN, 1963), pp. 35–49.

10 See Whitelock, Audience of Beowulf, p. 3; for other major works by her, see 'Anglo-Saxon Poetry and the Historian', TRHS, 4th ser. 31 (1949), 75–94; and English Historical Documents. Volume 1: c. 500–1042, 2nd edn. (London, 1979). Whitelock's running commentaries in this volume are among the most valuable historicist studies of Old English texts ever written.

11 Tolkien, 'Beowulf: The Monsters and the Critics', pp. 269 and 247–48, respectively.

12 R. Frank, 'The Beowulf Poet's Sense of History' in The Wisdom of Poetry, ed. L. D. Benson and S. Wenzel (Kalamazoo, MI, 1982), pp. 53–65 at 56.

13 F. C. Robinson, Beowulf and the Appositive Style (Knoxville, 1985), p. 6. For other important works in this vein of revisionist historicism, see K. O'Brien O'Keeffe, Visible Song: Transitional Literacy in Old English Verse (Cambridge, 1990); and S. Lerer, Literacy and Power in Anglo-Saxon Literature (Lincoln, NE, 1991). See also, from the historian's point of view, P. Wormald's important essay 'Bede, Beowulf and the Conversion of the Anglo-Saxon Aristocracy' in Bede and Anglo-Saxon England, ed. R. T. Farrell, British Archaeological Reports 46 (1978), pp. 32–95.

14 D. LaCapra, Soundings in Critical Theory (Ithaca, 1989), p. 192. On this same issue, see also H. White, Tropics of Discourse: Essays in Cultural Criticism (Baltimore, 1978), especially chapter 4, 'Historicism, History, and the Figurative Imagination'.

15 S. B. Greenfield and D. G. Calder, A New Critical History of Old English Literature (New York, 1986), p. 86.

16 G. N. Garmonsway, ed., Ælfric's Colloquy (London, 1965), p. 1; K. Crossley-Holland, ed., The Anglo-Saxon World: An Anthology (Oxford, 1984), p. 211. References to the text of the Colloquy are to the Garmonsway edition.

17 For Ælfric's use of this theory of trifunctionality, see the discussion in G. Duby, The Three Orders: Feudal Society Imagined, trans. A. Goldhammer (Chicago, 1980), pp. 102–8. For conditions of English monastic life in Ælfric's time, see J. Burton, Monastic and Religious Orders in Britain, 1000–1300 (Cambridge, 1994), chapter 1; and a few vivid pages in D. Knowles, Saints and Scholars: Twenty-five Medieval Portraits (Cambridge, 1962), pp. 19–22.

18 K. Sisam, 'The Compilation of the Beowulf Manuscript' in Studies in the History of Old English Literature (Oxford, 1953), p. 96. For his comments on

Judith, see p. 67. On the issue of the monsters and the manuscript see now A. Orchard, *Pride and Prodigies: Studies in the Monsters of the Beowulf Manuscript* (Cambridge, 1995).

19 See M. Irvine, 'Medieval Textuality and the Archaeology of Textual Culture' in *Speaking Two Languages*, ed. A. J. Frantzen (Albany, 1991), pp. 181–210 at 193. Irvine further explores the historicist resonances of grammatical tropes such as *compilatio* in his *The Making of Textual Culture: 'Grammatica' and Literary Theory, 350–1100* (Cambridge, 1994), especially pp. 272–460 for Anglo-Saxon England.

20 S. Justice, review of *Chaucer's England*, ed. B. Hanawalt, *Speculum* 69 (1994), 791.

21 Cox and Reynolds, 'The Historicist Enterprise', p. 29. On the historical relations between Old English studies and Nazism, see D. Townsend, 'Alcuin's Willibrord, Wilhelm Levison, and the *MGH*' in *The Politics of Editing Medieval Texts*, ed. R. Frank (New York, 1993), pp. 107–30. Readers should also consult the haunting paragraphs at the close of the Preface to Wilhelm Levison's *England and the Continent in the Eighth Century* (Oxford, 1946), pp. vi–vii. In them, Levison suggests his political reasons for writing on this subject while living in England as a refugee from Nazi Germany.

5

Oral tradition

ANDY ORCHARD

•

When King Alfred the Great (871–99) composed the Preface to his translation of the *Pastoral Care* of Pope Gregory, so inaugurating an ambitious programme of educational reform, he was careful to begin with a
formal third-person opening ('King Alfred sends greetings . . .') borrowed from Latin epistolary style, before slipping almost immediately
into the first person ('I'), and to pepper his prose with Latin-derived
themes and motifs drawn directly from the very books which he considered 'most needful for all men to know'. Alfred's debt to a literate and
Latinate tradition in this context is both clear and unsurprising, spiced
with the zeal of the newly converted; as Asser, his biographer, makes
clear, the king learned to read in stages, and perhaps never learned to
write.[1] Much of his troubled life was lived without the benefit of Latin
books, but with a deep devotion to the songs and poems of his native
tongue.[2] Such poems, characterized by formulaic phrasing and alliterative effects, ultimately derived from an oral tradition in the pre-literate
Germanic past, although by Alfred's time such poems had already been
collected in manuscripts, as an episode related in Alfred's own biography makes clear. Asser tells us how the young Alfred was enchanted by
the golden letters of a manuscript version of such vernacular songs, and
that his mother offered it to whichever of her sons could learn it by
heart. Alfred, at that time apparently illiterate, duly learned the book
from listening to it read out loud, recited the poems, and won his prize.
In such ways Alfred's own life echoes the consistent and complex interactions between orality and literacy to be found in the composition,
transmission, and performance of the literature of Anglo-Saxon
England.

As a mark of Alfred's continuing devotion to the native literature of his own people, it is intriguing to note the extent to which aural effects closely associated with vernacular verse are found in Alfred's own Preface alongside the traces of his Latin learning. So, for example, after an introductory passage decrying the current state of (Latin) education in England, Alfred outlines the problems and his proposed solutions in four 'paragraphs', each of which is prefaced by a formulaic phrase: 'Da ic ða ðis eall gemunde ða gemunde ic . . . Đa ic ða ðis eall gemunde ða wundrade ic . . . Đa gemunde ic hu . . . Đa ic ða gemunde hu' ('When I remembered all this I remembered . . . When I remembered all this I was amazed . . . Then I remembered how . . . Then I remembered how'). Precisely the same technique of employing repeated diction aurally to mark off sections of a text is used in Old English verse, where it is but one of a number of ways in which vernacular poets used repeated sounds and words to impose a pattern on their discourse.[3]

A particularly rich combination of aural effects is found, fittingly, in a further passage in the same Preface where Alfred imagines the response of earlier generations of Anglo-Saxons to the then-current state of educational decay:

Ure ieldran, ða ðe ðas stowa ær hioldon, hie lufodon wisdom 7 ðurh ðone hie begeaton welan 7 us læfdon. Her mon mæg giet gesion hiora swæð, ac we him ne cunnon æfter spyrigean, 7 forðæm we habbað nu ægðer forlæten ge ðone welan ge ðone wisdom, forðæmðe we noldon to ðæm spore mid ure mode onlutan. (Sweet, *Pastoral Care*, p. 5)

[Our ancestors, who held these places previously, they loved wisdom, and with it they won wealth, and left it to us. Here one can still see their tracks, but we do not know how to follow after them, and because of that we have lost both the wealth and the wisdom, since we were unwilling to bend down to the trail with our minds.

The whole force of the passage is contained in a barrage of aural effects such as alliteration, paronomasia, rhyme, and assonance ('lufodon . . . læfdon'; 'spyrigean . . . spore'; 'forlæten . . . onlutan'; 'wisdom . . . welan . . . welan . . . wisdom'), in which repetition or near-repetition of sounds and words plays a crucial role, all of which effects can be closely paralleled in the vernacular verse tradition.[4]

Alfred's concern throughout the Preface to balance the requirements of traditional and, we may assume, ultimately oral presentation with those of the new literacy mirrors a tendency evident throughout the literature of Anglo-Saxon England to blend and combine elements from both Latin and vernacular traditions. The difficulty of distinguishing between 'oral' and 'written' elements in Old English literature is therefore a fundamental one, and underlies a range of other tensions between opposing concepts which help to define the field, notably those between verse and prose, secular and religious, and vernacular and Latin; such tensions are inevitably reflected in a literature which depicts the transition from an illiterate and secular society, which based its traditions on poetry composed orally and passed on in memory, to one in which literacy was introduced by a Christian religion which depended on the Book for its authority, and which encouraged (and to a large extent controlled) the spread of reading and the written record.

For over a century and a half scholars have noted that Old English verse is fundamentally formulaic, relying heavily on stock and repeated phrases, and debate has focused on the precise nature, significance, and function of such repetitious diction. In a series of articles and books published between 1886 and 1897, for example, Gregor Sarrazin noted striking verbal correspondences between *Beowulf* and the signed poems of Cynewulf, eventually concluding that the latter was the author of the former.[5] Other work from the same period by Eduard Sievers, comparing Old English poetic diction (particularly that of *Beowulf*) with that of other Germanic verse traditions, was held to point to a common Germanic poetic language preceding the arrival of the Anglo-Saxons in England. Such pieces of research, and other studies like them, which carried the conflicting implications that the language of the *Beowulf*-poet was at once an ancient relic of the pre-literate past and had some connection with the writings of a clearly literate and Latinate author such as Cynewulf, who signed his name in runes for what appears to be primarily visual effect, were wholly submerged in the immediate wake of the widespread application of the so-called 'oral-formulaic' theory to Old English poetry in the 1950s and 1960s. The logic of the oral-formulaic theory, which relied on a much more precise definition of formulaic phrasing than had been applied previously, seemed irresistible to many in its force and simplicity: Milman Parry and his student Albert Lord had sought to demonstrate that Homer's *Iliad* and *Odyssey* relied heavily on repeated formulas (now defined as 'a group of words which is regularly employed under the same metrical conditions to express a given essential idea'), and that similar techniques of formulaic composition characterized the epic verses of illiterate Serbian poets in the twentieth century; therefore (the reasoning went) Homer too was an illiterate bard.[6] Such an argument − which, it should be noted, relies on analogy − has proved attractive to many scholars, who have disseminated the theory in many diverse fields: a recent annotated bibliography of oral-formulaic theory and research documents its spread into well over a hundred language areas. Given the relatively small size of the extant corpus, the availability of a range of concordances, and the more recent possibility of employing computers on machine-readable texts, it is perhaps unsurprising that Old English should have provided one of the most densely studied of those areas; Alexandra Hennessey Olsen has provided an exhaustive survey of the application of the oral-formulaic theory to Old English.[7]

In 1953 Francis P. Magoun enthusiastically applied oral-formulaic theory to the verses of *Beowulf*, and concluded that the *Beowulf* poet was an oral poet too, arguing that

the recurrence in a given poem of an appreciable number of formulas or formulaic phrases brands the latter as oral, just as the lack of such repetitions marks a poem as composed in a lettered tradition. Oral poetry, it may be safely said, is composed entirely of formulas, large and small, while lettered poetry is never formulaic.[8]

The faulty logic implied by the final sentence is revealing: notwithstanding the rashness of the assumption that 'lettered poetry is never formulaic' or the claim, which goes far beyond anything suggested by Parry or Lord, that 'oral poetry . . . is composed entirely of formulas', the implied chain of thought which runs 'oral poetry is (generally) formulaic: *Beowulf* is formulaic, therefore *Beowulf* is an oral poem' is as dangerous as supposing that 'cats (generally) have four legs: my dog has four legs, therefore my dog is a cat'. Notwithstanding the problems implicit in the over-strict (not to say dogmatic) application of oral-formulaic theory in Old English, the importance of Magoun's work in introducing the concepts implied by the approach cannot be denied. For an illustration of the extent to which the diction of *Beowulf* is demonstrably formulaic (in Magoun's sense of the term), we need look no further than a self-contained passage from the much-analysed opening lines (*Beowulf* 4–11), with some of the more obvious formulas in italics, and parallels cited:[9]

Oft Scyld Scefing   *sceapena þreatum,*
monegum mægþum   meodosetla ofteah,   5
egsode eorl[as],   *syððan ærest wearð*
feasceaft funden;   he þæs frofre gebad,
weox under wolcnum   weorðmyndum þah,
oð þæt him æghwylc   *ymbsittendra*
ofer hronrade   hyran scolde   10
gomban gyldan;   þæt wæs god cyning!

[Often Scyld Sceafing deprived hosts of enemies from many peoples of their mead-benches, terrified the warriors, after he was first found helpless; he experienced comfort for that; he grew under the heavens, throve in honours until each of his neighbours over the whale's riding had to listen to him, to pay tribute: that was a splendid king!]

Evidence:

4b	to scipe sceohmod *sceaðena þreate*	*Jul* 672
5a	*manigre mægþe* geond þisne middangeard	*Beo* 75
	manigum mægþa geond þysne middangeard	*Beo* 1771
6b	inwitniða *syððan ærest wearð*	*Beo* 1947
8a	*weox þa under wolcnum* and wriðade	*Gen A* 1702
	wod under wolcnum to þæs þe he winreced	*Beo* 714
	weold under wolcnum ond his wigge beleac	*Beo* 1770
8b	werodes wisa *wurðmyndum spræc*	*Ex* 258
9b	*ymbesittendra* ænig ðara	*Beo* 2734
10a	*geond hranrade* inc hyrað eall	*Gen A* 205
	ofer swanrade secean wolde	*Beo* 200
10b	þære þe þam hæðenan *hyran scolde*	*Dan* 135
	hu ge heofoncyninge *hyran sceoldon*	*El* 367
	heaðorinca gehwilc *heran sceolde*	*Met* 9.45
11a	*gombon gieldan* ond gafol sellan	*Gen A* 1978
11b	glædne Hroðgar *ac þæt wæs god cyning*	*Beo* 863
	Geatum wealdan *þæt wæs god cyning*	*Beo* 2390

That ten out of the sixteen half-lines here exhibit some kind of formulaic phrasing, and that nine of the seventeen lines of supporting evidence cited should derive from *Beowulf* itself, underlines the extent to which the *Beowulf* poet relies on the repetition of particular phrases, defined by the half-line. The conclusion that *Beowulf* is in some sense a formulaic poem seems inescapable, but Magoun's more sweeping conclusions about the utterly distinctive nature of oral-formulaic composition, by comparison with composition pen in hand, have, naturally, not gone unchallenged. Indeed, Sarrazin's work alone on the extent to which the clearly literate Cynewulf relied on repeated diction ought to have raised questions about the validity of such an assertion, as can be illustrated simply by analysing in the same way a passage from the beginning of Cynewulf's *Christ II* (*Christ B* 440–9a):

> Nu ðu geornlice   gæstgerynum,   440
> mon se mæra,   modcræfte sec
> þurh sefan snyttro,   þæt þu soð wite
> hu þæt geeode,   þa se ælmihtiga
> acenned wearð   þurh clænne had,
> siþþan he Marian,   mægða weolman,   445
> mærre meowlan,   mundheals geceas,
> þæt þær in hwitum   hræglum gewerede
> englas ne oðeowdun,   þa se æþeling cwom,
> beorn in Betlem.

[Now, you, illustrious man, earnestly seek in the spiritual mysteries with strength of mind, through the wisdom of your soul, so that you truly know, how it came about when the Almighty was born through virginal state after he chose as protecting vessel Mary, the illustrious lady, the flower of maidens, that angels arrayed there in white garments did not appear, when the prince came, a warrior into Bethlehem.]

Evidence:

440a	þæt ic geornlice gode þegnode	*Gen A* 585
	ond him geornlice gæstgemyndum	*Guth* 602
	ongan þa geornlice gastgerynum	*El* 1147
440b	giedda gearosnottor gæstgerynum	*Christ B* 713
	in godcundum gæstgerynum	*Guth* 248
	þam ic georne gæstgerynum	*Guth* 1084
	geonge gencwidum, gastgerynum	*And* 858
	ðus gleawlice gastgerynum	*El* 189
	ongan þa geornlice gastgerynum	*El* 1147
441a	þeoden mæra þines ahredde	*Gen* 2145
	þeoden mæra þe to gewealde	*Jul* 86
442a	on sefan snyttro nu is sæl cumen	*And* 1165
	on sefan snyttro heo to salore eft	*El* 382
	ðurh sefan snyttro searoðonca hord	*CPPref* 7
442b	... swice ær he soð wite	*MSol* 170
	miht ðu me gesecgan þæt ic soð wite	*And* 603

443a	*ða þæt geeode* þæt se eadega wer	*Gen A* 1562
443b	icest þine yrmðo *þa se ælmihtiga*	*And* 1190
	elne unslawe *ða se ælmihtiga*	*Guth* 950
	wel la ðu eca *and ðu ælmihtiga*	*Met* 4.29
	ac þonne se eca *and se ælmihtiga*	*Met* 11.74
444a	*acenned wearð* cyninga wuldor	*El* 5
	acenned wearð cyninga wuldor	*El* 178
	acenned wearð in cildes had	*El* 775
444b	ferde to foldan *þurh fæmnan had*	*Sat* 493
	ær me lare onlag *þurh leohtne had*	*El* 1245
	acennedne *þurh cildes had*	*Guth* 1361
447a	*þæt hy in hwitum þær* hræglum oðywden	*Christ B* 454
447b	hilderincas *hyrstum gewerede*	*El* 263
	þæt to þære blisse *beorhte gewerede*	*Christ B* 552
448b	eorlum oð exle *þa se æðeling het*	*And* 1575
	æscrof unslaw *þa se æþeling fand*	*El* 202
	witgena woðsong *þa se waldend cwom*	*Christ A* 46

This passage is clearly at least as formulaic (in Magoun's terms) as that from *Beowulf:* twelve of the nineteen half-lines exhibit some sort of formulaic usage, and it is interesting to note that many of the parallels cited come not simply from *Christ II* (*Christ B*) itself, but also from two others of Cynewulf's signed poems, namely *Juliana* (*Jul*) and *Elene* (*El*). Such repetition within the works of one poet demonstrates that extent to which individual poetic style can still be demonstrated even within a fundamentally formulaic tradition.

Cynewulf's singular address to his unnamed audience in this passage, *mon se mæra* ('illustrious man'), surely implies an authorial comment to a single reader, and therefore a text written for the eye, quite as much as his runic 'signature' later in the poem (*Christ B* 797–807), which has a purely visual effect. The whole tone of the passage is learned and Latinate, yet just as Christ is depicted here (as elsewhere in Old English verse) in the guise of a secular hero, a prince (*æþeling*) and a warrior (*beorn*), so too Cynewulf has clothed his sentiments in the traditional manner and diction of vernacular verse. Nor was Cynewulf the only literate Anglo-Saxon who chose to compose in what is presumably a traditional formulaic (and ultimately oral) style: it has been demonstrated not only that some Old English poetry which simply translates Latin material (and must therefore in some sense be considered literate) is also highly formulaic, but also that Anglo-Saxon poets writing in Latin, such as Aldhelm of Malmesbury (who died in 709 or 710) could equally rely on very similar formulaic methods of composition.[10] Collectively, such evidence underlines the main weakness of the designation 'oral-formulaic': formulaic poetry, contrary to what Magoun and others have asserted, need not be oral, although the technique of composition may derive from an ultimately oral tradition.

The extent to which the kind of oral-formulaic theory espoused by Magoun has been modified in its application to Old English is apparent from a number of the examples already cited, in which the 'evidence' adduced consists of no more than the repetition of a single word in a half-line of similar metrical shape. Such 'parallels' underline the important observation that oral-formulaic theory must be adapted to the individual traditions to which it has been applied: it has become apparent that Old English verse does not rely simply on the verbatim repetition of inflexible formulas, but rather on the recognition of related formulaic 'systems', generally centred on the fixed placement of a single word.[11] So, for example, the *Beowulf* poet only uses the word *gedryht/gedriht* ('troop') on the following six occasions:

æþelinga gedriht ('troop of princes')	*Beo* 118b
mid his eorla gedriht ('with his troop of warriors')	*Beo* 357b
ond minra eorla gedryht ('and my troop of warriors')	*Beo* 431b
mid minra secga gedriht ('with my troop of men')	*Beo* 633b
mid his hæleþa gedryht ('with his troop of heroes')	*Beo* 662b
mid þinra secga gedryht ('with your troop of men')	*Beo* 1672b

None of these half-lines precisely matches any of the others, and yet all seem clearly to reflect a formulaic system which places the word *gedryht/ gedriht* at the end of the b-verse, preceded by another (alliterating) noun in the genitive plural. Such a system, moreover, was again not restricted to retrospective and heroic verse, but could apparently be manipulated by literate and Latinate poets such as Cynewulf, who in his *Christ II* (*Christ B*) seems to have adapted the same system, on each of the three occasions on which he used the word *gedryht*:

his þegna gedryht ('his troop of thegns')	*Christ B* 457b
mid þas engla gedryht ('with his troop of angels')	*Christ B* 515b
mid þas bliðan gedryht ('with that joyous troop')	*Christ B* 519b

Still further modifications to what is plainly the same system are implied by the usage of the anonymous poet of *Christ III* (*Christ C*) who also uses the word *gedryht* on three occasions:

mid his engla gedryht ('with his troop of angels')	*Christ C* 941b
eadig engla gedryht ('blessed troop of angels')	*Christ C* 1013a
eadigra gedryht ('troop of blessed ones')	*Christ C* 1663b

The practical logic by which the formulaic secular concept of a 'troop of warriors' (*eorla gedryht*) should become a formulaic Christian 'troop of angels' (*engla gedryht*) is attractive, and once again, such comparisons of the use of particular formulaic systems by different poets strongly indicate the extent to which individual authors exercise freedom within the tradition; indeed, it is only by assessing precisely what a particular poet may owe to the formulaic tradition that his own contribution can be considered.

More recently, there has developed the growing realisation that such formulaic techniques of composition in Anglo-Saxon England were not restricted to verse: Old English that was quite clearly intended to be heard by an audience, such as the rhythmical 'prose' sermons of (the certainly literate) Archbishop Wulfstan of York, who died in 1023, can be analysed in precisely the same way as Old English verse, and demonstrably rely on the formulaic repetition of rhythmical phrasing.[12] Such an approach, which has been greatly facilitated by the availability of machine-readable texts and the possibility of swiftly generating concordances by computer, depends upon the recognition that, just as individual metrical units in verse (notably the half-line) can be recognised as formulaic, so too the two-stress phrases regularly found in certain kinds of regular rhythmical prose, such as that characteristically employed by Wulfstan, lend themselves to exactly the same kind of analysis. Moreover, just as Old English poetry demonstrates considerable repetition not merely at the level of the individual phrase, but also at several other levels of discourse, particularly that of the theme,[13] so too Wulfstan will often include in his sermons whole passages which are similar (but seldom identical) to others widely scattered in his works. One might compare, for example, the three following highly rhythmical and formulaic descriptions of Hell, each of which is littered with carefully wrought aural effects, such as alliteration and rhyme:

Dær is ece bryne grimme gemenced, and ðær is ece gryre; þær is granung and wanung and aa singal heof; þær is yrmþa gehwylc, and ealra deofla geþring. Wa þam þe þær sceal wunian on wite. Betere him wære þæt he man nære æfre geworden þonne he gewurde. Forðam nis se man on life þe areccan mæge ealle þa yrmða þe se gebidan sceal se ðe on ða wita ealles behreoseð; and hit is ealles þe wyrse þe his ænig ende ne cymð æfre to worulde. (Bethurum, *Homilies*, p. 126 [III.66–73])

[There is eternal burning grimly mingled, and there is eternal terror, there is groaning and moaning and always continual misery; there is every kind of humiliation, and a thronging of every kind of devil. Woe to the one who must dwell there in torment. It would be better for him that he was never born than that that should occur. There is no man alive who can tell all the humiliations which he must endure who wholly experiences those torments, and it is all the worse since no end ever comes in the world.]

Dær is ece bryne grimme gemenced, and ðær is ece gryre; þær is wanung and granung and a singal sorh. Wa þam þe þær sceal wunian on wite. Him wære betere þæt he æfre on worulde man ne gewurde þonne he gewurde. Nis se man on life þe areccan mæge ealle þa yrmða þe se gebidan sceal se ðe on ða witu ealles behreoseð; and hit is ealles þe wyrse þe his ænig ende ne cymð æfre to worulde. (Ibid., pp. 162–3 [VII.122–8])

[There is eternal burning grimly mingled, and there is eternal terror, there is moaning and groaning and always continual sorrow. Woe to the one who must dwell there in torment. It would be better for him that he was never made a man in the world than that that should occur. There is no man alive who can tell all the humiliations which he must endure who wholly experiences those torments, and it is all the worse since no end ever comes in the world.]

Dær is ece bryne grimme gemenced, and ðær is ece gryre; ðær is ece æce, and ðær is sorgung and sargung, and a singal heof; þær is wanung and granung; ðær is yrmða gehwylc, and ealra deofla geðring. Wa ðam ðe ðær sceal wunian on wite. Betere him wære ðæt he man nære æfre geworden ðonne he gewurde. Nis se man on life ðe areccan mæge ealle ða yrmða ðe se gebidan sceal se ðe on ða witu ealles behreoseð; and hit is ealles ðe wyrse ðe his ænig ende ne cymð æfre to worolde. (Ibid., pp. 230–1 [XIII.84–92])

[There is eternal burning grimly mingled, and there is eternal terror; there is eternal pain, and there is trial and tribulation, and always continual misery; there is moaning and groaning; there is every kind of humiliation, and a thronging of every kind of devil. Woe to the one who must dwell there in torment. It would be better for him that he was never born than that that should occur. There is no man alive who can tell all the humiliations which he must endure who wholly experiences those torments, and it is all the worse since no end ever comes in the world.]

Such a technique of thematic repetition, it should be stressed, with its rhythmical reworking of a familiar theme, is quite distinct from the kind of verbatim copying of written passages which is also found in the so-called 'cut-and-paste' homilies of late Anglo-Saxon England; indeed, the very fact that both techniques were evidently employed at about the same time underlines the extent to which the written and oral traditions could coexist.

The rhythmical and formulaic aspects of Wulfstan's style are of particular interest since they can be matched closely with those of more recent 'prose' authors who are demonstrably composing within a long-established and ultimately oral tradition, namely a group of African-American preachers, whose sermons have recently been studied in detail.[14] Close comparison of the techniques employed by both Wulfstan and these American preachers is instructive at a number of levels, even bearing in mind the dangers inherent in analogy. So, for example, many of the latter, such as the Reverend C. L. Franklin, regularly punctuate their extemporised and recorded sermons with what have been called 'bywords': parenthetic asides such as 'listen if you please' or 'I wish you'd pray with me', which permit the speaker to gather his thoughts for the next wave of speech. These bywords would appear to have a striking parallel in a range of parenthetic and formulaic asides such as the following, with which Wulfstan regularly peppers his sermons, and which may originally, perhaps, have served a similar function: 'gecnawe se þe cunne' ('let him recognize it who can': *Homilies* v.24, v.32; xxa.45, xxa.84; xxb.59, xxb.96; xxc.50, xxc.99); 'gelyfe se þe wille' ('let him believe it who will': *Homilies* vi.196; xiii.79; xxa.77; xxb.88; xxc.84); 'understande se þe wille' ('let him understand it who will': *Homilies* xc.114; xxa.80; xxb.92; xxc.95); 'understande se þe cunne' ('let him understand it who can': *Homilies* xxb.105; xxc.107); 'gime se þe wille' ('let him understand it who will': *Homilies* xi.99, xi.188; xvii.16; xix.84; xxb.11); 'soð is þæt ic secge' ('it is true what I am saying': *Homilies* ix.143; xi.137; xvii.65; xviii.74; xxa.33; xxb.39; xxc.187; xxi.10). Such parallels need not, of course, imply that Wulfstan extemporised his sermons in performance (although the possibility is intriguing); highly literate African-Americans working within the same tradition could compose in an equally formulaic way. The soaring peroration of Martin Luther

King's 'I have a dream' speech, delivered in Washington on 28 August 1963, is a masterpiece of rhythmical discourse orally delivered, but it also demonstrates the way in which a speaker well-versed in an oral tradition (as Dr King, an accomplished performer of extemporised speeches and sermons, assuredly was) can rework familiar themes in new ways; after quoting from the hymn 'My country, 'tis of thee' Dr King, who had at this point departed from his written notes, continued:[15]

So let freedom ring from the prodigious hilltops of New Hampshire.
Let freedom ring from the mighty mountains of New York.
Let freedom ring from the heightening Alleghenies of Pennsylvania.
Let freedom ring from the snow-capped Rockies of Colorado.
Let freedom ring from the curvaceous slopes of California.
But not only that.
Let freedom ring from Stone Mountain of Georgia.
Let freedom ring from Lookout Mountain of Tennessee.
Let freedom ring from every hill and molehill in Mississippi, from every
    mountainside, let freedom ring.
And when this happens, when we allow freedom to ring, when we let it ring
    from every village and every hamlet, from every state and every city, we
    will be able to speed up that day when all of God's children – black men
    and white men, Jews and Gentiles, Protestants and Catholics – will be
    able to join hands and sing in the words of the old Negro spiritual, 'Free
    at last! Free at last! Thank God Almighty, we are free at last!'
                                    (Washington, *Testament of Hope*, p. 220)

Quite apart from the obvious aural appeal and highly formulaic phrasing of such a climactic ending, it is important to realise the extent to which Dr King was simply reworking and recombining themes and phrases used over a considerable period. In another speech delivered almost seven years earlier, in Alabama in December 1956, Dr King had again quoted the same hymn, before continuing in a familiar (but not, we note, identical) vein:

This must become literally true. Freedom must ring from every mountainside. Yes, let it ring from the snow-capped Rockies of Colorado, from the prodigious hilltops of New Hampshire, from the mighty Alleghenies of Pennsylvania, from the curvaceous slopes of California. But not only that. Let freedom ring from every mountainside – from every molehill in Mississippi, from Stone Mountain of Georgia, from Lookout Mountain of Tennessee, yes, and from every hill and mountain of Alabama. From every mountainside let feeedom ring. When this day comes, 'The morning stars will sing together and the sons of God will shout for joy.' (Ibid., p. 144)

Although the ending is different, the build-up is recognisably the same. As with Wulfstan's varied depictions of Hell, the order of the elements presented is different, with at least one striking variant that must have depended on its similar sound: the 'heightening Alleghenies' of the Washington speech are here presented as 'mighty Alleghenies', whilst even the different ending (which, it might be noted, was itself recycled elsewhere) shares with the 'I have a dream' speech the notion of singing together. Even so, the famous conclusion of Dr King's Washington speech was itself anticipated in another address, in Pennsylvania in June 1961, which contains in two passages recognisable variants of the same theme:

One of the first things we notice in this dream is an amazing universalism. It does not say some men, but it says all men. It does not say all white men, but it says all men, which includes black men. It does not say all Gentiles, but it says all men, which includes Jews. It does not say all Protestants, but it says all men, which includes Catholics . . . I believe . . . that we will be able to emerge from the bleak and desolate midnight of man's inhumanity to man into the bright and glittering daybreak of freedom and justice. That will be the day when all of God's children, black men and white men, Jews and Gentiles, Catholics and Protestants, will be able to join hands and sing in the words of the old Negro spiritual, 'Free at last! Free at last! Thank God Almighty, we are free at last!' (Ibid., pp. 208 and 216)

A still closer variant is found in a speech given in Florida in December 1961:

Yes, this will be the day when all of God's children, black men and white men, Jews and Gentiles, Catholics and Protestants, will be able to join hands all over this nation and sing in the words of the old Negro spiritual, 'Free at last! Free at last! Thank God Almighty, we are free at last!' (Ibid., p. 207)

Such a technique of repeating themes with slight variation closely matches what can be observed widely in Wulfstan's works, and suggests the possibility that more detailed comparison of his (and other Anglo-Saxons') methods of composition with those of his African-American counterparts may prove productive in future for the study of Old English homiletic technique.

The value of such analogues lies in the emphasis they place on the role of performance in establishing the form and style of a text, and such examples illustrate an increasing tendency to look beyond the narrow confines of the oral-formulaic theory as first applied to Old English verse, by focusing attention on other forms of discourse from Anglo-Saxon England, and attempting to address the issue of formulaic expression as a communal vehicle for interpretation. To this end a number of recent studies of Old English have focused on precisely the element of the sound or 'vocality' in the performance and transmission of a text.[16] Such studies mark the transition of scholarly interest from the poet (concentrating on the formula as a method of composition) to the audience (where the interpretative impact of the formula is assessed). The story of the youthful Alfred's acquisition of a beautiful book of Old English poetry which he had learned and recited but could not read likewise serves as a reminder that the vitality of the Anglo-Saxon oral tradition is not to be measured simply in terms of composition, but also in transmission and (at least in some cases) performance.

Once the possibility is accepted that, as in the parallels drawn from the African-American tradition, 'oral' habits of mind can (and could) coexist alongside 'literate' ones, some exciting prospects for assessing the methods of transmission of medieval texts suggest themselves. A number of the key issues connected with the problem of assessing the role of orality or literacy in the transmission of texts can be seen in the Exeter Book Riddles, which in their highly formulaic phrasing and reliance on a range of aural effects on the one hand, and demonstrable debt to Latin models on the other, send out a number of conflicting signals about their ultimate debt to an oral or written tradition. Riddle 36, for example, the apparently simple text of which points to a complicated textual history, reads as follows:

Ic wiht geseah   on wege feran,
seo wæs wrætlice   wundrum gegierwed.
Hæfde feowere   fet under wombe
ond ehtuwe
monn·h·w·M·wiif·m·x·l·kf·wf·hors:qxxs·   5
    ufon on hrycge;
hæfde tu fiþru   ond twelf eagan
ond siex heafdu.   Saga hwæt hio wære.
For flodwegas;   ne wæs þæt na fugul ana,
ac þær wæs æghwylces   anra gelicnes   10
horses ond monnes,   hundes ond fugles,
ond eac wifes wlite.   Þu wast, gif þu const,
to gesecganne,   þæt we soð witan,
hu þære wihte   wise gonge.

[I saw a creature travelling along; it was marvellously adorned with wonders. It had four feet under its belly and eight ('monn·-h·w·M·wiif·m·x·l·kf·wf·hors:qxxs·') up on its back; it had two feathers and twelve eyes and six heads. Say what it was. It travelled the waterways, nor was it only a bird, but there was the likeness of every one of these: horse, man, dog, bird, and also the face of a woman. You know, if you understand speaking, what we know to be the truth: how the track of that creature goes.]

This perplexing riddle has been variously solved as, for example, 'sow with five piglets', 'pregnant horse and two pregnant women', 'waterfowl hunt'.[17] Most solutions view the creature as some sort of water-vessel, perhaps a four-oared boat with two sails (the four feet below and two wings mentioned), manned by four rowers (the eight feet above, eight of the eyes and four of the heads), with stem and stern carved in the shape of a woman and a dog (supplying the other two heads and four eyes). Traditional riddling formulas, which some (applying Magoun's assertions uncritically) have seen as indications of oral composition, begin and end the first section of the poem (lines 1–8): the phrase 'ic wiht geseah' ('I saw a creature') – or some variation on it – begins no fewer than eight of the Exeter Book Riddles (numbers 29, 34, 37, 38, 56, 68, 75, and 76), whilst the challenge 'saga hwæt hio wære' ('say what it was') or, more often, 'saga hwæt ic hatte' ('say what I am called') is found in sixteen other Riddles (numbers 1, 2, 3, 8, 10, 12, 19, 23, 35, 39, 62, 66, 73, 80, 83, and 86), always, however, at the conclusion of the poem. The further existence of a parallel closing formula, 'frige hwæt ic hatte' ('find out what I am called') in four other Riddles (numbers 14, 16, 26, and 27), together with the extraordinary addition of the first-person ('I') tag 'saga hwæt ic hatte' at the end of Riddle 86, which is otherwise entirely conducted in the third person ('it'), only underlines the utter conventionality of the diction expressed in Riddle 36, which incorporates a number of other phrases found elsewhere.

Taken together, such indications of formulaic composition might point towards the influence of an oral tradition (although, as we have seen, they do not necessarily indicate oral composition); but the appearance in the text of the apparently nonsensical line 5, which disturbs the alliteration and metre, clearly indicates at least one level of written transmission. As it stands, the line contains three recognisable Old English words: *monn* ('man'), *wiif* ('woman') and *hors* ('horse'), and presumably represents a not wholly unreasonable stab at a solution: if we assume that the horse is carrying its two passengers across water (as indeed we are told), then the reflection will provide the four legs underneath, eight on top, six heads and twelve eyes, leaving, however, the two feathers (or wings) and the dog unaccounted for. That this 'solution' is not wholly satisfactory suggests that it is not authorial. More than that, the Old English words seem to gloss three Latin words which here appear disguised by a common code, which renders each vowel by the following consonant in the Latin alphabet (so 'a' becomes 'b', 'e' becomes 'f', 'i' becomes 'k', 'o' becomes 'p', and 'u' becomes 'x'). According to this system, the three Latin words *homo* ('man'), *mulier* ('woman') and *equus* ('horse') should have become: 'hpmp-mxlkfr·fqxxs'. At some later stage, presumably, the Latin has been glossed – it is hard to see why the same person should wish to conceal his 'clue' in a Latin code and then supply the answer – and at this point other purely scribal corruptions seem to have been introduced, understandable only from a visual perspective: 'p' has been transformed into runic 'p' (= 'w'), with the second 'p' of (now) 'hpmp' merging with the initial 'p' of 'wiif'; the final 'r' of 'mxlkfr' has also been turned into a runic 'p' (= 'w'), presumably via an understandable confusion of 'r' in Insular minuscule script with 'p'; the 'f' of 'fqxxs' has become detached from the front of the word, apparently suggesting that the intrusive 'hors', originally a gloss, has by now become incorporated into the body of the word it was supposed to have been explaining, in much the same way as the whole of line 5 appears to have been copied into the body of the text from a marginal or interlinear gloss. Riddle 36 has clearly passed through the hands (and heads) of several Anglo-Saxons, some of whom have left their mark on the extant written text.

It is interesting to observe that with line 5 excluded, the riddle breaks easily into two equal parts of six lines each (lines 1–4a and 6b–7; lines 8–14), in which the first and highly formulaic section comprises a self-contained riddle marked off at beginning and end by traditional formulas, and the second section simply adds more detail. It might even be suggested that this second section is a later addition to an 'original' six-line riddle, in which case the extant Riddle in the Exeter Book reveals a still more complicated series of stages of transmission: a highly formulaic six-line riddle has been expanded by the same number of lines of 'help', as well as having a 'solution' suggested in Latin and in code ('hpmp·mxlkfr·fqxxs'). At some later stage, the enigmatic Latin itself acquired a gloss ('monn·wiif·hors'), and in the process of scribal copying mistakes were made. Eventually the resulting gobbledygook was copied (perhaps none too accurately) from an originally marginal or perhaps interlinear position into the text itself. Only written transmission (and that in a number of stages) can explain such progressive degeneration of what may once have been a text, which, if not orally composed, was in its 'original' form brief and formulaic enough not to require a written transmission.

The first two lines of Riddle 36, moreover, are repeated almost verbatim at the beginning of Riddle 68 ('ic þa wiht geseah on weg feran / heo wæs wrætlice wundrum gegierwed'), a curious situation which is, however, not unparalleled elsewhere in the Exeter Book. Riddles 31 and 32 both begin with the same rather unspecific sentence: 'is þes middangeard missenlicum / wisum gewlitegad, wrættum gefrætwad' ('This world is arrayed in various ways, adorned with ornaments'), and conclude with yet another formulaic ending, in which the audience is invited to guess 'hwæt sio wiht sie' ('what the creature is'), a phrase which, with minor variants, is found in no fewer than six Riddles (numbers 28, 31, 32, 39, 41, and 67). More intriguing still is Riddle 79, consisting of a single line, 'ic eom æþelinges æht ond willa' ('I am a prince's property and joy'), which looks suspiciously like a 'false start' for the opening line of Riddle 80, which begins 'ic eom æþelinges eaxlgestealla' ('I am a prince's close companion'). The apparent confusion of the graphically distinct *æht ond willa* and *eaxlgestealla* is difficult to explain in purely scribal or formulaic terms (although the word *eaxlgestealla*, or morphological variations of it, does comprise an entire half-line in *Beo* 1326a and 1714a; *El* 64a), and may suggest that other factors are operating. It is, for example, possible that the scribe is consciously or unconsciously 'improving' a received text from his own knowledge of the formulaic tradition, and there are certainly indications elsewhere in the corpus of such activity, which has been described as the result of what is termed 'residual orality'.[18] Unlike Riddle 36, however, we cannot be sure whether the work in question has been copied from a written exemplar, or has simply been (mis-)remembered. Such a process of what has been described as 'memorial transmission' is sometimes held to account for the minor and often rather quixotic differences that are occasionally found between Old English verse texts preserved in more than a single copy.[19]

So, for example, there are two distinct versions of Riddle 30, the solution of which appears to be 'cross'; the first is found in the Exeter Book on folio 108r, and reads as follows:

> Ic eom legbysig,   lace mid winde,
> bewunden mid wuldre,   wedre gesomnad,
> fus forðweges,   fyre gebysgad,
> bearu blowende,   byrnende gled.
> Ful oft mec gesiþas   sendað æfter hondum,   5
> þæt mec weras ond wif   wlonce cyssað.
> þonne ic mec onhæbbe,   ond hi onhnigaþ to me
> monige mid miltse,   þær ic monnum sceal
> ycan upcyme   eadignesse.

[I am flame-busy, at play with the wind, enveloped with glory, made one with the sky, eager for the journey hence, troubled by fire, a blossoming grove, a burning ember. Very often companions pass me from hand to hand, so that proud men and women kiss me. Then I rise up, and they bow down to me, many with mercy, where I shall increase for men the bounty of blessedness.]

A second, more direct, version of the Riddle is found on folio 122v of the Exeter Book, and, rather puzzlingly given that it has been copied by the same scribe, exhibits a number of minor differences, indicated here by italics:[20]

> Ic eom *ligbysig*,   lace mid winde,
> *w*[. . . . .]   dre gesomnad,
> fus forðweges,   fyre *gemylted*,
> bear[.] blowende,   byrnende gled.
> Ful oft mec gesiþas   sendað æfter hondum,   5
> *þær* mec weras ond wif   wlonce *gecyssað*.
> Þonne ic mec onhæbbe,   *hi onhnigaþ* to me
> *modge miltsum*,   *swa* ic *mongum* sceal
> ycan upcyme   eadignesse.

While some of these differences are undoubtedly trivial, it is the sheer number which must give pause, particularly since a number of them, particularly the sequence in line 8, seem, like the variant *æht ond willa* for *eaxlgestealla* noted in Riddles 79 and 80 above, to derive from aural rather than visual confusion. To attribute all such differences simply to sloppy copying (of which Exeter Book scribe is undoubtedly guilty in many places) seems rather strained; the variant *gebysgad* for *gemylted* in line 3 of the first version, for example, *could* be explained as a form of dittography after *legbysig* in line 1, but elsewhere the Exeter Book scribe simply repeats the entire word, rather than a single element of it, and such aural repetition of sounds is, as we have noted above, common-place in Old English poetry (as here 'winde bewunden'; 'fyre... blowende byrnende... sendað'). It seems more likely that the scribe has either 'improved' his text, or copied variant versions which were themselves the result of memorial transmission, or both.

The conflicting signals given out by Riddles 30 and 36 in the Exeter Book, of which one is certainly the product of a written transmission while the other may reflect some oral element, only highlight the poten-tial difficulties and contradictions inherent in any study of the oral tradi-tion in Anglo-Saxon England. Just as Alfred's prose Preface to his translation of the *Pastoral Care* (and indeed the historical facts of his life) manage to reflect the complex interactions between literacy and orality that are the hallmark of the literature of Anglo-Saxon England, so too the seemingly bookish metrical Preface, which may also be Alfred's work, exhibits many of the same traits:

> Þis ærendgewrit   Agustinus
> ofer sealtne sæ   suðan brohte
> iegbuendum,   swa hit ær fore
> adihtode   dryhtnes cempa,
> Rome papa.   Ryhtspell monig   5
> Gregorius   gleawmod gindwod
> ðurh sefan snyttro,   searoðonca hord.
> Forðæm he monncynnes   mæst gestriende
> rodra wearde,   Romwara betest,
> monna modwelegost,   mærðum gefrægost.   10
> Siððan min on englisc   Ælfred kyning
> awende worda gehwelc,   and me his writerum
> sende suð and norð,   heht him swelcra ma
> brengan bi ðære bisene,   ðæt he his biscepum
> sendan meahte,   forðæm hi his sume ðorfton,   15
> ða ðe Lædenspræce   læste cuðon.

[Augustine brought this message over the salty sea from the south, to the island-dwellers, just as the Lord's champion, the Pope in Rome, had com-posed it. Gregory, learned in spirit, surveyed many a proper text through his spirit's wisdom, a hoard of cunning thoughts. Thereby, best of Romans, most generous-hearted of men, most famed for his deeds, he won over most of mankind to the Guardian of Heaven. Afterwards King Alfred turned every word of me into English, and sent me south and north to his scribes, told them to make more such from the exemplar, that he might send them to his bishops, because some of them were in need of them, those who knew least Latin.]

Katherine O'Brien O'Keeffe has pointed out how even this apparently unpromising text, which assuredly depicts a situation scarcely paralleled elsewhere in extant Old English verse, nevertheless demonstrates considerable familiarity with its traditional diction and formulaic systems.[21] The transmission of the poem may also demonstrate some oral element, given the variant in one manuscript of the highly formulaic phrase *eorðbugendum* ('earth-dwellers'), which occurs on no fewer than twenty-nine occasions elsewhere in Old English verse, for *iegbuendum* ('island-dwellers') in line 3, and which may therefore reflect the residual orality of an individual scribe. More interesting still is the sudden change from the third person ('this message') in lines 1–10, which describe the Latin text, to the first person ('me') in lines 11–12, which depict the translation. Such a transformation, which, as we have seen, echoes precisely a similar change at the beginning of the prose Preface (and is indeed repeated in the metrical *Proem* to Alfred's translation of Boethius' *Consolation of Philosophy*), bears eloquent witness to the contrast in perspective between the literate Latin discovered in written books, and the immediate English of the spoken word. In other words, the Latin text requires to be read, the English to be heard. This simple contrast also highlights an important characteristic of the extant literature of the period, and a truth implicit throughout the entire preceding discussion: sometimes Anglo-Saxon books can speak, and we would do well to listen.

Notes

1 See further S. Keynes and M. Lapidge, *Alfred the Great: Asser's 'Life of King Alfred' and other Contemporary Sources* (Harmondsworth, 1983), p. 239, n. 46; K. O'Brien O'Keeffe, *Visible Song: Transitional Literacy in Old English Verse*, Cambridge Studies in Anglo-Saxon England 4 (Cambridge, 1990), pp. 81–4. All quotations from the Preface are from H. Sweet, ed., *King Alfred's West-Saxon Version of Gregory's 'Pastoral Care'*, 2 vols., EETS os 45 and 50 (London, 1871–2); I cite the version in the Hatton manuscript. On the change from third person to first, see now J. W. Earl, *Thinking about 'Beowulf'* (Stanford, CA), pp. 87–99, and above, pp. 119–20.

2 See P. Clemoes, 'King Alfred's Debt to Vernacular Poetry' in *Words, Texts,*

and Manuscripts: Studies in Anglo-Saxon Culture Presented to Helmut Gneuss on the Occasion of his Sixty-fifth Birthday, ed. M. Korhammer (Cambridge, 1992), pp. 213–38.

3 See further A. C. Bartlett, *The Larger Rhetorical Patterns in Old English Verse* (New York, 1935), esp. pp. 30–48 (her 'parallel pattern') and 49–61 (her 'incremental pattern'). So, for example, after a brief and self-contained opening passage, *The Wife's Lament* can be said to consist entirely of four 'paragraphs' (lines 6–14, 15–26, 27–41, and 42–53), each of which begins by describing a man (*min hlaford . . . hlaford min . . . mon . . . mon*) and ends by describing pain and longing (*longade . . . fæhðu dreogan . . . longaþes . . . langoþe*); indeed, such a structure effectively reveals the main theme of a poem which sensitively depicts the plight of a woman lurching between love and grief.

4 See further, for example, E. R. Kintgen, 'Echoic Repetition in Old English Poetry, especially in the *Dream of the Rood*', *NM* 75 (1974), 202–23; J. O. Beatty, 'The Echo-Word in *Beowulf*', *PMLA* 49 (1934), 365–73; R. Frank, 'Some Uses of Paronomasia in Old English Scriptural Verse', *Speculum* 47 (1972), 207–26. On the use of such aural effects in Old English prose in general, see J. Bately, 'The Nature of Old English Prose', in *The Cambridge Companion to Old English Literature*, ed. M. Godden and M. Lapidge (Cambridge, 1992), pp. 71–87, esp. pp. 83–4.

5 For an overview of these and other such studies, see A. H. Olsen, 'Oral-Formulaic Research in Old English Studies: I', *Oral Tradition* 1 (1986), 548–606 at 558–9.

6 The classic statements of the basic Parry-Lord theory are to be found in A. B. Lord, *The Singer of Tales* (Cambridge, MA, 1960); A. Parry, ed., *The Making of Homeric Verse: The Collected Papers of Milman Parry* (Oxford, 1971). For an overview of oral-formulaic studies, see J. M. Foley, *Oral-Formulaic Theory and Research: An Introduction and Annotated Bibliography* (New York, 1985).

7 Olsen, 'Oral-Formulaic Research in Old English Studies: I'; 'Oral-Formulaic Research in Old English Studies: II', *Oral Tradition* 3 (1988), 138–90; see too Foley, *Annotated Bibliography*, pp. 3–77. There are a number of invaluable tools for formulaic research in Old English, including J. B. Bessinger and P. H. Smith, *A Concordance to 'Beowulf'* (Ithaca, NY, 1969); J. B. Bessinger and P. H. Smith, *A Concordance to the Anglo-Saxon Poetic Records* (Ithaca, NY, 1978); A. diP. Healey and R. L. Venezky, *A Microfiche Concordance to Old English* (Toronto, 1980). The Dictionary of Old English Project, working in Toronto, has produced a comprehensive machine-readable corpus of Old English, which can be used in conjunction with a number of commercially available concordancing packages.

8 F. P. Magoun, Jr., 'The Oral-Formulaic Character of Anglo-Saxon Narrative Poetry', *Speculum* 28 (1953), 446–67 at 446–7. Magoun's paper has been reprinted many times, for example in D. K. Fry, ed., *The Beowulf Poet: A Collection of Critical Essays* (Englewood Cliffs, NJ, 1968), pp. 83–113.

9 F. Klaeber, ed., *Beowulf and the Fight at Finnsburg*, 3rd edn. (Boston, 1950). In general, reference to Old English poems is made according to the system suggested by B. Mitchell, C. Ball, and A. Cameron, 'Short Titles of Old English Texts', *ASE* 4 (1975), 207–21, and 'Short Titles of Old English Texts: Addenda and Corrigenda', *ASE* 8 (1979), 331–3.

10 For the formulaic quality of 'translation' poetry, see L. D. Benson, 'The Literary Character of Anglo-Saxon Formulaic Poetry', *PMLA* 81 (1966), 334–41; for Aldhelm, see M. Lapidge, 'Aldhelm's Latin Poetry and Old English Verse', *CL* 31 (1979), 249–314; A. Orchard, *The Poetic Art of Aldhelm*, Cambridge Studies in Anglo-Saxon England 8 (Cambridge, 1994), pp. 102–25. For Cynewulf, see further R. E. Diamond, 'The Diction of the Signed Poems of Cynewulf', *PQ* 38 (1959), 228–41.

11 On the concept of formulaic systems, see, for example, D. K. Fry, 'Old English Formulas and Systems', *English Studies* 48 (1967), 193–204; J. Niles, 'Formula and Formulaic System in *Beowulf*' in *Oral Traditional Literature: A Festschrift for Albert Bates Lord*, ed. J. M. Foley (Columbus, OH, 1981), pp. 394–415; and particularly A. Riedinger, 'The Old English Formula in Context', *Speculum* 60 (1985), 294–317.

12 See A. Orchard, 'Crying Wolf: Oral Style and the *Sermones Lupi*', *ASE* 21 (1993), 239–64. All quotations from Wulfstan are from D. Bethurum, ed., *The Homilies of Wulfstan* (Oxford, 1957).

13 B. Peabody, *The Winged Word: A Study in the Technique of Ancient Greek Oral Composition as Seen Principally Through Hesiod's 'Works and Days'* (Albany, NY, 1975), pp. 3–5, suggests five 'tests for orality', each at a different level of discourse. For Old English, Peabody's 'tests' have been applied to *Beowulf* by R. P. Creed, 'The *Beowulf*-Poet: Master of Sound-Patterning' in *Oral Traditional Literature* pp. 194–216; cf. Orchard, 'Crying Wolf', pp. 258–9; *The Poetic Art of Aldhelm*, pp. 112–19. In addition, there have been a large number of studies of the use of stock themes such as 'the beasts of battle' or 'the hero on the beach' in Old English poetry; see further the detailed discussion in Olsen, 'Oral-Formulaic Research in Old English Studies: I', pp. 577–88.

14 See B. A. Rosenberg, 'The Formulaic Quality of Spontaneous Sermons', *Journal of American Folklore* 83 (1970), 3–20; *The Art of the American Folk Preacher* (Oxford, 1970); 'The Message of the American Folk Sermon', *Oral Tradition* 1 (1986), 695–727. For a collection of such sermons, many of which are also available as recordings from Chess Records, see J. T. Titon, ed., *Reverend C.L. Franklin: Give Me this Mountain. Life History and Selected Sermons* (Urbana, IL, 1989).

15 See further S. B. Oates, *Let the Trumpets Sound: The Life of Martin Luther King, Jr.* (New York, 1982), p. 260. All citations of the works of Dr King are from J. M. Washington, ed., *A Testament of Hope: The Essential Writings and Speeches of Martin Luther King, Jr.* (New York, 1986).

16 For the concept of vocality, see particularly P. Zumthor, 'The Text and the

Voice', *New Literary History* 16 (1984), 67–92; A. N. Doane, 'Oral Texts, Intertexts, and Intratexts: Editing Old English' in *Influence and Intertextuality*, ed. E. Rothstein and J. B. Clayton, Jr. (Madison, WI, 1991), pp. 75–113; U. Schaefer, 'Hearing from Books: The Rise of Fictionality in Old English Poetry' in *Vox Intexta*, ed. A. N. Doane and C. B. Pasternack (Madison, WI, 1991), pp. 117–36; U. Schaefer, *Vokalität. Altenglische Dichtung zwischen Mündlichkeit und Schriftlichkeit*, Scriptoralia 39 (Tübingen, 1992); A. N. Doane, 'Editing Old English Oral/Written Texts: Problems of Method (With an Illustrative Edition of Charm 4, *Wiðfærstice*)' in *The Editing of Old English: Papers from the 1990 Manchester Conference*, ed. D. G. Scragg and P. E. Szarmach (Cambridge, 1994), pp. 125–45. On the distinctions between composition, transmission, and performance in an oral context, see particularly R. Finnegan, *Oral Poetry: Its Nature, Significance and Social Context*, 2nd edn. (Bloomington, IN, 1992). On performance, see J. M. Foley, *Immanent Art: From Structure to Meaning in Traditional Oral Epic* (Bloomington, IN, 1991); 'Word-Power, Performance, and Tradition', *Journal of American Folklore* 105 (1992), 276–301; *The Singer of Tales in Performance* (Bloomington, IN, 1995).

17 C. Williamson, ed., *The Old English Riddles of the Exeter Book* (Chapel Hill, NC, 1977), pp. 248–52 (his no. 34). The numbering system adopted here for the Riddles is that of the *ASPR*.

18 For the concept of 'residual orality', see in particular O'Brien O'Keeffe, *Visible Song*, pp. 8–22.

19 See particularly A. Jones, '*Daniel* and *Azarias* as Evidence for the Oral-Formulaic Character of Old English Poetry', *MÆ* 35 (1966), 95–102; A. Jabbour, 'Memorial Transmission in Old English Poetry', *Chaucer Review* 3 (1969), 174–90.

20 See further R. M. Liuzza, 'The Texts of the Old English *Riddle* 30', *JEGP* 87 (1988), 1–15.

21 O'Brien O'Keeffe, *Visible Song*, pp. 96–107.

6

The recovery of texts

PAUL E. SZARMACH

•

Et verbum caro factum est.

(John 1:14)

When the Fourth Gospel-Writer began his account with brilliant, Neoplatonic imagery, implying many related philosophical ideas about the origin of things, his interest was hardly textual criticism. Rather, the writer known as John sought to give expression to a recurrent Neoplatonic theme that eventually was woven into the recovery of texts from originary manuscript evidence: just as the divine had entered the corporeal world, so too had the words of authors descended from some special, irradiated literary sphere onto and into the flesh of animal skins, and just as the soul had entered the mundane, becoming corrupted and contaminated in the woeful descent, so too had the words of authors become corrupted and contaminated by successive transmission from archetype or exemplar, often but dimly perceived, to copy most sullied. The daemons in the transmission of text are most clearly the scribes who wound and torture words and texts in this Fall, and the redeemers most clearly are the editors who seek to restore readings to their original state. The process of restoration needed both theory and method beyond mere suppressed imagery, of course, and it was the nineteenth century, building upon its predecessors, that set about the task of ascertaining the author's words by methods that were positivist, scientific, and verifiable. Thus, generations before literary criticism became 'theoretical', i.e. self-conscious and reflective of its aims, methods, and presuppositions, textual criticism could be most theoretical indeed, especially in the recovery of Holy Writ or ancient texts. While the study of Old English texts, like the early study of medieval culture, is a sub-world pendant to the study of the classics in major ways, the self-conscious study of OE texts is ironically not very theoretical itself, for reasons discussed below, and it is only within the last decade or so, stimulated by a post-modern spirit of reevaluation, that the aims and methods of OE textual criticism have come under self-conscious scrutiny and the Neoplatonic bias against the scribes who transmit words been called into question. Indeed, what editors do and for whom they do it are now important questions, as how and why they do it have always been. In this essay I will suggest some of the classical inheritance of OE textual study, but I will focus more intently on the ways in which OE texts challenge presuppositions of textual criticism and present special problems. What is at stake is not only what we know about texts, but also how we know it. The old, apparently clear distinction between 'what a text says' and 'what a text means' is, as post-modern theorists help us understand, not quite so disjunctive, for determining what a text says is not a simple, objective, or scientific enterprise, but rather is already mediated by a tendency towards some instantiation of meaning. This discussion must begin with perhaps the major methodological divide in the classical heritage of medieval textual criticism.

The one and the many: optimism and recensionism

Although it must be stressed at the outset that there have been many variations in these two main traditions of textual criticism, editions of medieval texts have primarily either been 'optimist' or 'recensionist'.[1] In the 'optimist' tradition an editor presents the 'best' text of a given work. The standard edition of Chaucer's *Canterbury Tales*, for example, is the *Riverside Chaucer* (ed. L. D. Benson *et al.*, based on the edition by F. N. Robinson), an edition of the Ellesmere manuscript, which still holds sway because of its 'completeness' and its apparently early date, though recently the comparable Hengwrt manuscript has had similar optimist claims advanced for it. Those very dissatisfied with optimist editions (because of the logical circularity) usually argue that a genealogy of texts, or *stemma codicum*, must be established to sort out the (family) relationships of various witnesses in a 'recension'. Since recensionists often produce eclectic texts, that is, they attempt to recreate the author's text by choosing readings from various witnesses, they become liable to the optimist's charge that a recensionist text finally has no manuscript authority and that the Ellesmere text, for example, at least exists, was known, and was read. Some recent theorists of textual criticism would further emphasize that medieval transmission is a process, with the result that unless there is clear evidence of direct, authorial involvement, the record of transmission is only a record of scribal versions as such. Recensionists, it is often charged, assume a closed or uncontaminated vertical descent from an author's copy to the extant texts when, in point of fact, the uncontaminated text is rare and 'horizontal' relationships are common, occurring when a scribe has access to two traditions and blends both in producing his text. *Piers Plowman* may very well represent the worst case for horizontal relationships in English vernacular, offering several authorial versions according to common opinion and a trail of very enterprising scribes who sometimes join in the composition. These generally divergent schools, each ready to criticize the other, tend to converge in practice, as Edward J. Kenney says: 'The modern tendency is to acknowledge the validity of the [genealogical] method in principle while recommending a cautious empiricism in its application.'[2] Acknowledging the uniqueness of any manuscript text, one must agree with George Kane's eminently sensible appeal for 'open editions', that is, editions whose editors make clear from the outset their methods and follow them consistently in a spirit of full and open disclosure, so to speak.[3] Such a disarming move by an editor would at least result in redirecting criticism of an editor and his practice toward issues of validity and/or consistency, avoiding the issue of correspondence to the overall evidentiary picture because that issue will be a *given* or not, for the fit of the evidence will always be in context. But here too one can never escape second-guessing, which is akin to an indoor sport for critics of editors, as discussions of Klaeber's methods on ANSAXNET *passim* suggest.

The methodological purity implied in the optimist versus recensionist antinomy is for Old English studies often practically irrelevant and a theoretical bother. For the major poetic monuments there is but one copy for each text, with the result that editors of these texts must come forward as *de facto* optimists, following their own base text as best they can. The remarkable exception is Caedmon's *Hymn*, which exists in many versions ranging from comparative antiquity through later medieval times; other poems in multiple copies include the *Battle of*

Brunanburh and other, less familiar, *Chronicle* poems, and *Soul and Body I* and *II,* which are a related pair. The so-called canonical poems, which in formalist days occupied center stage in instruction and criticism, exist in sole copies (though, strictly speaking, all copies are 'unique') and, since most Old English literature students have experience with these sole texts, their understanding of textual criticism is accordingly limited by this experience. Even without the quicksand of variants coming from many witnesses, the editor still has to ask, what is the task at hand? Here the issue becomes interventionism; for example, when the text 'breaks down', what does the editor do? Of course, the epistemological question lurks here: how can you tell when there is a breakdown? Physical destruction, notably loss of a page or quire or obliteration in a line, make for easy occasions, but sooner or later an editor's judgment comes into play, hopefully and happily supported by consensus of past editors and generally the community of scholars.

The *Seafarer* is an excellent example of the editorial challenge, for the 'common reader' can make no sense of some parts and perhaps not much better sense of the over-arching whole. Lines 15–16, for example, show a problem involving alliteration and an apparent lost half-line:

> hu ic earmcearig   iscealdne sæ
> winter wunode   wreccan lastum,   15
> winemagum bedroren,
> behangen hrimgicelum;   hægl scurum fleag.

Likewise line 25 has a problem with alliteration:

> urigfeðra;   nænig hleomagum

and line 112 offers:

> þeah þe he ne wille w——fulne.

In his influential school-text edition Pope offers the reader a 'dagger', the conventional sign of a *locus desperatus* with the explanation: 'A dagger indicates a corrupt passage which the editor hesitates to emend.'[4] Pope's hesitation is honest. For readings that make no sense, emendation, i.e. correction, would appear to be the reasonable course of action, but emendation according to what authority or standard? Though knowledge of Old English alliteration and meter calls attention to a problem, all editorial tactics aimed at solving problems seem to fail. For the *Seafarer* there are no variant texts that can supply readings.

Comparable or similar texts there are, notably the so-called elegies of the Exeter Book and especially the *Wanderer*, but without a known author whose name can link these texts to satisfy the old classical standard whereby the special style or *curiosa felicitas* of an author may obtain (i.e. Hemingway is not Faulkner is not Joyce is not Woolf) only mere intuition seems left – or simple, but general, assertion of similarity. Nor can a concept of the whole of the poem, apart from authorial *curiosa felicitas*, assist, for how the *Seafarer* holds together, whether it has one speaker or two and whether the epilogue is an interpolation, are issues that have occupied literary critics for decades. Hardcore formalism, joined to old-style philology, has not produced the objective text despite the expressed and implied aims of their methods, proving ironically that the lines of the poem are not limbs of a dinosaur that can be used to construct other limbs. The situation is almost post-modern, for the text of *Seafarer* may be left to write itself or the audience may choose to write it. Pope chooses not to intervene in the text he presents except for normalization of spelling, offering suggestions and discussion in his notes. Pope's editorial method thus seeks to preserve the appearances of the only text he has, while rendering it intelligible on the best basis he can, meeting the Kane test of 'full and open disclosure' with relative completeness. In following the text he has at hand Pope clearly exhibits an orientation to empiricism, which is characteristic of editing Old English texts. This editorial state of affairs for Old English sole texts is common and standard.

For Old English prose texts the editorial situation tends to be different and, when placed against the tradition of the canonical poems, highlights the special textual nature of these poems. Sole prose texts exist, of course, but the field of discussion is much wider. To be sure, scholars would prefer to have many more identifiable prose writers who might even be known beyond abstract groupings according to style (e.g. 'Pseudo-Wulfstan') so as to situate works in time and place more easily, but by and large Old English prose texts more typically offer variant witnesses. Thus, recensionism, or more broadly the comparison of variants of a text, begins to have practical force. There is a happy exception in prose that deserves mention here, London, BL, Royal 7.C.XII, which contains Ælfric's *Catholic Homilies I [CH I]*.[5] Ælfric himself knew this manuscript, a statement that seems on the face of it absurd to a twentieth-century reader accustomed to current models of publication; but it is certain that Ælfric contributed notes to his own work, canceling passages and directing scribes, and thus can be seen as literally authorizing this manuscript version. There is no similar authorial act in poetry, unless one sees Alfred as an intervening poet in Oxford, Bodleian Library, Hatton 20. Yet the textual criticism of *CH I* cannot end here because there are other manuscript witnesses to this collection of homilies. The study of the textual traditions of *CH I* not only indicates the transmission of the homilies, and by inference their great influence in later Anglo-Saxon England, but also points out that Ælfric himself was a reviser of his own work. For Ælfric publication, so to speak, was a process, not an event. Ælfric's documented commitment to revision makes the idea of 'ascertaining his words' a very fuzzy concept indeed, similar to the *Piers Plowman* problem or the multiple editions of Walt Whitman's *Leaves of Grass*.

The comparison of variant witnesses to a prose text creates many analytical situations where recensionism as a method seems right, real, and efficacious as well as illustrative of implied recensionist themes. The anonymous prose of the Vercelli Book (Vercelli, Biblioteca Capitolare CXVII [Ker 394]) offers twenty-three prose pieces, some of them sole witnesses, but many existing in a context of multiple witnesses. Vercelli xx offers an excellent recensionist exercise, for there are two other versions of the same text, one in Cambridge, Corpus Christi College (CCCC) 162 and one in CCCC 303.[6] A threesome allows for the desirable 2:1 split, a split desirable because it fulfills the recensionist aim to classify and distinguish families or groupings, particularly (as here) isolating one witness with some clarity against the others. Here the desired result is achieved because, 'mere' spelling variants such as *i/y* and *ð/þ* aside, very often textual variation will be CCCC 162 and CCCC 303 against Vercelli. These variations begin with the homiletic opening, *Mine gebroðra ða leofestan* against *Menn ða leofestan*, significant also because it might indicate influence of a different school of composition, and continue with variation at a comparable verbal level, that is, noteworthy differences but not earth-shaking. Thus, for the purposes of editing, the witnesses form an identity and do not, happily, seem to exhibit any significant messy, horizontal contamination. In this threesome it is clear that CCCC 162 and CCCC 303 are not direct copies of Vercelli xx, but is the later CCCC 303 a copy of CCCC 162? In CCCC 162 there are interlinear and other corrections, and CCCC 303 does not necessarily follow them. The likelihood is that cccc 162 and cccc 303 share an exemplar that does not survive, thus fulfilling another latent dream of recensionism, the recreation or postulation of a non-extant witness. In this quasi-recensionist analysis of the three witnesses one may feel uneasy about too much logical or scientific rigor in a human process where scribal weariness or inattention can explain failures to copy directly, or inclinations to write automatically in certain situations despite what is actually in front of the eyes. One must admit to a little intellectual cheating as well: other evidence beyond textual comparison establishes the useful chronological sequence Vercelli, cccc 162, cccc 303 so that the temporal descent is clear; then too, cccc 162 is a Canterbury book, probably St. Augustine's, and cccc 303 a Rochester book, all thus within the Kentish cultural-religious milieu. This Kentish connection then has a kind of backward reference to Vercelli, which, despite its minor diverging paths, can be seen with increasing probability as a Kentish book. In comparisons with variants to other prose pieces Vercelli seems to be an isolate as well, notably in the versions of the Martin *vita* where the Blickling and Junius versions often read against Vercelli, providing a 2:1 split in another, codicologically different, part of the Vercelli Book.[7] There is something emotionally and psychologically satisfying in finding Vercelli alone in a stemma, a situation replicating its peculiar current geographical home in a cathedral library in a northern Italian city far away from the Anglo-Saxon heartland. Does geography inspire textual analysis behind the scenes?

The preceding paragraph, one must hasten to note, gives emphasis to Vercelli in the complex of Vercelli–cccc 162–cccc 303. If the injunction is to edit the Vercelli Book, which is important to edit for reasons of literary history, then one necessarily chooses Vercelli xx as the base text and the point of reference. Logically, one can choose any of the three prose texts as a base. Thus, cccc 162, art. 36 could be the base text, say, if literary Canterbury were the purpose behind the commission to edit, or cccc 303, art. 44 if later literary OE or regionalism were the aim or the purpose. Indeed, Cross and Bazire use cccc 162 as the base for their edition of this homily as much for practical, publishing reasons as because of the unsuitability of cccc 303 owing to its linguistic and spelling difficulties. Intrinsically or abstractly, one could not really argue that there is a 'best' text in this threesome. There is a 'best' text for a particular purpose; but a corrected base text, which would come close to an optimist edition in its effect, could actually serve any purpose if it were accurate in detail and clear in presentation.

The reference to 'intellectual cheating' above needs even further explanation. The recensionist exercise here described would appear to operate in the Neoplatonic realm of *uerbum*. In actuality the recensionist analysis draws aid and comfort from the knowledge of material conditions outside of the idealized verbal relationships. These material conditions of textual production now, for many scholars of texts, must be a significant part of the discussion involving the recovery of texts, for there is significant meaning in them. The phrase 'material conditions' seeks to emphasize the codex book or manuscript as object, and it is the book in its physicality, or the book as body, that commands attention: just as the soul comes in a body, so too does a text come in physical form. Materialist concern for the book as object was always embedded in the study of texts, but it was always of secondary interest. Codicology was seen as a distant cousin of literature. The concern with the book as object can, for example, lend an economic dimension to literary history. How many cows or sheep did it take to create the *Beowulf* text in its present form? The answer to this question might point to, say, a well-endowed monastery that implicitly did not see a conflict between Ingeld and Christ in the scriptorium. The arrangement of pages, hair side versus flesh side, is a codicological feature that, as is well known, has general applicability to dating and some relevance to literary history as an indication of the absence of continental ideas of book production, where scribes tended to match hair side with hair side, or flesh side with flesh side, to achieve a form of visual uniformity. Layout and design features can have a more pointed effect on discussion. To return to Vercelli–cccc 162–cccc 303: the Vercelli Book is a compilation of booklets that easily betray at least three major origins, thanks in part to the use of different styling in headings (for example, titles in red or in black square capitals), whereas the two Corpus manuscripts indicate programmatic layout and design features through specific uniformity in the use of color and script.[8] Again, but now in the comparison of books as objects, Vercelli is an isolate, perhaps implying some form of personal book as opposed to a book with a public, liturgical function as a text for reading. Versions of the *Anglo-Saxon Chronicle* offer further examples of how seeing the text as object affects meaning. The BCD versions of the story of Æðelflæd of Mercia are two-to-one textually, where BC seem to represent an earlier version of the story, more readily pointing to an antecedent text, and D a later 'leveling'of incident and emphasis, more in line with the apparent dynastic impulse of the House of Wessex and the concept of the *Chronicle* as a narrative with a grand sweep.[9] The B and C scribes present their texts differently enough in the treatment of annal numbers, for example, but they both use annal numbering as a kind of bracketing device that sets off the story of Æðelflæd. BC are 'against' D in this important feature of layout and design. As Fred Robinson has stressed, the text's *mise en page* contributes to the context of understanding.[10]

To intervene or not to intervene is still the practical question for an editor of Old English texts when the text fails. When Vercelli xx loses a leaf, supplying the words lost from cccc 162 makes easy sense, given the relative transmissional superiority of cccc 162. When less extensive breakdowns occur (as in the *Seafarer*) and there are no variants to supply readings, Pope's option to note and discuss with open hesitation is not the only one. One logical extreme is clearly to leave the text of the *Seafarer* all by itself, offering no intervention in the text and, theoretically at least, no emending discussion and only nihilist discussion. Pope does not quite intervene, but he wants solutions to problems. The interventionist option is to conjecture a reading based on whatever secondary evidence can be adduced or on whatever knowledge the editor can bring. The non-interventionist position may tend towards a diplomatic edition, where the editor tries to present 'what is on the diploma', transliterating and noting all scribal activity, as Zupitza attempts to do in the EETS facsimile edition of *Beowulf*, which offers a transcription opposite a photographed page.[11] For many this form of activity is not the product of the editorial process, but rather more like a state in the careful progression towards an edition. The ongoing project Anglo-Saxon Manuscripts in Microfiche Facsimile, while successful in its aim to bring manuscripts to larger audiences as cheaply as possible, carries within it a view that the manuscripts and their scribes are the only real authority. The interventionist position heads in the opposite direction, arguing that editing is a scholarly activity that requires knowledge and judgment operating over evidence and not simply recording it on page or film or, now, computer screen. At the 1990 Manchester conference A. N. Doane and Michael Lapidge represented the opposing views: Doane argued for the intellectual sovereignty of scribes and Lapidge called for the return of the classical standard of conjectural emendation.The differences were sharp, the debate vigorous, and the intellectual state of affairs astonishing, for these themes have been recurrent in the enterprise of scholarly editing since the origins, but never quite so clear and stark as in the Doane–Lapidge exchange on the editing of Old English.[12]

Instability of texts

The foregoing discussion of broad theoretical orientations and some of their problems can only be a contribution to the decline and fall of the Absolute. Several generations of discussion have clarified some issues, but solutions to problems are less easy to come by. For the audience of editions (or the readership) the knowledge of the tendencies of textual criticism make for a form of meta-reading or meta-criticism when a text is encountered. Just as readers of Old English dictionaries no longer receive them like documents from Sinai, so too readers of texts must likewise accept editions as contingent documents. 'Trust the tale, not the teller', an old bromide of fiction criticism, must for OE texts be rephrased less elegantly to something like 'we don't know what the tale is or whether we have one, and we are not about to hear you, the editor, without some tough questions about what you are doing and how you are doing it'. Edited texts are unstable in the philosophical sense, and an acceptance of this state of affairs, informed by knowledge of the editor's dilemma, can prevent error and acknowledge ambiguity or contingency in final interpretation. Three examples may illustrate the far-reaching effects of textual criticism as an exercise in textual instability.

The first editor of Ælfric's *Catholic Homilies*, Benjamin Thorpe, used Cambridge, University Library, Gg. 3. 28 (Ker 15) as the basis for his edition.[13] For the Second Series of *Catholic Homilies* particularly, the choice is very sensible: among the twenty-seven or so manuscripts that give evidence for *CH II* this manuscript emerges as the most authoritative one. This working and workable conclusion does not come without several nagging difficulties, perhaps the most problematic being the question of textual identity. Thorpe offers forty-five homilies for *CH II*, when Ælfric explicitly says in his Preface that he has issued two series, now called *CH I* and *CH II*, each of forty pieces. It is not within the scope of Thorpe's edition to offer any discussion of this apparent discrepancy. The modern editor of *CH II*, Malcolm Godden, is quite open about the problem, pointing it out at the beginning of his Introduction and citing his argument for the arrangment that he offers whereby the apparent forty-five homilies become forty, the desirable number hallowed by Gregory the Great's own collection. Godden joins together five homilies that Thorpe had treated as separate. This expedient solution to save the appearances of an authoritative text, however, necessarily inspires a series of other questions. Certainly the first question, perhaps somewhat rude, is can Ælfric count?, or less rudely, does Ælfric display a casual attitude towards the whole collection despite his otherwise documented anxiety over the transmission of his work? Or does this most authoritative manuscript begin to lose some authority, evincing the status of at least a second stage beyond Ælfric's authorial version where Ælfrician control disappears? While the focus of these questions is on Ælfric, there is another set of questions about the literary artifact. Has Ælfric – or has Godden – created a new homiletic form in these five combined homilies where, for the liturgical occasion, Ælfric offers 'a composite homily'? Such a generic hybrid would be in line with Ælfric's general experiments in genre and style but would not, in effect, have been seen to exist before Godden's 1979 edition because Thorpe's enumeration precluded it. One can indeed make a literary case for the composite homily. Thus Godden II.xviii, formerly Thorpe II.xix and II.xx, may function like a narrative diptych. The first part is an account of the finding of the True Cross and the second an account of the martyrdom of Alexander, Eventius, and Theodolus. What unifies the two parts is the image of the Cross, perhaps, but there is a thematic unity when the two parts are seen as complementary studies on the relation of *saeculum* and *ecclesia*. This new prose genre might have more sophistication than twentieth-century readers may wish to allow Ælfric and his audience, and there are questions about how this work would function in a liturgical context; but Godden's enumeration of homilies opens up a set of new literary topics. Similar questions about where a text ends and where a text begins exist in the Lives of Saints, as indeed they do for, say, the riddles in the Exeter Book.

While the differing treatments of *CH II* show how on a large strategic level of text editing an editor can influence meaning quietly, similarly on a more local textual level editorial decisions can have wide ramifications. For the current literary moment perhaps no more charged reading of a text may exist than that of *Beowulf* 1931b and its 'Modþryðo'. There seems to be no particular disagreement over what the text says. The Zupitza-Davis transcription may stand, here presented from the equivalent of line 1925 (London, BL, Cotton Vitellius A.xv, fol. 172r [175r], ll. 10–20):

> ...bold wæs
> bet-lic brego rof cyning hea healle
> hygd swiðe geong wis wel-þungen þeah ðe
> wintra lyt under burh-locan gebiden
> hæbbe hæreþes dohtor næs hio hnah
> swa þeah *ne to gneað gifa geata leo-
> dum maþm-ge-streona mod þryðo wæg
> fremu folces cwen firen ondrysne
> nænig *þæt* dorste deor ge-neþan swæsra
> gesiða nefne sinfrea * þæt hire an-dæges
> eagum starede ac him wæl-bende.

Klaeber's edited version of this passage is:

> Bold wæs betlic,   bregorof cyning,   1925
> hea[h on] healle,   Hygd swiðe geong,
> wis welþungen,   þeah ðe wintra lyt
> under burhlocan   gebiden hæbbe,
> Hæreþes dohtor;   næs hio hnah swa þeah,
> ne to gneað gifa   Geata leodum,   1930
> maþmgestreona.   Modþryðo wæg,
> fremu folces cwen, firen' ondrysne;
> nænig þæt dorste   deor geneþan
> swæsra gesiða,   nefne sinfrea,
> þæt hire an dæges   eagum starede;   1935
> ac him wælbende   ....[14]

Zupitza-Davis would appear to represent the state of the manuscript (though hyphens, for example, are used which are not in the manuscript), and the equivalent of edited 1931b is three verbal units: 'mod þryðo wæg'. The simple question is, are these three verbal units three words or a compound (name) and a word (verb). It is not the intention here to rehearse all the scholarship and to offer a new interpretation, but rather to indicate simply what is at stake, which is nothing less than the existence of a female character in the poem. Klaeber's view of the passage supports what has become, arguably, the mainline interpretation of the line and the passage, which goes this way more or less: in an aside the poet presents a contrast between a positive figure, Hygd wife of

Hygelac, and the dreaded Modþryð, who has men put to death for gazing upon her until Offa 'tames' this murdering shrew. But just as there are various adjustments to this mainline view that allows the character to exist, there is a minority opinion that, uncomfortable with 1931b as a collection of verbal units, sees other options possible, including a set that seeks to diminish, if not outright eliminate, the character. Thus, Wrenn has argued that *modþryðo* means 'pride' and that the passage has only an oblique reference to the shrew, translating the passage (here quoted with Wrenn's brackets and his italics): 'The forward queen of the people [the lady corresponding to the Drida of the *Vitae duorum Offarum* of c. 1200] showed pride (*mod-þryðo*), terrible wickedness.'[15] Whereas previous editors of this passage brought philology, history, paleography, and folklore to bear on this text as well as an expressed or implied aesthetic, any present editor has to be aware of the feminist theme of 'erasure'. To find an interpretation other than the mainline one runs the risk of participation in erasure and all that such a criticism implies. Likewise, any interpretation based on the mainline view of the text has to acknowledge that received opinion is not unanimous and that a grand interpretation using this passage as proof does not enjoy a full *consensus omnium*. The scribe seems confident in his writing: there is no direct, apparent physical difficulty in the manuscript, but what does the scribe really mean?

An equally problematic possibility of erasure haunts the opening of *The Wife's Lament*. The Exeter Book (Exeter Cathedral 3501, Ker 116), fol. 115v, offers

> Ic þis giedd wrece   bi me ful geomorre,
> minre sylfre sið.

The feminine singular forms, *geomorre* and *minre sylfre* referring back to the speaker of the poem, identify the voice as gendered feminine. Most critics agree that a woman is speaking, though it must be acknowledged that we know very little about the poem, and the grammatical gender could allow for, say, an allegorical figure rendered in feminine grammatical form. There is a *consensus omnium* that the poem as a whole is obscure, thus offering little clear contextual support for this very clear manuscript reading. The possible existence of a female voice means that the poem could be the earliest such poem in the Middle Ages, antedating by hundreds of years a more readily documented later medieval tradition. Here the dynamic between exception and 'rule', or between the horizon of expectations and the text at hand, operates with special effect. According to this line of thinking, because the evidence for female-voicing is generally sparse in this period or contra-indicated by all that can be known with certainty, the thoughtful editor must emend to the masculine, restoring the presumptive cultural framework to the scribally impaired poem. But the Exeter Book clearly offers what it offers, and except for a few hardy Anglo-Saxonists, all other commentators agree that the feminine forms should remain. The opening of *The Wife's Lament* really then offers a special example of the editorial principle *lectio difficilior*, i.e. 'the harder reading [is to be preferred]', which acknowledges that scribes tend to level or smoothe out what they receive and render and, when they do not so level or smoothe out a text, the apparently harder reading is in fact the correct one. At this time in the history of the subject, where writing on the theme of erasure of women has revealed so many larger implications for cultural history and the conduct of scholarship, it is easy to accept this 'harder' reading.

The special case: oral literature

If there is one area where Old English literary studies as a whole have made a signal contribution outside of their own precincts, it is in the description and understanding of the oral tradition (see chapter 6 above). This contribution has its impact on textual criticism as well, for the setting down of oral texts, which makes sound into something material, is so basic an adjustment of medium that it has to be seen to affect undertanding in a primary way. Early on in the discussion of oral poetry it was not unusual to find a document-driven observer who would claim that because the poems were written down, they were no longer oral, and indeed even interpreters seeking the oral matrix would deny the existence of a transitional state between oral and written poetry, a position allowing methodological purity but seeming to fly in the face of all cultural experience. Once oral theorists would grant that transitional literacy was a real and actual state, then at least some manuscripts could be seen to have transitional features reflecting that state. The materializing of Old English oral literature now seems a comparatively new area of investigation, but some broad outlines are beginning to emerge.[16] As has been suggested above in the discussion of recensionist possibilities in Vercelli–CCCC 162–CCCC 303, the physical nature of manuscript layout and design is meaningful. The comparative poverty of visual clues in a manuscript could be attributed to an oral consciousness. Those conditioned in print culture would, for example, expect a three-deck banner headline on the front page of *The New York Times* to point to the story of most importance; the reader does not choose the two-line advertisement in six-point print on the bottom of the page to be indicative of journalistic emphasis. Likewise paragraph indentations in English nonfiction books, if composition manuals are correct, signal a complete unit of thought; capitalization marks proper nouns, and the various marks of punctuation indicate relationships of thought. The visual cues provided in Old English manuscripts, particularly punctuation and capitalization, prove very vexatious. Some manuscripts, such as the Vercelli Book, offer a wide range of capitals, and in the running text offer small capitals, which until the advent of word processors was not an option available to the individual who had only a typewriter. Old English punctuation may assist oral delivery – it would appear so in some cases – but the idea of a sentence necessarily beginning with a capital is an intellectual notion rather difficult to maintain as a rule or precept in the recovery of texts. Even if one seeks to dismiss this line of argumentation – that a lack of visual clues indicates transitional literacy – by claiming that what is indicated here is simply primitive book design, as is to be expected at the beginning of the tradition of the vernacular book, the point is that it is 'primitive' book design because it does derive from an oral tradition.

But there is even more at stake than the question of visual cues. If the scribe sought to freeze-frame oral literature by writing it down, so too does the modern editor of oral literature mediate the process of recovery by offering a snapshot where a moving picture seems necessary. Oral literature is surely process literature: there is no one and sole ideal text, only a set of sub-texts likely to be fuzzy at the edges and, when in multiple versions, stretched out over time and place. Characteristically, the editors of *Beowulf* impose print-culture conventions on a text that shows oral origins. While the Modþryð passage discussed above was presented as a case of editorial variance, the root of the variance in that instance is word separation and division, a problem that arguably derives from oral tradition where segmentation of verbal units cannot occur by spacing, of course, but rather from speech patterns. One might also observe that sentence division and paragraph separation are also print-culture impositions, as the editors *en masse* show in practice at almost every chance. Add to this mix different punctuation traditions in German and in English: Klaeber's use of a dash *and* a comma together continue to puzzle American students taught that such a collocation of punctuation marks is impossible, and the punctuation Förster uses in the Vercelli Homilies seems very strange indeed. The realization that *uerbum caro factum est* can only ultimately undermine editions that ignore the physical text is the major conclusion here. In bringing forward oral poetry modern editors and their readers must be aware that there is another level of mediation beyond those which a lettered transmission history imposes.

Poetry has always been primary in early studies and prose secondary, with the result that developments in the study of prose almost always follow those in poetry. The question of the material text, particularly as illustrative of the oral tradition, has not yet been raised fully in the study of prose-text traditions. (In fact, the oral dimension of Old English prose seems, for many, a non-subject, for the absence of a metrical demand makes analysis problematic.) The Cynewulf and Cyneheard episode in the Anglo-Saxon Chronicle needs close study from this perspective, if the episode is really derived from oral tradition as so many believe. From the perspective of oral tradition, Godden's choice to offer manuscript punctuation in his edition of *CH II* is a masterstroke. In his brief discussion of editorial procedures and conventions Godden states that he follows manuscript punctuation, but does not explain why. This replication of manuscript forms may assist the study of *CH II* as an intersection of oral and book culture, unmediated in the edition. The role of Latin punctuation practices and liturgical punctuation would have to be reevaluated and reconsidered. What would have to be delayered is Godden's choice to offer his own word-division and paragraphing. Still, the hardy interpreter, armed with the knowledge that there was an oral tradition in Old English literature that had its impact on the written tradition and displayed its characteristics in a material way, may yet be able to describe the oral sources of Ælfric's prose style and his material texts.

Towards an electronic future for editing

Within the last decade the potential of computers to assist the editing process has been well on the road to realization.[17] The future prospect is that manuscript and book culture will yield to electronic culture, while physical text will yield to virtual text. What can the computer do to assist the recovery of texts? At the moment the given benefits seem to be most clearly practical. A computer edition can present more evidence, more efficiently and more cheaply, than a printed text. The technical successes of 'The Electronic *Beowulf*' project have produced a digitized facsimile that exceeds quality standards of any printed photographed facsimile; this facsimile is in a sense even better than the original because it can show more than the human eye can see in the original, thanks to various lighting techniques. Texts that exist in many and complicated variants (which, as indicated above, is not the typical case in Old English studies), can now offer them all, and perhaps the 'partial edition' of a large or complicated text will begin to disappear as a genre. But more information has its downside as well, for in some cases undifferentiated information can be daunting and confusing, and the non-expert may still have questions unresolved while facing files of data.

One certain area of difficulty will be the role of the editor as judge. Because there is ultimately no real practical limitation on the material contents of an edition, the editor could become a mere inputter of information with a tendency towards deferral of judgment to the reader. A case in point is the rhythmical prose of Ælfric. The scholarly question is, what is the nature of Ælfric's rhythmical prose, which seems to be Ælfric's own independent stylistic innovation? Pope prints Ælfric's rhythmical prose as metrical lines, Needham as regular prose text; Godden follows manuscript punctuation, and Old English scribes and their practices may be brought into the discussion as well. An editor editing Ælfric's rhythmical prose electronically would not need to make a choice, as Pope, Needham, and Godden did, but could display all the choices as options for the reader to choose, thus abnegating judgment. Here one might wish to argue that the computer always offers a hierarchical tyranny, or at least sets up data in certain ways, refusing, say, to process an order for flowers because no telephone number is given to complete the data field; but at the level of choice described here the data field does give traditional editors what they want and does so more efficiently. The presentation of all the evidence or all the examples need not preclude editorial judgment, but it does appear that the reader will enter the editor's domain and exercise independent judgment.

On the strategic scale of editorial activity, where editions are conceived, no pertinent example is extant. It might, therefore, be useful to sketch the likely shape of a scholarly edition intended to take advantage of all available technology. 'Old English Online Editions' (OEOE), a project under development by a broad-based group of Anglo-Saxonists, is an attempt to offer texts in prose or poetry in electronic form.[18] As an experimental project, the collective of editors is planning to offer small, self-contained works, or discrete units from larger works, so as to test the potential scope of electronic editions and to encounter exemplary problems of electronic editing, presumably to offer exemplary solutions. The work that an editor will do will replicate the process of understanding and discovery that has been traditional. The first stage is the engagement with the primary evidence, namely, the witness(es) to the text. Each editor will consult the manuscripts and also work with a digitized facsimile of the text and its variant witnesses (where appropriate), which one might consider to be forensic evidence. The success of 'The Electronic *Beowulf*' and the Kontron-Roche digital camera suggests that with multiple light-source possibilities and image-processing programs digitized technology can far outstrip regular photography and in many cases personal, visual inspection of a manuscript, for the digitized camera can discriminate more in pixels than the human eye can. The process of interpretation of that evidence begins with diplomatic transcriptions and continues through the representation of extant edited texts, which in their layout and design of a text, assisted by punctuation and capitalization, might be considered the first grand level of intervention. It is at this level, of course, that much literary or historical interpretation begins. The OEOE editor will then supply explanatory notes and with the aid of the *Dictionary of Old English* (*DOE*) and in consultation with the *DOE* staff offer the lexical resources necessary for verbal understanding. The editor will assemble a package to include other necessary evidence for contextual understanding, such as visual or visual-material evidence (e.g. representations of material artifacts). The package will include major critical or scholarly articles or excerpts from books, chosen to reflect current, best scholarship. Thus, the editor will consider the needs of the audience in a unique way: rather than restrict information because of the limits of book-print technology, an OEOE editor will emphasize the maximum amount of intellectual choice for the user up to and into the process of interpretation. George Kane's call for 'open editions', by which he meant an open declaration of method and procedure, will then be consistently followed; OEOE will extend the notion of editorial openness even further than clarity and consistency of method, for the audience will have either unmediated or open evidence. One further advantage of technology confers an extra responsibility on the OEOE editor. Since online publication is a process and not an event, there will be the easy opportunity to continue to add, change, and adjust an edition. The OEOE editors undertake to stay with their texts beyond version 1.0 of their edition, at this point in the plan for at least five years, in order to allow for the continuing development of the understanding of the text. In this sense no edition will ever have a *Nachleben*, as Klaeber's edition of *Beowulf* does, for a text will always be dynamic. To adopt computer language, the product of these intentions — the reader must note the future tense in the discussion — will be an archive, not a book-print edition. From this point of view the product will contain five grand categories: text, glossary, intertext, graphics, and bibliography. (Technology makes possible the inclusion of other categories, too, such as sound, video, animation, and various possible analytical applications.) Quite obviously, there are technological assumptions in this plan: a willing user, knowledgeable in technology and in the subject with access to appropriate machinery and with the desire to ingest more information than hitherto available for a given text. Again, technology promises speed, efficiency, access, capacity: here it forecloses needs for library resources and travel to manuscript *fontes*.

Whatever the future will promise and whatever the past has accomplished, there would appear to be certain constants. Perhaps the best expression of these constants appears in M. H. Abrams's discussion of the coordinates of literary criticism.[19] Abrams distinguishes four major elements: the artifact, the artist, the audience, and the art. To apply these ideas to the recovery of texts, which is indeed the *ars artium*, for it is *prior* to all other arts, one would change the terms to: the edition, the editor, (retaining) the audience. The history of the art suggests that the practitioners have stressed different elements at different times. Sometimes the objective, verifiable reality of the artifact has had the emphasis, existing almost without the human dimension as an idealized form; sometimes the creative, or biased, editor has moved to the fore, directing meaning intrusively; sometimes the receivers of the artifact have tugged and pulled at the other elements, demanding a role for their contributions as respondents to form or intention. If the computer is the wave of the future, then the user/reader will have his/her day, and democracy, not expertise, will rule.

Notes

1 The literature on textual criticism, particularly in its formulation for the Latin and Greek tradition, is immense. For the medievalist a start towards the bibliography is L. E. Boyle's useful *Medieval Latin Palaeography: A Bibliographical Introduction* (Toronto, 1984), particularly pp. 298–316, containing 137 items, many on the optimist v. recensionist issue. L. Bieler's *The Grammarian's Craft: An Introduction to Textual Criticism*, 3rd edn. (New York, 1965) (= Boyle no. 1956), would be a good start, as would be E. J. Kenney's entry 'Textual Criticism' in *Encyclopedia Brittanica, Macropedia* 20, 15th edn. (New York, 1994), pp. 614–23. 'Textual Criticism' as such represents but a small portion of S. B. Greenfield and F. C. Robinson, *A Bibliography of Publications on Old English Literature to the End of 1972* (Toronto, 1980), items 758–72, which may suggest, as implied below, that Old English textual criticism is often embedded in the discussion of specific texts; cf. the Greenfield-Robinson section on '*Beowulf*: Textual Criticism'. The annual bibliographies of the *Old English Newsletter* and *Anglo-Saxon England* cover Old English and Anglo-Latin matters since 1972. Apparently the first book-length treatment of the topic is the collection of papers from the 1990 Manchester Conference, D. G. Scragg and P. E. Szarmach, eds., *The Editing of Old English* (Cambridge, 1994). See also J. R. Hall, 'Old English Literature' in *Scholarly Editing: A Guide to Research*, ed. D. C. Greetham (New York, 1995), pp. 149–83, which offers many useful historical comments.

   The role of editing is now caught up with the issues imported to medieval studies from post-modern theoretical concerns. See S. Nichols, 'Philology and its Discontents' in *The Future of the Middle Ages*, ed. W. D. Paden (Gainesville, FL, 1994), pp. 113–41; L. Patterson, 'The Return to Philology' in *The Past and Future of Medieval Studies*, ed. J. Van Engen (Notre Dame, IN, 1994), pp. 231–44; D. C. Greetham, 'Textual Forensics', *PMLA* III (1996), 32–51, which is part of a special-topic issue, 'The Status of Evidence'.

2 Kenney, 'Textual Criticism', p. 619.

3 G. Kane, 'Outstanding Problems of Middle English Scholarship' in *The Fourteenth Century*, ed. P. E. Szarmach and B. S. Levy, *Acta* 4 (1977), 2–4; now reprinted in the collection of Kane's articles, *Chaucer and Langland: Historical and Textual Approaches* (Berkeley, 1989), pp. 228–41.

4 J. C. Pope, ed., *Seven Old English Poems*, 2nd edn. (New York, 1981), p. 33. The text of the *Seafarer* occupies pp. 33–8, and I follow Pope's treatment of it. The question of multiple speakers in *Seafarer* may be the 'classic' example of

textual uncertainty in Old English studies and, as is well known, Pope himself espoused and retracted the view that there were multiple voices.

5 N. Eliason and P. Clemoes, eds., *Ælfric's First Series of Catholic Homilies*, EEMF 13 (1966).The editors' introduction, esp. pp. 19–22, discusses Ælfric's interventions and annotations.

6 The set of texts commonly known as Vercelli xx has in the last two decades received comparatively great attention. See D. G. Scragg, ed., *The Vercelli Homilies*, EETS, os 300 (1992), pp. 329–46; P. E. Szarmach, ed., *Vercelli Homilies IX–XXIII*, Toronto Old English Series 5 (1981), pp. 77–82; J. Bazire and J. E. Cross, eds., *Eleven Old English Rogationtide Homilies*, Toronto Old English Series 7 (1982), pp. 25–39 (now reprinted as King's College London Medieval Studies 4 [1989]); and P. E. Szarmach, 'Vercelli Homily xx', *Mediaeval Studies* 35 (1973), 1–26 with corrections in 'Revisions for Vercelli Homily xx', *Mediaeval Studies* 36 (1974), 493–4. These two articles, which discuss manuscript relations in detail, stand behind the treatment here.

7 See *The Vercelli Homilies*, ed. Scragg, pp. 289–309; *Vercelli Homilies IX–XXIII*, ed. Szarmach, pp. 57–67.

8 For general descriptions of the manuscripts see Ker, *Catalogue*, nos. 38, 57, 394. D. G. Scragg, 'The Compilation of the Vercelli Book', *ASE* 2 (1973), 189–207, sets forth the evidence for Vercelli.

9 See my essay, 'Æðelflæd: *mise en page*', forthcoming in *Words and Works: Studies in Medieval English Language and Literature in Honour of Fred C. Robinson*, ed. P. S. Baker and N. Howe (University of Toronto Press, 1997).

10 F. C. Robinson, 'Old English Literature in Its Most Immediate Context' in *Old English Literature in Context*, ed. J. D. Niles (Woodbridge, Suffolk, 1980), p. 11; now reprinted in Robinson's *The Editing of Old English* (Oxford, 1994), p. 3 and in *Old English Shorter Poems: Basic Readings*, ed. K. O'Brien O'Keeffe, Basic Readings in Anglo-Saxon England 3 (New York, 1994), pp. 3–4.

11 J. Zupitza, ed., *Beowulf*, EETS os 245 (1959; rpt. 1967), 2nd edn. with note by N. Davis.

12 The ASMMF project, general editor P. Pulsiano (Binghamton, 1994–); A. N. Doane, 'Editing Old English Oral/Written Texts: Problems of Method' in *The Editing of Old English*, ed. Scragg and Szarmach, pp. 125–45; Michael Lapidge, 'On the Emendation of Old English Texts', ibid., pp. 53–67. Part of the interchange between Doane and Lapidge concerns the idea of the author, which has now become a major theme of post-modern scholarship. See M. Foucault, 'What is an Author?' in *Language, Counter-Memory, Practice*, ed. with an introduction by D. F. Bouchard and trans. by F. Bouchard and S. Simon (Ithaca, NY, 1977), pp. 113–38, and R. Barthes, *The Rustle of Language*, trans. R. Howard (New York, 1986), pp. 49–55. While an anti-humanist strain of post-modern analysis would seem to do away with the existence of authors, Old English scholars typically do not have them at

all. As a result, Old English studies may serve as a blind, intellectual test for some of the assumptions and conclusions of the post-modern desire for a world without authors.

13 B. Thorpe, ed., *The Homilies of the Anglo-Saxon Church*, 2 vols. (1844–6), II. The modern edition is M. Godden, ed., *Ælfric's Catholic Homilies, The Second Series: Text*, EETS ss 5 (1979).

14 F. Klaeber, ed., *Beowulf and the Fight at Finnsburg*, 3rd edn. (Boston, 1950).

15 C. L. Wrenn, ed., *Beowulf*, rev. edn. (London, 1964), p. 215.

16 K. O'Brien O'Keeffe, 'Editing and the Material Text', in Scragg and Szarmach, eds., *Editing Old English Texts*, pp. 147–54; cf. Doane, as cited in n. 12.

17 The new technology, if one is to subscribe to George Landow's analysis, is very post-modern when it comes to hypertext packages, in its congruence with the ideas of Derrida, Barthes, Foucault, and Benjamin, among others. See G. P. Landow, *Hypertext: The Convergence of Contemporary Critical Theory and Technology* (Baltimore, 1992). For an overview and analysis of Old English and computing, see chapter 9 below.

18 With a joint administrative base at Western Michigan University and West Virginia University, the project committee comprises: P. S. Baker, P. W. Conner, A. diPaolo Healey, K. O'Brien O'Keeffe, K. S. Kiernan, M. P. Richards, D. G. Scragg, and P. E. Szarmach. A. Prescott is liaison for the British Library.

19 M. H. Abrams, *The Mirror and the Lamp* (London, Oxford, New York, 1971), pp. 6–7.

7

At a crossroads: Old English
and feminist criticism

CLARE A. LEES

•

Evocative of choice, change, and even conflict, crossroads can be uncomfortable places. For some, feminism has been crossing Old English,
or passing it by, for some time now; for others, the variety of contemporary feminisms and related post-modern theories – postcolonialism, performativity, border theory, subjectivity, and queer theory, for example –
are themselves such diverging roads that it is hard to see how they converge with the discipline of Anglo-Saxon studies. In connection with the
map of the relation between feminist criticism and Anglo-Saxon studies,
moreover, there is one additional problem: the territory has barely been
charted. Mapping involves consensus, and this consensus is as absent
from the general area of feminist criticism in the humanities as it is from
our own discipline. Feminism challenges our comfortable presuppositions about reading Old English texts: it asks difficult questions about
our scholarly relationship to the period we study; it pays attention to the
silences and omissions of our habitual methods by demanding a place in
a field that once seemed constructed so as to ignore it; and – most
uncomfortable of all, perhaps – it questions the past as well as the
present and future. In short, by challenging so thoroughly the ideologies
that inform our study of the past, feminism draws attention to its own
ideological status as a practice committed to revision and reform.
Feminism is after all a politics, not just a hermeneutic, and therefore
troubling – sometimes to its adherents as well as to its opponents.

   The 1993 *Speculum* volume, *Studying Medieval Women: Sex, Gender,
Feminism*, offers a prominent example of the current uneven relation
between feminist approaches and medieval disciplines. Nancy F.
Partner begins her Introduction with a brief apologia for the general

neglect of women's contributions to past cultures in order to usher in, somewhat belatedly and problematically, the arrival of feminism in medieval studies: 'The reasons which account for the recorded history of the political, social, religious, and aesthetic strivings of our mammalian species being so overwhelmingly dominated by only one of its two sexes have turned out, on repeated examination, to be so shamelessly thin and brittle that there is almost something comical about it, in a nasty bad-joke sort of way.'[1] It is possible that the record of the history of the relations between the sexes is comical from Partner's perspective, but her humorous embarrassment in the face of the past is an odd preface to one of the most important recent developments in medieval studies. Indeed, the special issue is itself an important witness and contribution to feminist work, illustrating not only its range but also how debate about feminist theories and methods is integral to it. Partner's own essay, ambiguously titled 'No Sex, No Gender', refers to one such debate, about the relation of sex to gender, and her work usefully highlights the strong emotions that feminism generates, both within and without feminist circles. Feminist medievalists are faced with a choice, in sum, and one familiar to many other feminists: how to participate dialectically in the two worlds of conventional disciplines and feminist theory and praxis. These two worlds are hardly commensurate, and each generates its own allegiances, conflicts, and tensions. Rather than refuse to take chances in new and uncomfortable territory and thereby deny commitment either to medieval studies and Old English within it or to feminism, let us explore the lay of this land in order to pose the more vital questions feminist practice has to offer. Since feminist criticism is interested above all in multidisciplinary ways of interpreting written texts, this chapter examines the relation of feminist work to the Anglo-Saxon period in terms of its cultural, not merely literary, significance, and then offers a brief example of a feminist approach to one particular Old English poem, *Elene*.

Feminist origins and omissions

Feminist criticism, especially in its more radical and literary forms, shares with other post-modern theories a certain skepticism about narratives of origins. The notion of the origin, we learn, is itself a fiction; originary narratives are constructed around illusory desires that address the present more than the past. Yet for precisely these reasons, origins are seductive, compelling, and powerful, especially in a field such as Anglo-Saxon studies, which continually finds itself placed at one such origin or another: the beginnings of English society or the beginnings of English literature, to name but two. In fact, feminist Anglo-Saxonists participate in the problematic status of the origin by reviewing its illusions and its desires in our own stories of the relation between feminism and Old English. Although it is certainly premature to write the history of feminism in Anglo-Saxon studies because this history is even now only in the making, I offer a preliminary sketch of the story so far.[2]

Given the masculinist structure of much of the disciplinary history of Anglo-Saxon studies and the dominance of patriarchal desires in Anglo-Saxon society itself, it comes as no surprise that there have been few attempts to place feminist concerns at any of the origins of the discipline, or indeed women at the beginning of Anglo-Saxon culture. Anglo-Saxon originary myths, such as that of Hengst and Horsa, recorded by male authors like Bede and manipulated by patriarchal aristocratic dynasties like those of the Kentish and West Saxon royal families, commemorate the male line. This origin, then, is emphatically masculinist, and the 'mothers' of the origin exist only as the other, omitted or suppressed, side of the coin. That there *were* women who did contribute to the making of English culture is well known; that there are also women scholars who have been instrumental in forging the emphases of the discipline of Old English is equally well known. The point, however, is that the institutional structures of the discipline and of its object of study, Anglo-Saxon culture, have often combined so as to prevent bringing into focus analysis of the role of women in the formation of culture.

In response to these institutional structures of both discipline and society, there emerged, particularly in the middle of the 1980s, a first 'phase' of work on women. Jane Chance, Christine E. Fell, and Helen Damico, for example, explored celebrated and exceptional women such as Hild, Emma, or Aethelthryth, or their fictional counterparts, such as Judith and Hildeburh, whose achievements seemed equivalent to those male figures already well discussed by scholarship. This approach sought a female hero equal in stature to a Beowulf, a female religious of equal importance to a Bede, for example. The evidence of the exception – the female aristocrat, land-holder, queen, abbess, or saint – was used to advance the argument that Anglo-Saxon society was relatively more egalitarian with regards to women than post-Conquest England. The so-called 'golden age' for Anglo-Saxon women emerged.

To give women prominent in the cultural record their due was an important first step towards a more general recognition of female achievement in Anglo-Saxon society. With hindsight, however, the problems of such an approach began to emerge. By adopting the structure of traditional historiography, this first phase found itself writing the history of famous women ironically analogous to that history of famous men so criticized by the feminist movement. Anglo-Saxonists had yet to address other feminist options for writing history, such as the complementary projects of writing women's history and of reviewing patriarchy, which were being explored at precisely the same time elsewhere in the humanities. Addressing the validity of the concept of patriarchy itself, especially in this highly stratified society, and the problematic status of powerful women in those cultural institutions that consolidated and advanced patriarchy, would be a necessary next step.[3]

There are other ironies. The argument in favor of Anglo-Saxon egalitarianism is itself an old one, inextricably entwined with the disciplinary origins of Anglo-Saxon studies, which in the eighteenth and nineteenth centuries regularly opposed the enlightened nature of Anglo-Saxon society to its subsequent Anglo-Norman counterpart or vice versa.[4] Early accounts of exceptional women, such as those by Chance and Fell, rely heavily on this argument. In them the processes of an evidently patriarchal culture remain unexplored, and the historical evidence for Anglo-Saxon women is evaluated against another patriarchal culture – post-Conquest England – whose structures are quite different, without recognition of the asymmetry of the comparison. As a result, this methodological approach can only go so far: there are only so many exceptional women, only so many female literary figures, who can be assimilated either to the paradigms of the discipline or to the institutional structures of the society it studies.

The strengths and weaknesses of this approach are best illustrated by the first, and thus far only, anthology of essays devoted to the study of women in Anglo-Saxon England, *New Readings on Women in Old English Literature*.[5] As the editors point out in their Introduction, these essays – drawn from eras both prior to and contemporary with the active phase of feminist work in the academies – sit uncomfortably with most of its premises. Feminist issues often seem marginal to this retrospective – and re-constructed – conversation about women in Anglo-Saxon England, which is largely focused on issues of female power, without consideration of the societal structures within which such power operates. The conversation is conducted firmly within the conventional structures of Anglo-Saxon studies and confirms, rather than challenges or reshapes, them. At stake here is the notion of difference; unless feminist methods make a difference to the ways we study our period there is no practical point to their use.

The story of feminism in Anglo-Saxon studies is more complicated, however, than the *New Readings* anthology suggests. The year that saw the publication of *New Readings* also saw the publication of a brief bibliographical survey of feminism in Old English by Helen Bennett, myself, and Gillian Overing, which was itself the successor to an earlier, more focused, critical survey by Helen Bennett. Both sought to develop the conversation about the disciplinary relationship between feminism and Old English by centering it upon critical examination of the problems and potentials of these methodologies. Helen Bennett concentrated on the exclusion and/or problematic inclusion of women and feminist work in *The Year's Work in Old English Studies*, while the collaborative 'Gender and Power: Feminism and Old English Studies' assessed the impact of feminist thought on three major areas in Old English – history, literature, and language – highlighting the conflict between such disciplinary divisions and the interdisciplinary nature both of feminist studies and of Old English itself.[6]

As these essays noted, feminist work in Anglo-Saxon studies was changing. The number of feminist and feminist-related studies in fact continues to grow steadily, often in response to the first phase of 'exceptional' women. Identification of women prominent in the cultural record has given way to examination of the kinds of prominence of exceptional aristocratic women, the nature of their agency, and their (occasional self-) representation. The issue of the absence of other women, alongside that of other men, in the period is in the process of demystification. That is, critical analysis does not accept that the absence of certain men and women from the cultural record is a necessary given, but asks instead whether Anglo-Saxon sociocultural relations, and their reconstruction by scholarship, have contributed to this invisibility. In addition, the discrete paradigms of social history, literature, or religion, for example, are now revealing their interrelatedness in studies that focus instead on issues of culture and representation. Debate thus continues around issues such as female power and the nature of the 'golden age', but examines the assumptions of their premises. These more recent conversations about gender in Anglo-Saxon England also demonstrate the increasing reach of feminist and feminist-related Anglo-Saxon studies by remodeling not only their object of inquiry – the Anglo-Saxon period – but also their audiences. Feminist work now finds its place in and alongside other periods of medieval studies – in anthologies such as the *Speculum* special issue, *Speaking Two Languages*, and *Class and Gender in Early English Literature* – and it participates in post-modern debates about language, genre, textual editing, authorship, and historiography, to name but a few topics.[7]

History, methodology, difference

Taken together, the *New Readings* anthology and more recent feminist scholarship yield important insights into the problems of working with feminism in Old English. These problems crystalize around two related questions: first, how to preserve the historical difference of the Anglo-Saxon period, as well as the fruits of well-established historical methodologies, as a basis for feminist work within the period; and second, how to maintain productively the necessarily uneven relation between the main strands of contemporary feminist thought and the main strands of Anglo-Saxon criticism. A good example of the interrelatedness of both of these issues is offered by the Introduction to *New Readings* as well as that of the *Speculum* volume, both of which are haunted by a legitimate sense of the belatedness of their work in relation to feminist studies in the humanities in general, even as they present studies of individual aspects of women's history.

It is worth pausing to consider the general significance of this belatedness. Feminist work develops at different paces as a necessary consequence of the different nature of the periods, cultures, and disciplines within the humanities. In the case of Anglo-Saxon studies, the first phase of work on women established the importance of feminist work for the discipline. Subsequent work has built upon this phase and indicates current and future directions. As a result of this increasing body of work, feminists are now in a position to assess the different emphases of Anglo-Saxon studies in comparison with the feminisms of post-Conquest periods. At the same time, feminist Anglo-Saxonists continue to explore feminism's relationship to other theoretical and methodological approaches within Anglo-Saxon studies.

Central to this project is the reconceptualization of the meanings of 'history' and 'culture', so as to take account of (and in some cases highlight) the force of gender relations in their formation. At its most basic, such rethinking means embracing the principal theoretical insight of feminist scholarship: that women, as well as men, produce and use culture, sometimes in similar ways, more often in quite different ones. Such a model therefore also demands the recognition of historical difference. Simply put, Anglo-Saxon gender relations and their cultural representations cannot be separated from the sociohistorical circumstances that co-create them. The nature of this historical difference has two further implications. First, the difference of the past from the present means that our present discrete paradigms for studying Anglo-Saxon culture are, and will continue to be, challenged and revitalized by interdisciplinary models. Second, the recognition of difference creates a space for feminist critics to debate the often presentist assumptions of mainstream gender theorists. Metaphorically, this might be understood as a dialectical conversation between voices of the past and those of the present. Although there is a widespread tendency among both conventional and contemporary theorists in medieval studies to emphasize the textual production of culture, with some impressive results, a more broadly anthropological and material approach has the additional value of placing women as well as men at the center of their culture.[8] Culture, after all, is a matter of men and women.

One link in this chain of gender relations, past and present, in Anglo-Saxon culture is forged by reviewing the formation and history of the discipline itself. Women have always been present in originary narratives — whether of the culture or the discipline — although their presence has sometimes been elided, erased, forgotten, or not fully assessed. The rewriting of the genealogy of Anglo-Saxon studies is well underway, however, and has succeeded in bringing to prominence some of the earlier female students of the subject. Of major importance is the work of Elizabeth Elstob, whose own concern for the interrelationship between past and present, formulated as that between language and voice, led her to produce the first post-Anglo-Saxon grammar of Old English in the 'mother' tongue (1715), which was specifically designed as a teaching text to promote Anglo-Saxon amongst women. In the nineteenth century, Vida Scudder also stressed the integration of cultural study with teaching, as Allen J. Frantzen has recently reminded us. Similarly, Mary Bateson's important study of the phenomenon of early medieval double monasteries (1899) opened up new areas of cultural investigation that are still being pursued by feminist and non-feminist historians alike. Other women, less prominent by virtue of their representation as mere translators, have bequeathed an equally important inheritance by translating many of the major Anglo-Saxon texts for male editors of the Early English Text Society.[9]

Many of these women worked in fields or used methods counter to those dominant in their own age, although their work has been recognized subsequently as foundational for various aspects of the discipline: language, teaching, transmission, and religious culture, for example. Other women who gained considerable prominence as Anglo-Saxon scholars earlier in the twentieth century – Dorothy Whitelock, Margaret Goldsmith, Dorothy Bethurum, Rosemary Woolf, to name but a few – are rightly valued for their work although its relation to women's history, or feminist concerns now, has yet to be analyzed. Connecting the woman to the work may be one way to restore a focus on female contributions to the formation of the discipline, paving the way for an assessment of a female genealogy of Anglo-Saxon studies. One new question for future research is therefore how far the scholarly work of female Anglo-Saxonists, some of which was often undervalued by their contemporary male colleagues, can be characterized as 'women's work', 'feminist' or even protofeminist, and in the process reclaimed by feminists within the larger narrative of women's history. Indeed, one strand of contemporary feminist theory urges the necessity of both biography and autobiography as an important vehicle for highlighting the nature of female desire as it crosses both public institutions and private selves.[10]

Women's work within the discipline of Anglo-Saxon studies can lead to a more thorough analysis of women's work within Anglo-Saxon society and culture. A good example of this is the career of Mary Bateson, whose determination to reconstruct the significance of early medieval double monasteries, and thereby the importance of the female religious, led her to resist more conventional approaches to the subject in favor of alternative methodologies. The impact of Bateson's work cannot be overestimated; the most fully developed body of archival and theoretical work on women in Anglo-Saxon remains that of the female religious, and recent studies such as that by Stephanie Hollis continue the tradition. Hollis's gendered reading of Bede recovers the patriarchal desires of this major figure of Anglo-Saxon culture, nuancing our understanding of the asymmetric representation of the participation of both men and women in the production of religious culture.[11]

Hollis's careful rereading of the archive, based as it is on both conventional and feminist methods of research, provides one important model for future studies. Reading against the grain of patriarchy also advances the project of reconceptualizing the historical difference of Anglo-Saxon culture, highlighting both the nature of patriarchy itself in specific historical formations and the nature of individual participation within it. Studies that inquire into the nature of Anglo-Saxon laws, kinship structures, and the gendered nature of social institutions further clarify this difference. If the gendered division of labor – men produce, women reproduce – has in the past led to the invisibility of women in those areas of Anglo-Saxon life often most valued now (the arts, for example), then the recognition of this description of the formation of culture as a gendered ideology can begin the project of revaluing women's work. We need look no further than the well-known account of Alfred learning Anglo-Saxon poetry at the instigation of his mother, Osburh, to understand the ways in which women produce as well as reproduce. In other words, cultural understandings of motherhood can help fill out our sense of how culture is produced at the knees of a royal mother as well as in the monastic scriptorium. In fact, female nurturing of culture is most often a matter of masculine representation in that scriptorium: only by reading against the desires of such representations as Asser's can we begin to speculate about those other female desires concealed within them. Viewed from the perspective of some contemporary feminist theory, which argues that experience of the body is always cultural (or rather, only available for analysis within the discursive aspects of culture), the revaluation and restoration to visibility of women's reproductive work in Anglo-Saxon England forms a useful reminder of the changing significance of the physical female body across cultures. In a society troubled by disease, plague, and war, subject to high levels of mortality, the dangers of childbirth, and poor harvest yields, one body that matters is in a very real sense female.

The physical body is one site in Anglo-Saxon culture across which many conflicts for identity are played out. Trade in female bodies quite literally consolidated the kin-structures of ruling families; the perhaps analogous trade in body-parts of dead women formed an important strand of the cult of saints. Women's work in this culture is embodied, and in many ways, both symbolic and literal. Contemporary feminist theory, however, stresses quite rightly how often an emphasis on embodiment leads to entrapment, with women valued only for their reproductive capacities. One way to balance this implication of the gen-dered ideology of labor is to explore as well the implications of repre-sentation and – as one aspect of representation – performativity in the construction of gender. It is in fact no easy matter to distinguish between the material body and cultural representations of it, as Judith Butler reminds us in *Bodies That Matter*, even though the material body must always be present in our thinking so as to underline the limits of the power of representation.[12]

To reconceptualize the meaning of culture and find a place within it for Anglo-Saxon women, we need to weigh the emphases of feminist historians on the nature and construction of the family and women's agency – as mothers, wives, daughters, and sisters – against the repre-sentations of female agency or subordination in what is often called the public spheres of society, cultural or social. In fact, where Anglo-Saxon society is concerned, these spheres of social action cannot easily be separated into public and private.[13] Family life *is* public, social and cul-tural; the lives of the women we do know about are bound up with those of their families, and these families, so often, are ruling and upperclass. If there is a private, domestic world where the interests of class and gender are managed differently, then our sources are largely silent about it. Indeed, more useful than the binarism of public and private as a method of social and cultural analysis may be the intersection of class and gender interests. To pose just two pressing questions on the agenda of future feminist research: how many Anglo-Saxon 'mothers' gain prominence in the cultural record by virtue of the family interests they advance? How much of female experience remains unrecorded because it does not represent the interests of those classes with access to cultural forms of representation? Moreover, by highlighting the methodological problems of recovering female agency and experience, we are dealing not only with the presence of women in the record, but also with their absence.

Gender, genre, and identity

A methodology that attends to the nature of the absence and presence of women in the historical record has far-reaching implications for more conventional areas of cultural study. It is often remarked, for example, that the poetic heroic world of the Anglo-Saxons renders the world of the female and that of the family practically invisible; so too that of 'other' men. Only recently, however, and in direct response to the new emphasis on gender representation, has this poetic world been cut down to size. Roberta Frank's brilliant study of the heroic corpus, for example, not only stresses the slender evidence with which the literary critical imagination of the last fifty or so years has worked, but also demystifies its almost exclusively masculine interest: 'Germanic legend', she reminds us, 'seldom eulogizes the figures it condemns to historic action, and its themes are the stuff that fantasies of younger brothers are made of.'[14] The Anglo-Saxons indeed paid the poetic price of their increasing struggle to reinvent and maintain their fantasies of a cultural Germanic identity as the centuries passed. By the time that a *Beowulf* for example is recorded, there emerges a strongly idealized representation of a masculine warrior culture that may in fact never have existed, certainly not in Anglo-Saxon England. And yet this idealization is distinctively English, with at best a conflicted relationship with similar genres in the related Germanic literatures. Analyses of the aristocratic masculinity specific to the Anglo-Saxon heroic world contribute to the reshaping of our claims for the cultural significance of those poetic texts that have so long dominated the modern canon. The study of masculinity, although now only in its infancy, is one important element of a feminist project, of course, for it allows us to look again at female representation within and without the canon at the same time as it reminds us of the constructed and gendered aesthetics of the canon itself.

Work by Frank and others on the constructed nature of the heroic world and its masculinist reflexes problematizes not only the relation of this art to the social world within which it is produced and received but also the specific nature of its female representation. Anglo-Saxon female poetic representation is constrained within the heroic world by the poetic and psychological strategies with which it elicits and manipulates identification with a masculine aristocratic warrior ethic. While identification with the hero is highly complex (who would want to be a Beowulf?), and not all men are heroes, women too are represented as differently 'other' to the main concerns of warrior life. In a similar way, we have begun to look again at the issue of female signification in the elegies, where the physical and psychological states of exile that inform this poetry are rendered anew when read through the filter of gender.

It is well known that female-voiced elegies such as *The Wife's Lament* have parallels in other Germanic literatures, such as the so-called *Frauenlieder*. By the same token, female representation in the heroic literatures — martial and religious — is assessed in relation to figures from the Old Norse sagas. In all of these cases, however, critical claims have been pressed too far, without noting the specific differences between these apparently similar genres. To put the matter bluntly, the chief virtue of the comparison of the female-voiced Anglo-Saxon elegies with related continental genres such as the *Frauenlieder* is the poverty of the Anglo-Saxon examples. We can hardly hope to build claims for the specific nature of female voice and psychology in Anglo-Saxon literature on the basis of a couple of examples, and perhaps this is the point: if we are to read the elegies as one place in the poetry where the internal psychological state of the individual matters, then it follows that in Anglo-Saxon England that individual is male, even when, or perhaps especially when, that voice is universalized. Pertinent examples are the warrior voice of *The Wanderer*, and the peculiarly literal and metaphoric voice of *The Seafarer*. Located in the intersection between gender and genre, the female voice of, for example, *The Wife's Lament* has to be accommodated within, or abjected from, the conventions of the male.[15]

The constraints of genre on gender and representation in Anglo-Saxon England have implications for a much wider issue. One current critical trend in post-Conquest fields — whether those of the medieval, Renaissance, or Enlightenment periods — is the search for the origins of western subjectivity as a uniquely individual, private, interior state and identity. Feminist criticism complicates this search considerably, since it regularly points to the difficulty of identifying, let alone analyzing, a distinctly female subjectivity within patriarchy. While this critical problem has yet to be fully explored by Anglo-Saxonists, there is already sufficient evidence to suggest what Anglo-Saxon England might contribute to this debate. Post-Conquest critics often associate notions of individual subjectivity with the formation of public and private domains, which are frequently read as gendered spaces. The absence of a clearly delineated sense of either social or cultural space in the Anglo-Saxon period with which to begin to map public or private, masculine or feminine, domains suggests that there is no evidence for such interiority in Anglo-Saxon England. Other evidence compounds the problem. Confession in this period is largely public, and only tangentially Augustinian, for example. Notions of authorship are not associated with our post-Conquest (often Romantic) concepts of individuality but are instead largely anonymous and ungendered; that is to say masculinist, pseudonymous (therefore universal or transcendental of self), and associated with the clerical orders or with the cultural construction of the (always already) male *scop*. Representation of the individual – male or female – is deeply embedded in the idealized cultural codes of Christian community or heroic society. Reading for the subject, in other words, often means reading against modern notions of the individual and recognizing the historical alterity of Anglo-Saxon identity.

This is not to argue for any sentimental idealization of Anglo-Saxon identity as community, however. To the contrary, identity – whether social or literary – is, to say the least, conflicted and is forged as much by ideologies of gender, rank, kin, and belief as by genre. The competing demands of such ideologies, none of which is ever totally dominant, form the asymmetric patriarchal matrix within which identity is produced. Small wonder, then, that critical opinion is deeply divided about even the idea of the agency of Eve, for example, the nature of whose problematic desire (or will) in *Genesis B* forms one axis along which we can assess the relation between identity, gender, and representation within this period. In contrast with humanist notions of the individual, the parallels between Anglo-Saxon structures of identity, formed within a matrix that includes class and gender ideologies as well as cultural representation and post-modern theories of the self, are superficially striking but cannot be pressed too far. One obvious difference between post-modern and Anglo-Saxon notions of gender and identity is the emphasis in the former on sexuality and on paradigms of heterosexuality and homosociality. Anglo-Saxon England is a period marked by its apparent cultural lack of interest in sexuality, indicating that sexuality, identity, and gender are differently constructed cultural discourses in this period. The factors of belief and community so important to notions of Anglo-Saxon identity, by contrast, are generally elided by post-modernist and feminist theories of the subject. In other words, the study of Anglo-Saxon identity has much to contribute to post-modern discussions of similar phenomena, reminding us of the limits of contemporary theory as well as of the alterity of the past.

Elene's voice

One genre in which we can clearly see the alterity of gendered notions of the subject is the poetic saint's life, which presents an intriguing, culturally distinctive blend of female subjects, violence, heroic convention, Christian intent, and dynamic relation between Latin pre-text and Old English poetic reception. These generic features are peculiarly marked, or rather problematically attenuated, in Cynewulf's *Elene*. As a narrative of the finding of the True Cross (the *Inventio crucis*) the misleadingly titled *Elene* offers poetic insight into a piety of considerable popularity in Anglo-Saxon England: the cult of the Cross.[16] The poem is therefore a most peculiar saint's life, both in the English and Latin versions, being not so much about one saint or even two (Elene and Judas, renamed Cyriacus) as about the sacred history of an icon, the Cross, whose feast-day provides one of the climaxes of the narrative.

Elene, however, conforms to the conventions of hagiography whereby what matters is not the saint but the significance of the phenomenon of sanctity to the Christian community. Accordingly, the icon of the Cross is revealed and interpreted to us via three figures, Constantine, Judas, and Elene, not to mention the iconic poet himself. The relationship between these figures provides the drama of the poem as each unfolds to the audience the power of the Cross. The conversions that demonstrate the figural power of the Cross in the poem — Constantine's, Judas', and, more arguably, the poet's (Cynewulf's) — do not include that of Elene, and it is Judas who is the more obvious candidate for sanctity (as the title of the Latin versions witness). Judas' conversion to Christianity actually leads to the miraculous revelation of the whereabouts of the Cross. The poem's perspective thus embraces temporal history within a figural frame of sacred history and accordingly locates sanctity in the relations between men (Constantine, Judas, the poet), women (Elene), and icon (the Cross, God). Where, within this generic map of relations both human and divine, can we locate Elene and her justly celebrated voice? Feminist criticism has tended to concentrate on Elene alone and the importance of her speeches, which are positioned at the center of the narrative, and represent some of the lengthiest speeches by a woman in the poetic corpus.[17] Yet Elene is not the only subject of the poem, nor perhaps, given the poem's dual focus on Judas and the Cross, the most important. In terms of the plot, however, Elene provides the link between Constantine, Judas, and the Cross, while in both literal and symbolic terms her representation offers a nexus for the poem's thematic interests. She is, in short, overdetermined as an Anglo-Saxon poetic female figure. One feminist reading of the poem would seek to understand the nature of this overdetermination and to explore further the significance of Elene's gender and agency. A good place to start is with an analysis of her representation and its analogues in early medieval literary culture.

Free of the conventions of prose hagiography, which demand a title and an occasion for delivery, thereby producing a clear focus of subject on the *inventio* in the English prose analogues of the story, Cynewulf's poetic narrative complicates and amplifies the structure of his inherited material in sophisticated ways. It is well known, for example, that in the first section of the poem Cynewulf unlocks his wordhoard in order to create an Anglo-Saxon epic, complete with set pieces of sea-voyages and battles. The poem thus finds itself constrained by the generic demands of Anglo-Saxon heroic poetry at the same time as it negotiates the paradigms of hagiography. This generic manipulation, in turn, enhances and complicates our notions of the significance of gender in the narrative. Constantine, as the anxious military leader poised on the threshold of Christian revelation and reward (as well as military success), becomes in part assimilable to other heroic male figures in the canon. His difference – that of faith – comments poignantly on figures such as Hrothgar and Beowulf who are not projected from the heroic world of the mythical past into the Christian world of sacred history. The representation of Elene appears to be rooted in a similar poetic technique, beginning as she does as a heroic *guðcwen* entering Greece at the head of a triumphant host in search of the Cross (line 254). The

catch, of course, is that Elene is the only Anglo-Saxon heroic aristocratic woman, or *ides*, distinguished in such a way, and her host is to say
the least somewhat redundant: Elene fights no battles, unlike Constantine; struggles with no devils, unlike Judas; and is herself granted no
revelations of the divine, bearing witness instead to those granted to
Judas.

If we broaden the terms of our investigation beyond the poem itself,
the puzzling nature of Elene's gendered representation becomes even
clearer. For one thing, although she is identified as an *ides*, the exact
nature of her relation to other poetic aristocratic women is problematic,
as I have already suggested. Nor is Elene usefully comparable to other
female figures in the hagiographic tradition, prose or poetry. Elene faces
no trial of her virginity – symbolic or literal – and suffers no physical
torture or passion. Hers is no *imitatio Christi*, and she cannot be read
convincingly as a female *miles Christi*, like Juliana, for example. In fact,
as Rosemary Woolf noted years ago, Elene's combative judicial challenges of Judas resemble most closely 'an inverted passion, in which the
ruler is the Christian and the prisoner the pagan'.[18] This complicates the
audience's or reader's identification with her quite considerably. At
times, our sympathies lie more readily with the tortured Judas, whose
imitatio is far more accessible. This is an effect of which Cynewulf may
have been aware, for he reiterates Elene's blessed nature, her rightness,
her admirable plain speaking, and her eagerness for truth throughout.
Cynewulf's interest in Elene is clear; how to understand that interest
drives any feminist reading of the poem. Has Cynewulf forged from the
intersection of two genres – heroic and hagiographic – an Anglo-Saxon
Christian female epic and in doing so exposed, perhaps unconsciously,
the gender implications of such a move? That is to say, no woman could
actually form, in an unconflicted fashion, the heroic subject of such a
poem.

The proposition that *Elene* points to the constraints and limitations
on the representation not merely of Elene but of women more generally
in Anglo-Saxon poetry – the conflicts, in other words, between genre
and gender – is an attractive one, largely because our attempts to understand Elene herself are conducted so negatively. The negative argument
is always a problem in Anglo-Saxon studies, since so much of our evidence has been lost and since, in the case of female representation, the
evidence extant is so sparse. Nonetheless, in the case of Elene, the list of

negations is striking. In fact, she first enters the poem negatively, characterized by Cynewulf (in a neat reworking of conventional male heroic understatement) as not wishing to resist Constantine's commands:

> Elene ne wolde
> þæs siðfætes   sæne weorðan,
> ne ðæs wilgifan   word gehyrwan,
> hiere sylfre suna,   ac wæs sona gearu. . . .   (219b-22)

[Elene did not wish to be reluctant about this journey, nor to despise the word of the ruler, her own son, but was immediately ready.]

Subject to Constantine's desire, and his surrogate or rather subordinate for the rest of the poem, Elene's own identity as heroic mother, or even aristocratic queen, remains largely untapped and redundant. To be sure, Cynewulf sprinkles his poem with the appropriate female epithets – heroic and religious – but such terms gesture toward generic, and within them class, boundaries rather than enhance Elene's own characterization. The effect oddly empties and flattens her representation as a woman and attenuates her agency on the literal and heroic levels. As we have already seen, feminist work in Old English often focuses on the nature of female agency, especially that of aristocratic women; the paradoxical prominence of Elene in the poem, given the complex nature of her agency, is a good example of the kinds of problems feminist criticism addresses.

Another example of the conflict between genre and gender can be detected in Cynewulf's reworking of Elene's speeches to Judas. Critics of the poem tend to agree that these remarkable passages, in which Elene chastises the Jews for their sins and their secrets as she pursues her son's desire (now her desire too) for the Cross, owe nothing to the heroic genre of flyting, even though Judas himself seems to anticipate this generic identification in his reported account of his father's words (443b). Gender and genre support this position: Elene's words cannot resemble heroic flyting first because she is a woman (flyting is a male activity in the Anglo-Saxon heroic corpus), and secondly because their content is religious, not martial and vaunting. And yet it is hard not to read these passages as flyting, not only because Judas later uncannily reproduces a similar verbal battle with the devil (898b-955), but also because in Elene's case Cynewulf has set up the necessary heroic conditions. Elene first faces the Jews surrounded by her martial retainers, signaling the required potential for battle: later she alone faces Judas and offers him a choice, which is both heroic and religious (259-81; 598-608). The result is a flyting that is not a flyting by a woman who, by virtue of her gender, is a most unusual hero. In other words, the transposition of heroic culture into religious material, so common in Anglo-Saxon England, highlights the problematic nature of Elene's female religious heroism.

In this regard, to compare Elene to the world of Norse literature with its selection of taunting women who, displaced from the sphere of direct action, fight instead with words is helpful, though not in the ways we first suppose. For Elene is no woman inciting violence and revenge on behalf of her kin – unless we grant that Elene's kin are not just Constantine but the Christian community, and that her revenge is not for her son but for the Son, Christ. In fact, however, the language of family resonates much more strongly in Judas' account of the transmission of Jewish wisdom and lore across the paternal generations than in Elene's speeches (436-535).[19]

The feminist question of what it means that Elene is a woman turns out to be highly complex. In the examples of the poem's generic affiliations and the difficulty of classifying Elene within them, it becomes clear that, counter to (especially feminist) common sense, Elene's gender, her femaleness, while generically unique, matters very little on the literal level of the poem. Female gender is so thoroughly naturalized that it carries little signifying weight: Elene is a mother and an *ides*, but neither role is explored: her agency is that of her son. In addition, the nature of her heroism is constrained as much by generic convention as by the subjects of the poem: remember that the Cross and Judas are stressed as more important by the narrative. A feminist reading of the poem thus faces a paradox: on the one hand, Elene is prominent in the poem, especially by virtue of her powerful words; on the other hand, an analysis of the conventions of her representation reveals the limited nature of her autonomy, her agency.

In fact, where female gender matters – signifies – is on the figural level of the poem. For Elene is not just a woman but also the figure of *Ecclesia*, as Thomas D. Hill has convincingly suggested.[20] Hill is a little uncomfortable with this suggestion, however, detecting in Cynewulf's fashioning of the historical (literal) persona of Elene few of the discrepancies in that of Judas. In other words, it is precisely the problematic representation of Elene that leads Hill to make discussion of Judas (who represents not only the historical person but also Judaism and the Jews) carry the burden of his argument about the poem's allegorical significance. Only secondarily does Hill reconsider Elene. From a feminist perspective, however, only Cynewulf's exploitation of the allegorical significance of Elene as *Ecclesia* explains Elene's paradoxical representation on the literal level of the text. The flattened significance of her gender and the oddity of her highly repetitive and stylized speeches make it clear that her own (Constantine's own) desire to find the Cross is of lesser importance than the reenactment of the historical rejection of Judaism and the reeducation of Judas into Christianity.

There is of course a fine irony (not wholly of Cynewulf's making) in the conventional representation of *Ecclesia* as female; the figure of the chastizing, powerful and wise mother occludes the real conditions of women within the institution of the church and idealizes their social roles as mothers. Elene's own role as mother is hardly explored in the poem, as has already been suggested. The irony is enhanced when we recall that it is in this figural role of the maternal church that Elene – as female – assumes the power to redefine the identity and significance of Judas and the Jews. Gender is here pressed into service as a boundary over which to negotiate and thereby create the abjection of the racial and masculine otherness of the Jews, in very physical terms (remember Elene's torture of Judas). To put it another way, the Jews are more powerfully 'other' in Anglo-Saxon culture than women. On the other side of the equation, Elene's subjection to Constantine, whose agency she also performs throughout the poem, maintains the masculine social order intact. Without doubt, part of Elene's compelling presence in the poem is an effect of this dual process, since she acts as guarantor of both symbolic and social orders. The price is the emptying out of the feminine at the literal level and its redeployment at the figural, which is used to position these masculinist structures.

Viewed in this light, Elene's central speeches, whose static nature contrasts with the unfolding and therefore temporal dramas of both Constantine and Judas, are iterations of the atemporal power of the Christian faith. Power, especially the power of faith, thrives on the maintenance of boundaries: think of all those struggles between the body and the soul, for example. Elene's speeches, in their insistent repetition of the rightness of Christianity, are iterations or citations, in Judith Butler's sense of the terms, but they do not iterate gender, instead using gender to iterate belief. Hence, gender and belief are conflated in the image of the maternal *Ecclesia*. What is produced by this process of conflation is not a heterosexual subject, governed by the constraints of heteronormativity that we might recognize from Butler's theories of performance in the formation of identity, but a Christian subject. This subject — Judas and not Elene, who is never formally converted in the poem — is formed in part from a resignification of gender, as well as ethnic, categories for both Jewish son and heroic mother, figured as Judaism and Christian *Ecclesia* respectively. The process of resignification does not mean that gender does not matter in the poem, however, but that gender relations, masculine and feminine, matter differently in a Christian symbolic order. The final key to this difference lies in the nature of divine knowledge and its relation to human knowledge in the formation of the believing subject, which is the poem's main theme.

Both Judas and Elene, in fact, are put in the position of knowing and not knowing: Judas knows history without knowing that it is but a veil for sacred history, and Elene does not know where the Cross is but knows the historical errors of the Jews. The difference between these two positions is enacted in the debates of Elene with Judas as a conflict between literal and spiritual knowledge. As the figure of *Ecclesia*, Elene is the institution that preserves God's law, spiritual knowledge. Gender is here remetaphorized as an image of the boundary between those who know they are subject to divine truth and believe, figured as feminine, and those who do not know and therefore do not believe until that truth is revealed to them, figured as masculine. As the historical woman and not the figure of the church, however, Elene *in addition to Judas* requires that knowledge to confirm her faith. Accordingly, Elene is given the gift of wisdom after the discovery of the nails of the Cross (lines 1142–3) in a move that points up the slippage between literal and allegorical figuration, since the already wise and learned *Ecclesia* would have no need of such a gift. As Hill points out, the literal and allegorical levels of a poem, though simultaneous, are never synonymous, and the redundancy of the gift on the allegorical level highlights its importance to the historical woman. What is enacted as a conflict between masculine and feminine positions at the allegorical level is shared by both at the literal. Elene's literal desire, in short, conflicts with her spiritual type, which may explain why in the poem, though not the English prose analogues, Elene is hardly direct in asking Judas the whereabouts of the Cross.

As the poem moves to closure and coda, however, the representation of Elene returns to the literal level, as she returns to her son and establishes the feast-day of the *Inventio*. At this stage, the figure of the poet displaces Elene, since he too receives divine wisdom, and thereby with it, for him though not for Elene, the gift of poetry (1236–51a). Thus Elene performs a final service of mediating divine knowledge in the poem to its expression and performance outside it, just as she acted before as the mediator between Constantine and Judas.

My reading of Elene points to how both gender and genre intersect in her representation as a Christian figure, and how the significance of that figure is further nuanced by exploring the connections and disconnections between allegory and gender. In other words, a feminist approach does not replace a more conventional exegetical treatment, such as that by Thomas Hill, but complements and complicates it. Feminist theory helps elucidate how gender also plays an important role in the resignification of Elene. At the same time, Elene offers one example of how such theory (in this case, Butler's concepts of performativity and citation) must be rethought in the face of such massive cultural differences as the nature of belief. Hill correctly identifies the aesthetic of Cynewulf's poem as iconic. The poem recreates the Cross as an icon for worship, and as one stage in that process Elene herself assumes the position of icon, *Ecclesia*: static, resolute, unwavering in her faith. The use of the poetic convention of the beautiful *ides*, who similarly commands our attention, to signify this icon on the literal level makes perfect sense as long as we do not mistake this literal level for the spiritual. It is difficult not to be ambivalent about Elene, perhaps because the conversion of a woman into an iconic object, revered as the spiritual sign of *Ecclesia*, is achieved at the price of that historical woman as subject.

Although this reading of *Elene* operates within the familiar territory of literary analysis, it intersects with those broader issues of feminism in Anglo-Saxon culture that I explored in the first half of the essay by exploring the relation between gender, genre, and the formation of belief in culture. A feminist inquiring into any cultural document of the Anglo-Saxon period will find herself asking about the woman in or absent from the text, and about her relation to that woman – not at the expense of other interdisciplinary questions about origins, genre, subjectivity, aesthetics, and gender, but perhaps because of them.

Notes

1 *Studying Medieval Women: Sex, Gender, Feminism*, ed. N. F. Partner, *Speculum* 68 (1993), 305–8 at 305.

2 The fullest examination of the concept of origins in relation to the discipline of Anglo-Saxon is that of A. J. Frantzen, *Desire for Origins: New Language, Old English, and Teaching the Tradition* (New Brunswick and London, 1990). See also G. R. Overing and M. Osborn, *Landscape of Desire: Partial Stories of the Medieval Scandinavian World* (Minneapolis and London, 1994) for a study of the relation between landscape and origins.

3 J. Chance, *Woman as Hero in Old English Literature* (Syracuse, 1986); C. Fell, *Women in Anglo-Saxon England and the Impact of 1066*, with C. Clark and E. Williams (Oxford, 1984), especially for her comments on the so-called 'golden age'; and H. Damico, *Beowulf's Wealhtheow and the Valkyrie Tradition* (Madison, 1984). Discussion of the problems of traditional historiography from the standpoint of women's history and culture was a major feature of feminist thought of the 1970s and 1980s (as it is now); a useful example is J. Kelly-Gadol, 'The Social Relations of the Sexes: Methodological Implications of Women's History', *Signs* 1 (1976), 809–23, repr. in *The SIGNS Reader*, ed. E. Abel and E. K. Abel (Chicago, 1983), pp. 11–25. The notion of 'golden ages' (still a matter of debate for the Anglo-Saxon period, to judge from A. Hennessey Olsen's 'Old English Women, Old English Men: A Reconsideration of "Minor" Characters' in *Old English Shorter Poems*, ed. K. O'Brien O'Keeffe, Basic Readings in Anglo-Saxon England 3 [New York and London, 1994], pp. 65–83), has been most recently challenged in the medieval period by J. M. Bennett, 'Medieval Women, Modern Women: Across the Great Divide' in *Culture and History 1350–1600: Essays on English Communities, Identities, and Writing*, ed. D. Aers (Detroit, 1992), pp. 147–75.

4 For this general phenomenon see C. A. Simmons, *Reversing the Conquest: History and Myth in Nineteenth-Century British Literature* (New Brunswick and London, 1990).

5 *New Readings on Women in Old English Literature*, ed. H. Damico and A. Hennessey Olsen (Bloomington and Indianapolis, 1990).

6 H. T. Bennett, 'From Peace Weaver to Text Weaver: Feminist Approaches to Old English Literature', *Twenty Years of the 'Year's Work in Old English Studies'*, ed. K. O'Brien O'Keeffe, *OEN Subsidia* 15 (1989), 23–42; H. T. Bennett, C. A. Lees, and G. R. Overing, 'Gender and Power: Feminism and Old English Studies', *Medieval Feminist Newsletter* 10 (1990), 15–23.

7 *Speaking Two Languages: Traditional Disciplines and Contemporary Theory in Medieval Studies*, ed. A. J. Frantzen (Albany, 1991); *Class and Gender in Early English Literature: Intersections*, ed. B. J. Harwood and G. R. Overing (Bloomington and Indianapolis, 1994).

8 For examples, see S. Lerer, *Literacy and Power in Anglo-Saxon Literature* (Lincoln, NE and London, 1991); K. O'Brien O'Keeffe, *Visible Song: Transitional Literacy in Old English Verse* (Cambridge, 1990); and, more generally, B. Stock, *The Implications of Literacy: Written Language and Models of Interpretation in the Eleventh and Twelfth Centuries* (Princeton, 1983).

9 It is a pleasure to find Elstob included in G. Lerner's feminist history, *The Creation of Feminist Consciousness* (New York and Oxford, 1993), pp. 36–8; see also V. W. Beauchamp, 'Pioneer Linguist: Elizabeth Elstob (1683–1756)', *Papers on Women's Studies* 1 (1974), 9–43; and Frantzen, *Desire for Origins*, pp. 52–3, 60–61. For Vida Scudder, see Frantzen, *Desire for Origins*, p. 106. Mary Bateson is discussed by S. Mosher Stuard, 'The Chase After Theory: Considering Medieval Women', *Gender and History* 4 (1992), 135–46. There is no study of the women who worked with the editors of the Early English Text Society, who are otherwise acknowledged in the prefaces to various editions; see, for example, W. W. Skeat's acknowledgement of the Misses Gunning and Wilkinson in translating various *Lives* for his edition of *Aelfric's Lives of Saints*, 2 vols., EETS os 94 and 114 (London, 1890, 1900; repr. as 1 vol., 1966), II, pp. liv–lv.

10 See, for example, S. Felman, *What Does A Woman Want? Reading and Sexual Difference* (Baltimore and London, 1993); and *Life/Lines: Theorizing Women's Autobiography*, ed. B. Brodzki and C. Schenck (Ithaca and London, 1988).

11 S. Hollis, *Anglo-Saxon Women and the Church* (Woodbridge, Suffolk, 1992).

12 For Anglo-Saxon notions of mothering, see C. A. Lees and G. R. Overing, 'Birthing Bishops and Fathering Poets: Bede, Hild, and the Relations of Cultural Production', *Exemplaria* 6 (1994), 35–65, with discussion of Asser at 60–1. J. Butler's theories of performance are first elaborated in *Gender Trouble: Feminism and the Subversion of Identity* (London and New York, 1990) and then subsequently refined in *Bodies That Matter: On the Discursive Limits of 'Sex'* (London and New York, 1993); for my discussion of *Elene* later in this essay I rely principally on Butler's most recent work. Of related interest is E. J. Burns, *Bodytalk: When Women Speak in Old French Literature* (Philadelphia, 1993).

13 As J. Nelson also notes in 'Women and the Word in the Earlier Middle Ages', *Women in the Church*, ed. W. J. Sheils and D. Wood, *Studies in Church History* 27 (1990), 53–78.

14 R. Frank, 'Germanic Legend in Old English Literature' in *The Cambridge Companion to Old English Literature*, ed. M. Godden and M. Lapidge (Cambridge, 1991), pp. 88–106 at p. 88. See also J. Harris, 'Love and Death in

the *Männerbund*: An Essay with Special Reference to the *Bjarkamál* and *The Battle of Maldon*' in *Heroic Poetry in the Anglo-Saxon Period: Studies in Honor of Jess B. Bessinger, Jr.*, ed. H. Damico and J. Leyerle (Kalamazoo, MI, 1993), pp. 77–114; and C. A. Lees, 'Men and *Beowulf*' in *Medieval Masculinities: Regarding Men in the Middle Ages*, ed. Lees (Minneapolis and London, 1994), pp. 129–48. For a broader discussion of masculinity in Old English texts, see A. J. Frantzen, 'When Women Aren't Enough' in *Studying Medieval Women*, pp. 455–71.

15 For discussion of the signification of heroic women, see G. R. Overing, *Language, Sign, and Gender in 'Beowulf'* (Carbondale and Edwardsville, IL, 1990), pp. 68–107. For a related discussion of the elegies see H. T. Bennett, 'Exile and the Semiosis of Gender in Old English Elegies' in *Class and Gender in Early English Literature*, ed. Harwood and Overing, pp. 43–58.

16 *Cynewulf's 'Elene'*, ed. P. O. E. Gradon (London, 1958) includes discussion of the cults of the Cross and sources, pp. 15–22. As yet, no direct source for Cynewulf's version has been identified, so I make only general comments about the sources. For English prose analogues, see M.-C. Bodden, ed. and trans., *The Old English Finding of the True Cross* (Woodbridge, Suffolk, 1987); Ælfric's 'V. Non. Mai. Inuentio Sanctae Crucis', *Ælfric's Catholic Homilies: The Second Series Text*, ed. M. Godden, EETS ss 5 (1979), 174–6; R. Morris, ed., *Legends of the Holy Rood*, EETS os 46 (London, 1871; repr. New York, 1969); and A. S. Napier, ed., *History of the Holy Rood Tree*, EETS os 103 (London, 1894; repr. New York, 1973).

17 For example, A. Hennessey Olsen, 'Cynewulf's Autonomous Women: A Reconsideration of Elene and Juliana' in *New Readings on Women*, ed. Damico and Olsen, pp. 222–32.

18 For discussion of Elene as a problematic *ides*, see P. Belanoff, 'The Fall (?) of the Old English Poetic Female Image', *PMLA* 104 (1989), 822–31; see also Rosemary Woolf, 'Saints' Lives' in *Continuations and Beginnings: Studies in Old English Literature*, ed. E. G. Stanley (London, 1966), pp. 37–66 at 47. The implications of J. Hill's 'The Soldier of Christ in Old English Prose and Poetry', *Leeds Studies in English* n.s. 12 (1981), 57–80, are that women may occupy a role analogous to that of the *miles Christi*, as in the case of Juliana, although no formal identification of the woman as such appears in the poetry.

19 For a discussion of the Norse analogues, see Olsen, 'Cynewulf's Autonomous Women', pp. 225–7. *Elene* is ruled out of consideration as heroic flyting in W. Parks, *Verbal Dueling in Heroic Narrative: The Homeric and Old English Traditions* (Princeton, 1990), p. 7.

20 T. D. Hill, 'Sapiential Structure and Figural Narrative in the Old English *Elene*', *Traditio* 27 (1971), 159–77.

8

Post-structuralist
theories: the subject and the text

CAROL BRAUN PASTERNACK

•

Jacques Derrida identifies in the history of western philosophy a point
of rupture, at the time of Freud, Nietzsche, Heidegger, and Saussure,
'when the structurality of structure had to begin to be thought'. At this
point, structuralism began. Derrida himself, Jacques Lacan, Roland
Barthes, Julia Kristeva, and Michel Foucault marked another rupture in
the late 1960s and early 1970s with the publication of their ground-
breaking work, which formed an intellectual core for the sexual, social,
and political revolutions of the time.[1] At that point, post-structuralism
began. Since then this theoretical perspective has been largely resisted
by Anglo-Saxonists, perhaps because its theoretical diction and syntax
have seemed to obscure matters that had seemed clear enough before
post-structuralist interventions, and perhaps because the theories have
seemed to be more concerned with their own post-modernist era than
with the Middle Ages. Though certain strains of post-structuralism have
been criticized as ahistorical (and some of the theories can be practiced
that way), post-structuralist theories can provoke new historical analyses and can provide questions and methodologies that shed new light on
Old English texts and Anglo-Saxon cultures, in part because their interventions do disturb the seeming clarity with which medieval texts have
represented their world to modern scholars. More than anything else,
post-structuralist theories help us look at the texts not as direct representations of culture but as participants in the construction of meaning
for Anglo-Saxon culture and society, and thereby in the construction of
the culture and society themselves.

Structuralism, particularly Ferdinand de Saussure's *Course in
General Linguistics*, enacted the originary break from thinking that

texts directly represent culture or society, for this book expressed the idea that meaning in language is constructed rather than natural, and is constructed differently for each language and culture. Especially influential was his idea that language generates meaning through its own system of differential relationships rather than through any natural links between words and the objects or ideas to which they refer. He showed that distinctions of sound differ from one language to another in a system conceptualized in terms of 'minimal pairs'; for example, *file* and *vile* are distinct in sound and meaning in Modern English even though they would not have been in Old English, where /f/ and /v/ were not distinct phonemes. Hence, although the perceived sound of a word results partly from physiology, it also acquires its distinctiveness from the system of differences particular to a language. The system of differences generates the signification. Each word is a 'sign' composed of 'signifier' (the 'sound image') and 'signified' (the concept). The link between them is arbitrary, and even the concept exists only in relation to other concepts in the language: 'it is quite clear that initially the concept is nothing, that is only a value determined by its relations with other similar values, and . . . without them the signification would not exist.' The same principle applies to lexical and grammatical meanings. For example, Saussure contrasts the lexical 'values' of French *mouton* and English *sheep* in that *mouton* refers to the animal on the hoof or on the table while *sheep* refers only to the animal on the hoof, differing from *mutton*, the food. Similarly, the present-tense inflections in Old English signify something different from present-tense inflections in Latin because Latin distinguishes present and future but Old English does not.[2]

Understanding the 'structurality' of language as a 'structure', to return to Derrida's phrase, provided a model for understanding the 'structurality' of cultures. So Claude Lévi-Strauss, the preeminent structural anthropologist, mapped cultures in terms of the oppositional qualities that their practices expressed. Hence, a culture would have practices that one could characterize as 'raw' and practices that one could characterize as 'cooked'; it was necessary for both to exist to give each other meaning through their difference.[3] This method of analyzing makes it seem logical that a culture, a society or even a single document would not express purely one element or another but oppositions in relationship.

Structuralist analysis, then, undermines the nationalist ideas that dominated nineteenth-century studies of Old English texts. Much of that work was founded on the belief that language, history, and moral value were integral in a culture, so that for German scholars a text in an early Germanic language, such as *Beowulf*, would naturally represent the early national spirit, and parts of that text representing a contradictory spirit would be analyzed as an inauthentic accretion, 'Christian coloring' on an originally pagan expression.[4] But from a structuralist perspective, *Beowulf* is neither a pagan text with Christian coloring nor a Christian text with pagan coloring but one in which Christian and pagan attitudes and practices have meaning through their oppositional difference. Further, the differential relation, as it is expressed in this text, contributes to the systematic opposition of Christianity and paganism as it is expressed in other practices in the culture and acquires meaning through that cultural matrix, in which other oppositions play a part as well (male and female, inside and outside, courage and cowardice, and so on).

Post-structuralist theories, then, are based on these concepts: that rather than any natural, universal, or divinely ordained set of principles, the relational structure of thought generates meaning, and that structures of thought are structured into and by the linguistic system of a culture and so can be analyzed as texts. The following pages will concentrate on the foundational moments of post-structuralism and their implications for Old English criticism in particular theories that suggest ways of reading culture through texts: Derrida's deconstruction; Barthes's and Kristeva's semiotics and textuality; Lacan's psychoanalytic theory of the subject; and Foucault's study of culture. One second-generation theorist, Fredric Jameson, will provide a way to read texts for cultural conflict and change.

Deconstruction and the textual basis of perception

Jacques Derrida took the first bold step beyond structuralism by asserting that the structure of thought and its 'reality' are textual in their definitions and can be analyzed as such. While people, wars, food, and famine exist in material dimensions, human perception is structured through linguistic systems, and so human understanding of the material and the immaterial are textual and any cultural artifacts – archeological remains, visual arts, manuscripts – are read as texts. This philosophical position suits the study of Anglo-Saxon culture in that texts are literally almost all that remains. Deconstruction, Derrida's method for interpreting systems of thought and the texts that embody them, provides a way of reading the structures of the texts and then questioning the structures to discover what was unthinkable in them and hence a motivating force in generating these structures.

Like structuralism, deconstruction initiates analysis by laying out a text's conceptual systems in binary fashion, identifying oppositional differences. Derrida's philosophical insight motivates the next steps. He argued in 'Structure, Sign, and Play' that western philosophical traditions have provided centers for these binaries in order to stabilize an otherwise indefinite play within the system, so that 'God', 'Nature', 'Man', or some other 'transcendental signified' indicates the value of one binary over another, such as the rational over the emotional or the civilized over the primitive. This center, not intrinsic to the structure, makes the system of thought seem a universal or natural or sensible system of meaning. Deconstruction identifies this center as a 'supplementary' imposition of a certain meaning and also identifies a term or terms that do not comply with the binary oppositions, 'something which escapes these concepts and certainly precedes them – probably as the condition for their possibility'. The oppositional system, then, by design, puts the 'common ground' in the realm of the 'unthinkable': it puts forward an 'irreducible difference' and so defers the unthinkable that underlies it (hence his term *différance*, which plays on the two senses of *différer*, to be different and to defer).[5] Thus, the critic attempts to distance herself from the structure of the text rather than identify with it. She does not attempt to reiterate its meaning in new words and clarify its unity and harmony, as a New Critic would, but to identify the system of meaning and think past those who participate in it to what is unthinkable in the system.

So John P. Hermann, in *Allegories of War: Language and Violence in Old English Poetry*, analyzed the language used to characterize the spiritual victory of the soul over the assaults of the devil. He used philological and exegetical methods to spell out the oppositions the poetry established between such categories as *Ecclesia* and *Diabolus*, and the violent, military metaphors used to establish the oppositions. He then deconstructed the oppositions by showing that, while the texts privilege the metaphorical violence associated with *Ecclesia*, a portion of the literal resists transformation and points to the common ground of violence that undermines the 'irreducible difference' between *Ecclesia* and *Diabolus*. As Hermann reflects in concluding his analysis of *Exodus*: 'Pleasure at the destruction of an enemy can be restricted to spiritual joy only by sanitizing an attitude that can always resurface in historical hostilities and encounters. Pleasure at the destruction of the enemy is made safe, even holy, through such textual processes.'[6]

This deconstructive analysis of language takes us to the analysis of cultural systems of thought, and instead of affirming the structures created through the texts, we question that one side of the binary is holier than the other. Deconstruction shakes us loose from the sense that any concepts, such as those concerning holiness, social relations, or gender, are God-given, universal, or natural. By doing so, it frees us to examine how such concepts are structured specifically within Anglo-Saxon culture.

Semiotics and textuality

In *S/Z* Roland Barthes asserted that the '"I" which approaches the text is already itself a plurality of other texts, of codes which are infinite' and that its subjectivity 'is merely the wake of all codes that constitute me'. In that book, he demonstrated the process in which someone deploys those codes to perform the 'labor of language' that is reading.[7] Some codes have specifically to do with literary convention, others with such cultural knowledge as geography, manners, and religious doctrine. Semiotics is the study of such sign systems. 'Textuality', the network of codes associated with literary discourse, has been especially interesting to post-structuralists, in particular the concepts of 'the author' and 'the work'. The post-structuralist theories of textuality interact with the newly revived interest in editing and the material text, in ways that are very interesting for Anglo-Saxonists. In fact, these theories help to explain conflicts between modern ideas about author and work and the physical facts of Old English texts that have troubled their interpretation for some time.

In *Séméiotiké* Julia Kristeva, like Barthes, describes the reading process as a 'dialogue' of two 'discourses', of the 'addressee' and of the 'subject of the narration'. The addressee 'transforms the subject into an *author*'. While the reader may understand the text to be a work which the author originated, it is in fact 'a mosaic of quotations' brought into play through the discourse that the reader brings to the text. In this way of thinking, 'The notion of *intertextuality* replaces that of intersubjectivity, and poetic language is read as at least *double*'; that is, Kristeva characterizes reading as a dialogue between texts, rather than between author and reader, in which meaning is generated ambiguously, both from the present context of a word or phrase and from the other contexts that the reader brings into play.[8] One implication of her theory and Barthes's is that the text's operation differs radically depending on the texts and codes that the reader brings into the dialogue. As Michel Foucault explained in 'What is an Author?', other social elements enter into the author's construction, such as copyright law, belief in individuality and originality, and the practice of labeling texts with an authorial name and distinguishing title.[9] Of course, a person exists who puts words on paper, but the meaning of that person is generated within a complex system of signs and is culturally specific. The concept of the 'work' is intimately related to the 'author' because the work acquires its aspect of particularity in part through the idea of originality, which characterizes the idea of the author as well.

Anglo-Saxonists have been interested in certain cultural and literary codes. We have analyzed the cultural codes that make the comitatus function, such as the *beot* or boast, and have used that analysis to 'decode' such scenes as Ælfwine's exhortation in *The Battle of Maldon* that the men remember the boasts they made when they passed the mead cup (211–14). In our attempts to understand the functioning of variation, kennings, and meter, we have been deciphering codes in the discourse of Old English verse. But we have only just begun to explore key concepts of author, work, reading subject, and their relation to the letter of the manuscript. My recent work contributes by examining the code of the 'implied tradition', which functions in the place of the implied author in modern literary discourse.

The code of the 'implied tradition' is generated from and affects the reading of a number of features of Old English verse.[10] For one thing, the verse's formulaic language does not point to particularities of expression and thought for a text's narrating subject, and it echoes no individual text but an indefinitely large set of similar expressions in an indefinite number of texts. In addition, texts appear in manuscripts as sequences of verse, divided by large capital letters and clusters of punctuation, without title or authorial name to assert their separateness. Furthermore, these verse sequences themselves are composites of stylistically differentiated movements. All of these features contribute to a remarkably transparent and active intertextuality. Where modern intertextuality works in conjunction with author and work so that its quotations of other texts are either obscured (in order to maintain the illusion of originality) or are understood as allusions to other particular texts that unlock the meaning of the present text,[11] the intertextuality in Old English verse works in conjunction with the implied tradition such that the 'mosaic' consists not of 'quotations' but of traditional expressions that allude to any number of other texts and validate the text's meaning. The 'ambiguity' or 'doubleness' that derives from the use of a previously uttered expression in the present context need not be resolved into the correct meaning for a present author or work, but can remain in play insofar as both texts are perceived as participating in the tradition. In addition, the stylistically distinct movements allow the sections in a verse sequence to play against each other through their own networks of intertexts, and the only partial separation in a manuscript of one verse sequence from another (for example, *Christ III* from *Guthlac*) extends the play.

If a reader employs this code of the implied tradition – in other words, if he functions as the addressee implied by the text – he engages in a different dialogue with the text from that generated through codes of author and work. For example, instead of struggling to define once and for all the boundaries of individual poems, such as whether or not the Vercelli Book presents one poem about Andreas and another about the fates of the twelve apostles perhaps written by a poet named Cynewulf, the reader engages in the purposively dialogic construction of his experience in the textual tradition. Also, this reader does not struggle to defend the harmonious unity of such works as *The Wanderer* or *Beowulf*, but engages with the intertextual ambiguities generated through the diverse movements in these textual sequences.

Anglo-Saxonists have recognized for a long time that Old English verse is intensely and extensively traditional, and the critic has customarily praised verse not for its original formulation of a thought, that sense that the idea has never before been captured by such a perfect choice of words, but for the power generated by the deep, traditional resonances of the phrase in its present context. And the field's long-term interest in sources has debunked any myths of original inspiration. But the post-structuralist insight that the meanings of signs are generated within a system specific to a culture can help us make sense of this traditionality in ways that are more consistent with the whole range of evidence at hand. Because this traditional, authorless system constructs the narrating subject in a radically different way from modern literature, investigating that construction would reveal historical changes in 'signifying practices' and in subjectivity itself.

The post-structuralist subject

Jacques Lacan's theories of psychological identity provide a framework for historicizing the subject through analysis of linguistic systems. Lacan rethought Freud through Saussurian linguistics. He accepted the arbitrariness of the link between the signifier and the signified in the sign and also the social and cultural basis of any linguistic system, taking that arbitrariness as a bar that separates them and as symbolic of the gulf dividing desire itself from the language that the subject uses to express his desire. To explain the individual drama that leads to this division, Lacan reconfigured Freud's Oedipal crisis in such a way that the father's intrusion in the mother–child dyad is the intrusion of the Name-of-the-Father; that is, of the symbolic order itself. In order to speak its separateness and subjectivity, the infant child's perception of unity with the mother must be broken, and the child must speak its needs, repressing the desire for that unity. It then constitutes itself in separateness, through the 'Symbolic Order'. The repressed does emerge, of course, in the unconscious; but there, too, language is the signifying structure in the symbols that emerge in dreams, in the metonymy that displaces the desire so as to avoid its censorship and in the metaphor that superimposes one signifier over another that would more directly point to the actual signified. In sum, it is through the language of one's culture that one becomes an individual and a social being, and through that same language that one has any connection (though it remains a disconnection) with one's being and the Other from which one is alienated and which one desires.

Because Lacan links the Symbolic with the Name-of-the-Father and hence with the masculine and the 'Imaginary', the pre-symbolic stage of undifferentiated unity, with the (m)Other and hence with the feminine, his work has engaged feminist thinkers. Kristeva, Hélène Cixous, and Catherine Clément, among others, have pushed that differential association in order to develop a concept of feminine language that values the qualities of the Imaginary and also builds on the idea that those who do not participate in the Symbolic are marginalized as 'hysterics', and that consequently non-masculine women have been marginalized. In Old English criticism, Patricia Belanoff uses the concept of feminine language to address the difficulties and interpretive resistances in *Wulf and Eadwacer*, drawing on Kristeva's concept of the 'semiotic'; Gillian Overing uses the concept of the hysteric, as developed by Cixous and Clément, to address the fact that all the women in *Beowulf*, except Wealhtheow, are speechless and powerless within the 'masculine economy' of the poem; and Helen Bennett uses the concept of woman's exclusion from the symbolic order to discuss the silence of the female mourner in *Beowulf* as well as the attempts by masculine critics to fill in the silences of the damaged manuscript.[12] Though these analyses provoke new ways of understanding the function of gender in Old English texts, developing them in a larger cultural context might significantly alter their conclusions. Not only does the symbolic nature of language itself necessarily present a barrier to the textual representation of the feminine, but all representations of women's voices and silences in Old English texts were necessarily filtered through the monastic scribal culture, which, at least by the tenth century, was unquestionably masculinist.

Lacan's theories do, however, give us a toehold for investigating at least masculine subjectivity in Anglo-Saxon England. Since subjectivity is constituted through language and also through 'the letter', texts offer us some access to that subjectivity and its differences from the modern Western European subject. According to Lacan, both the language of a culture and its 'discourse' establish a tradition and establish the culture's basic structures, and those structures are subject to radical, historical change. He cites the Reformation and Freudianism as such ruptures, exemplifying 'that the slightest alteration in the relation between man and the signifier . . . changes the whole course of history by modifying the moorings that anchor his being'.[13]

Lacan's theories, then, put special pressure on language – lexicon, structure, and medium. One vast territory we might investigate is the part language played in the conversion of the Anglo-Saxons to Christianity, because this set of changes must have been as profound as the Reformation and Freudianism. We might, for example, revisit the idea that in his story of Caedmon Bede represents the conversion of heroic diction to Christian and oral discourse to written. Although most have conceived of this process as a straightforward addition of new to old, Lacan's work implies that this conversion of old forms to new content and medium would also have been a conversion of subjectivity, of the identity of the subject who composed the verse and the subjects who became such through their use of this new symbolic order. My analysis of *Beowulf* (below, pp. 182–9) will show that the new uses of diction and new medium could not simply have supplemented the old: rather the new Christian symbolic restructured the lexicon, fundamentally contradicting the heroic. This analysis will also show that writing was an integral part of the new symbolic order and contributed to the loss of the old.

An archeology of culture through texts

Post-structuralist methodologies can be applied to individual texts: one can deconstruct the systems of thought in *Beowulf*, analyze the functions of codes in *The Battle of Maldon* or characterize the subject's struggle in language in *Wulf and Eadwacer*. But these theories also all encourage us to use methods of linguistic and textual analysis, pushing us towards a broader study of 'signifying practices' within Anglo-Saxon cultures. Michel Foucault's 'archeology' of cultures and Fredric Jameson's methods for reading the 'political unconscious' in texts can provide frameworks for such studies.

As the title of his theoretical work, *The Archaeology of Knowledge*, suggests, Foucault's great innovation was to study an archeological layer of history in order to describe a matrix of artifacts 'as they existed' rather than in terms of the development of political or economic or philosophical structures. He recognized that particular 'conditions of existence' or 'rules of formation' govern the artifacts that can be produced and their meaning, and he was interested in describing those rules, or 'statements', as one would describe a linguistic system.[14] Recognizing such rules means, of course, recognizing that the individual is not an autonomous subject but is subjected within a discursive formation. It also means that one cannot understand a political, philosophical, or other sort of text primarily in relation to what preceded or followed it in time, because its meaning is governed within its time: indeed, identical sentences can have different functional meanings within different archeological matrices.

As any student of manuscripts knows, the sentence 'I wrote this' in the margin of a tenth-century folio means something different from the same sentence in the introduction to a twentieth-century book: the first is an assertion about making letters on a page, not about originating ideas and sentences. To understand this sentence and the function of other artifacts – actual sentences, texts, events – one needs to observe them within their discursive formation according to the statements that govern their functioning. In the discursive formation of tenth-century English manuscript culture, some statements include: 'scribes write the letters of texts'; 'writing may include determining punctuation'; 'writing Old English verse may include substituting formulas for those in the exemplar being "copied"'; 'manuscripts do not designate authors for vernacular verse'; 'manuscripts do not designate titles for vernacular verse'; and 'a series of capital letters may mark a new section in a verse sequence'.

To get at the discursive formation and determine its sentences, one describes artifacts within their contexts. For students of Old English texts, this principle means describing texts within their manuscript contexts, observing what is actually there on the pages. Katherine O'Brien O'Keeffe's work on Old English verse texts in *Visible Song* follows this method, introducing statements about scribal functions particular to the inscription of the vernacular verse by describing the manuscripts as artifacts, comparing versions of a text, attending to layout, to punctuation, and to variants in formulaic expression. Her analyses are controversial because they recognize that the discursive formation of Old English manuscript verse was distinct to its era and place and did not hold the same statements about textual stability, originality, and authorship that modern book culture does, or that medieval Latin manuscript culture did.[15]

As Foucault states in the fourth chapter of Part III, the artifacts and statements that were enunciated and somehow passed on did not constitute all productions and ideas of the era, but have survived because they were rare, valued commodities; and, further, their existence depended and depends on certain material and institutional conditions, including the book and the library. In *Desire for Origins*, Allen J. Frantzen has followed Foucault in arguing that modern scholars need to be aware of the ways in which academic institutions have affected our picture of Anglo-Saxon culture. In addition, one can study the 'material techniques' that initiated and preserved the statements that we now take as representative of Anglo-Saxon culture. On this basis, Martin Irvine addresses the Parker manuscript of *The Anglo-Saxon Chronicle* and within that *The Battle of Brunanburh*. In his analysis, the manuscript compilation itself contributed to the ideology of an English nation, and *Brunanburh* within that context served the West Saxon dynasty by evoking a 'heroic past' for its kings and representing Athelstan as the leader of a consolidated English force.[16]

This sort of specificity in the production of texts leads to another topic: understanding the 'gaps', the 'absences' and the 'limits' in the 'dispersion' of artifacts and statements. We might consider the church, in conjunction with the noble court, as instrumental in the production of texts in Anglo-Saxon England and how its institutional and ideological interests selected the statements that have survived in time. Although Foucault opposes investigation of the repressed, it would be worthwhile to imagine what segments in society might have uttered and practiced statements that did not serve the institutional needs of those who made books and libraries. Certainly the church, like other social institutions, had a specific ideology and material interest to pursue that made certain statements worthy of expense and others unworthy. The effect of those practices has been to exclude from history, that is, from textual knowledge of the past, certain classes and interests of Anglo-Saxons.

Perhaps the best way to glimpse these excluded groups is through theories that deconstruct texts to discover the issues or ideas avoided by those producing the texts. Fredric Jameson's theory of *The Political Unconscious* provides a useful framework. Although he believes that in history real things happened to people in real ways, like Derrida he does not believe that we have any direct access to these experiences, and so concentrates on the analysis of texts. Like Lacan he understands the subject to be constituted in its social and linguistic activity. While he resembles Foucault in conceiving the subject as subjected by the social and ideological formations of its society, his analysis allows for conflict, exclusion, and change within a history of material events and the ideologies that engineer them and their meanings. As a Marxist, he focuses on social contradictions created by class differences and differences between old and new social formations, and he reads literary texts in particular as participating in those conflicts. 'Cultural artifacts' are 'socially symbolic acts' in that they resolve on the 'imaginary' plane the 'real' contradictions that continue to trouble the society. But even the imaginary resolution is not complete: one can detect fissures and slippages that point to the text's 'logical scandal' or 'unthinkable', repressed within the political unconscious of those producing the text.[17] Because in Anglo-Saxon society textual production itself emerged from the Christian mission, it was by its very nature a participant in that ideology which was attempting to change the structure of Anglo-Saxon society and culture. That fact makes Old English texts rich territory for investigating a political unconscious.

The Anglo-Saxon subject in *Beowulf*

As critics have long recognized, *Beowulf* presents a narrative that looks back at a pagan Germanic past, but presents its heroes in terms more congenial to its Christian Anglo-Saxon audience by portraying them as respecting a single, all-powerful God. In its other aspects, most critics have assumed that the text represents early Germanic practices, for example, funeral pyres, burial with treasure, and oral story-telling. The work of the last century has been to understand how the parts of the text work harmoniously to present a single vision of the heroic past and its significance for its Anglo-Saxon audience. The following post-structuralist analysis will question that harmony by first observing how it was constructed and then probing the fissures, slippages, and contradictions in its construction. The lexicon of the text will be at issue because language is a contested territory within which the culture and the subject are constructed. The media of oral discourse and manuscripts also will play a part because it was through the medium of writing that the Christian Anglo-Saxon subject came into being, and consequently these distinct sign systems supported the conflicting ideologies of the missionary culture and of the culture targeted for conversion. In this analysis, the very translation of oral-heroic discourse into manuscript was a political act of conversion.

The following dicussion, then, examines the construction of an Anglo-Saxon subject within the Christian, manuscript culture. This construction resolves, in the imaginary world of *Beowulf*, the contradictions between the heroic ethos and Christian ideology and between their media of expression, the oral performance and the manuscript. In this attempt at transforming an essentially pagan heroism into a Christian text and practice, the narrative also figures the loss of the heroic and of its oral milieu, a loss that is necessary to the construction of the Christian subject.

Throughout almost all of *Beowulf*, the Danes and the Geats are represented as both heroic and Christian, the text melding the virtues of both ideologies into a single, praiseworthy manner of acting and speaking. As many scholars have previously argued, this combination is important because in representing the Danes and the Geats the text also represents the Anglo-Saxons to themselves. The text declares the alignment of the Danes with the Christian God when it introduces Heorot and its opposing force, Grendel. Though in their representation the Danes have no knowledge of Christianity as such, the text defines Heorot as the place where the scop declared that *se ælmihtiga* created the earth, sun and moon, and life for all creatures, where men lived joyfully and *eadiglice*, a term often used to mean 'blessedly' as well as 'happily' (89b–100a).[18] Heorot's blessed condition exists in opposition to Grendel, the excluded being who dwells in the dark. He is the narrative occasion for the identification of the hall with the creation song (see 87b–9a and 99–101). Furthermore, his exclusion is also the Creator's doing: Grendel has occupied the moors 'siþðan him scyppend forscrifen hæfde / in Caines cynne' ('since the creator had proscribed him in the kin of Cain', 106–7a). Beowulf will fight this creature with God's support: as Hrothgar puts it, he hopes that *halig god* has sent him *for arstafum* (381–2; *stæf* means 'support' and in other contexts 'letter', and *ar* means 'benefit' or 'grace'; so the phrase translates 'out of kindness' or 'by God's grace' and carries writing as an intertextual resonance).

The inscribed text of *Beowulf* also represents these heroic-Christian figures as participants in an oral culture. The text represents them in an oral mode of discourse, through stories about what they do and have done, and it also thematizes this process in its representation of story-telling itself. Indeed, the text makes all story-telling happen through oral performance, the medium culturally associated with maintaining the heroic ethos, and covers over any contradictions between writing and the perpetuation of that ethos and between writing and orality.[19] The text presents several scenes of story-telling. The scene in which a teller celebrates Beowulf's victory over Grendel is so convincing in its details that scholars have mined it for evidence of story-telling practice, finding references to variation, alliterative meter, and harp playing (867–915). Other representations of gidds and tellers include the scop's creation song (89b–98); the gidd of Finn, Hildeburh, and Hnæf (1063–160a); Beowulf's account of Hrothgar as one who recites gidds (2105–10); Beowulf's stories about his own adventures; the gidd of the old man whose son hangs on a gallows (2446b–8a); and references to other mourning songs about Grendel's ravages (151a), Hildeburh's loss (1118a), and Beowulf's own death (3150a, 3172a).

The narrative itself pretends to work through oral discourse, beginning with its traditional opening:

> Hwæt, we Gardena   in geardagum,
> þeodcyninga   þrym gefrunon.   (1–2)

[Listen! we have heard about the glory of the Spear-Danes, of the kings of nations, in distant days.]

Here, *gefrunon* points to asking or hearing as the source of information and *we* places the present audience as listeners to that tradition. In addition, many times the narrator steps in to verify a detail with an assertion, 'I have heard' (see the uses of *gefrignan* and *hyran* in 38a, 62a, 1196b, 1197, 2163a, 2172a, 2752a, 2773a). These expressions place his discourse in line with that of Beowulf, Hrothgar, and other story-tellers within the narrative.

In the one scene where writing does appear, as *runstafas* on the ancient hilt that Beowulf brings back from the mere, the written merges with the spoken, and the inscription serves as object as much as text. The 'beginning of ancient strife' which was 'written' on the sword hilt connects it with the Christian world of books (1688b–9a), but the description of the *runstafas* as having

> rihte gemearcod,
> geseted ond gesæd,   hwam þæt sweord geworht
> . . .   ærest wære   (1695–7a)

[properly marked, set down and said by whom that sword . . . was first made]

associates 'marked' and 'set down' with 'said'. Seth Lerer interprets this passage as representing a scene in which Hrothgar reads, privately as an individual;[20] but Hrothgar gazes on the hilt in the same way that he stares at Grendel's head, when at the end of his sermon he thanks the eternal lord 'þæt ic on þone hafelan heorodreorigne / ofer eald gewin eagum starige' ('that I on that bloody head, after the old strife, stare with eyes', 1780–1): the head, seemingly, is just as significant to him of the ancient battle as the sword hilt. Beowulf, much later, at the end of his life, will gaze on the gold from the dragon's hoard as his inspiration to speech, and *sceawode* and *starie* will again be the words that indicate the act (2793 and 2796). So the hilt with its writing appears as a spectacle from the depths of time, a show of the monstrous.

These are the fictive resolutions of the text, to align the heroic with the Christian ideals and to declare this new heroic an oral tradition consonant with the Bible. But cracks appear in this attempt, and these fissures and slippages point to contradictions between an older oral-heroic social formation and the written-Christian formation attempting its conversion.

The greatest fissure in the heroic–Christian amalgam appears where the narrative is explaining the inability of Hrothgar and his advisors to devise an adequate response to Grendel's ravages. It states that many often sat in council to decide the best action against the *færgryrum* ('sudden terrors', 174a). When they repeatedly promise sacrifices at the temples of idols ('Hwilum hie geheton æt hærgtrafum / wigweorþunga'), the concept of the idol appears twice, in *hærg* and *wig* (175–6a). In the following verses, the narrative makes explicit what was wrong with this recourse: they were praying to a *gastbona* ('spirit-killer', 177a), and in doing so they 'hæþenra hyht helle gemundon' ('had in their minds the hope of heathens, hell', 179) and did not know *metod*. The next five verses define this governor or god in Christian terms as *dæda demend, drihten god, heofena helm*, and *wuldres waldend*. A pair of gnomic assertions concludes the fitt and clinches the lesson: there will be woe for the one whose soul is shoved into the embrace of fire and well for the one who seeks protection in the embrace of the Father (183b–8). Certainly here the Danes are heathens turning their backs on the *alwealda* that Hrothgar (and Beowulf) acknowledge elsewhere.

Critics have usually attempted to explain away the contradiction this passage poses in the representation of the Danes, or harmonize it thematically. But a post-structuralist reading takes such a contradiction as pointing to something the text is attempting to cover up, an idea that is scandalous within the text's dominant binary, which in *Beowulf* makes the heroic godly and the hero's opponents ungodly. The scandal here is that the Danes fundamentally do not differ from Grendel. An intertext points us to that scandal. The statements that the Danes 'oft gesæt / rice to rune' and 'helle gemundon' ('the high-ranking frequently sat at council' and 'they thought of hell', 171b–2a, 179b) echo the description of Grendel's moors as a place where 'helrunan hwyrftum scriþað' ('those skilled in the mysteries of hell [or, those in the councils of hell] move about', 163). This echo makes Grendel and his fellow *hel runan* (written separately in the manuscript, as is frequently true of compounds) an intertext for the Danes in council, so that they and their ravager for the moment are both opposed to the Christian God. Since, as the excursus recognizes, the Danes are pagans, this identification is logical; but in terms of the normative characterization of Danes and Geats, it must also be unintended, a slip revealing a scandal within the resolutions the text is attempting and a 'political unconscious' that the text is working hard to cover over.

In that unconscious alternative to the system of thought posed in the text, hero and opponent are morally one and the same. This possibility appears when we examine terms used to name the hero of the gidd, *wrecca* and *aglæca*. *Aglæca* characterizes Grendel and the dragon and *aglæcwif* Grendel's mother, but *aglæca* also characterizes Sigemund (893a), both Beowulf and the dragon together (2592), and, in two instances, ambiguously either Beowulf or his monstrous opponent, in the first possibly Grendel (739a) and in the second possibly mere-monsters (1512a). Klaeber struggles in his glossary to keep a clear distinction between hero and opponent, identifying the same term as, on the one hand, 'wretch, monster, demon, fiend', and, on the other, 'warrior, hero'. But, as George Jack recognizes in his edition, 'fierce assailant' indicates the common ground for all the referents.

The *aglæcan* are also *wreccan*, and this word and etymologically related terms point even more clearly to an oral-heroic paradigm in which hero and opponent fall within a single concept, the fierce outsider who is the subject of song. Klaeber glosses *wrecan* as 'drive, force'; 'drive out'; 'recite, utter'; 'avenge'. 'Recite' seems to be the odd definition out here. Bosworth-Toller explains the connection between 'recite' and the other meanings of the word by stating '*to drive out* words, *to express* in words, *utter, recite*' (*s.v. wrecan*, 1b); hence, it is the expulsion of air and sound from the mouth that makes it similar to 'drive out'. But it is also worth noting that virtually all of the examples that Bosworth-Toller cites for 'utter, recite' relate to formal oral discourse, specifically to *gidd* and *sang*, as in *Beowulf*, when there are celebrations in Heorot after Grendel's defeat: 'Þær wæs sang and sweg . . . gid oft wrecen' ('there was song and music . . . tales frequently recited', 1063–5). The lexicon, then, connects tale, uttering, and exile. The various terms that have to do with revenge, avenging, punishing by exile, or exile itself are most often references to a social situation. Hrothgar suffers *nydwracu* ('violent persecution' [Klaeber, *s.v.*], or perhaps 'compelled exile from his hall', 193a) because of Grendel's attacks on Heorot; Beowulf plans *wræce* ('revenge', 2336b) against the dragon; Herebeald's death at the hands of his brother Hæthcyn will be *unwrecen* ('unavenged', 2443a); Grendel's mother is his *wrecend* ('avenger', 1256b) and Beowulf tells Hygelac that she *gewræc* ('avenged', 2121a) her son. Exile and revenge, then, are the conditions worth recounting in tales. Furthermore, the *wrecca*, the 'exile, adventurer, hero' (Klaeber, *s.v.*), is one about whom tales are told: in *Beowulf*, the term names Sigemund, Hengest, and Eanmund. The text attempts to convert this sign system, however, when the narrative syntactically links the Creator's proscription of Grendel into Cain's race with the vengeance he wrought against Cain by exiling him:

> . . . him Scyppend   forscrifen hæfde
> in Caines cynne–   þone cwealm gewræc
> ece Drihten,   þæs þe he Abel slog;
> Ne gefeah he þære fæhðe,   ac he hine feor forwræc,
> Metod for þy mane   mancynne fram.   (106–110)

[the Creator had proscribed him among the race of Cain – that death the eternal Lord avenged, because he [Cain] slew Abel. He [God, *pace* Klaeber] did not rejoice in that feud, but He banished him far away from mankind, the Ruler on account of that sin.]

Whereas *wrecan* and its related terms imply that the exile and the hero of a story are dangerously close to being the same thing, this passage, which is setting the terms of the story, defines the exile as God's enemy in contradiction to this heroic milieu.

The contradiction between oral story-telling and the writing of the manuscript is buried somewhat deeper in the political unconscious. Writing breaks into the fiction of orality in two places. The connection between the Christian paradigm of the hero and writing emerges in the above passage in the term *forscrifan*. This loanword from Latin *proscribere* links Grendel's exile among Cain's kin to writing, and the text coopts *gewræc* and *forwræc* from oral-heroic discourse to explain the word and the event, implicating them in the Christian paradigm. Similarly, although Hrothgar gazes on the sword hilt that Beowulf retrieves from the mere as on an object signifying Grendel's defeat (see 1677–86), it has on it the biblical origin of God's feud with his enemies and so ties the oral-heroic Grendel into that biblical lineage. This writing can come back from the deep to be read, and therein lies its power: even if Hrothgar does not read it, the *Beowulf* text does write the hilt's content for Anglo-Saxon readers.

In contrast, the oral-heroic world depends on memory and community for its perpetuation. When Hrothgar's thane celebrates in verse Beowulf's victory over Grendel, the introduction to the story-telling (867b–882) emphasizes 'saying', 'recounting', memory, and personal connections. The king's thane is

> guma gilphladen,   gidda gemyndig
> se ðe ealfela   ealdgesegena
> worn gemunde.   (868–70a)

[A boast-laden man, mindful of tales, one who remembered a great many, a multitude of old sayings.]

The text even spells out the chain of remembrance: the thane spoke what 'he heard tell from Sigemund concerning courageous deeds' (875–6a), things not widely known except by Fitela, whom he 'desired to tell' (880b). When that chain breaks, the story is lost, but manuscripts survive.

The *Beowulf* text creates the fiction that it perpetuates the oral-heroic tradition, but instead it signifies a new Christian heroic that through the power of writing overwhelmed the oral-heroic. An intertext of 'on ðæm wæs or writen / fyrngewinnes' ('on that was the origin written of ancient strife', 1688b–9a) gestures toward this truth. As Frantzen points out, this *writen* resonates much later as an intertext for *forwrat*, the term used when Beowulf cuts into the dragon's belly (2705a). Klaeber glosses the first as the past participle of *writan*, 'cut, engrave (write)', and the second as preterite third singular of *forwritan*, a hapax legomenon meaning 'cut through'. As Frantzen states, the intertexts are linked by the act of carving, and tie together death and writing.[21] Although Frantzen is pursuing an abstract connection, writing was a material fact that was instrumental in a culture in which the godly were opposed by the ungodly, not one in which dragon and hero were both *aglæcan*. Writing killed that sort of dragon through failure of memory when the human links described in the Sigemund episode were lost but the manuscript endured. The last forty pages of the *Beowulf* manuscript narrate the loss of Beowulf, the dragon, and the hoard, culminating in Beowulf's pyre, which contains the dragon's hoard. This long leave-taking may unconsciously lament the loss of the heroic culture in the face of the manuscript. From a Lacanian view, such an act of mourning would be necessary in constructing a new Anglo-Saxon subject, subjected by the manuscript culture of Christianity.

Notes

1 J. Derrida, 'Structure, Sign and Play in the Discourse of the Human Sciences' in *Writing and Difference*, trans. A. Bass (Chicago, 1978; originally published as *L'écriture et la différance* [Paris, 1967]), pp. 278–93 at 280. See Derrida, *On Grammatology*, trans. G. C. Spivak (Baltimore, 1976; originally published as *De la grammatologie* [Paris, 1967]); J. Lacan, *Ecrits* (Paris, 1966); for a selection in English translation see *Ecrits: A Selection*, trans. A. Sheridan (New York, 1977). Lacan's publications go back to 1937 with 'Le stade du miroir comme formateur de la fonction du Je', 'The mirror-stage as formative of the function of the I as revealed in psychoanalytic experience', and the majority are from the 1950s. See also R. Barthes, *S/Z*, trans. R. Miller (New York, 1977; originally published as *S/Z* [Paris, 1970]); J. Kristeva, *Séméiotiké* (Paris, 1969) and *La révolution du langage poétique* (Paris, 1974), Kristeva's doctoral thesis, published in English translation and abridgement as *Revolution in Poetic Language*, trans. M. Waller (New York, 1984). See also, M. Foucault, *The Order of Things*, trans. A. Sheridan (New York, 1970; originally published as *Les mots et les choses* [Paris, 1966]) and *The Archaeology of Knowledge*, trans. A. Sheridan (New York, 1969; originally published as *L'archéologie du savoir* [Paris, 1969]).
2 F. de Saussure, *Cours de linguistique générale* (1916), trans. W. Baskin, *Course in General Linguistics* (London, 1960), pp. 115–17. See P. Bauschatz, *The Well and the Tree* (Amherst, MA, 1982) for an example of a structuralist description of medieval Germanic culture related to its system of tenses.
3 C. Lévi-Strauss, *Le cru et le cuit* (Paris, 1964); *The Raw and the Cooked*, trans. J. and D. Weightman (New York, 1969).
4 See E. G. Stanley, 'The Search for Anglo-Saxon Paganism' (Cambridge and Totowa, NJ, 1975); A. J. Frantzen, *The Desire for Origins* (New Brunswick, NJ, 1990); also D. G. Calder's critique, 'The Study of Style in Old English Poetry: A Historical Introduction' in *Old English Poetry: Essays on Style*, ed.

D. G. Calder (Berkeley, CA, 1979), pp. 1–65; and C. T. Berkhout and M. McC. Gatch, eds., *Anglo-Saxon Scholarship: The First Three Centuries* (Boston, 1982). On *Beowulf* see F. A. Blackburn, 'The Christian Coloring of *Beowulf*', *PMLA* 12 (1897), 205–25, and L. D. Benson, 'The Pagan Coloring of *Beowulf*', in *Old English Poetry: Fifteen Essays*, ed. R. P. Creed (Providence, RI, 1967), 193–213.

5 Derrida, 'Structure', pp. 283–4 and 293.

6 J. P. Hermann, *Allegories of War* (Ann Arbor, MI, 1989), p. 89.

7 Barthes, *S/Z*, pp. 10–11.

8 J. Kristeva, section of *Séméiotiké* (1969), translated as 'Word, Dialogue and Novel', ed. T. Moi, *The Kristeva Reader* (New York, 1986), pp. 34–61, at 45 and 37.

9 M. Foucault, 'What Is an Author?' in *Textual Strategies*, ed. J. V. Harari (Ithaca, NY, 1979), pp. 141–60.

10 For a full discussion of the ideas and evidence alluded to here, see C. B. Pasternack, *The Textuality of Old English Verse*, Cambridge Studies in Anglo-Saxon England 13 (Cambridge, 1995).

11 See M. Riffaterre, 'The Intertextual Unconscious', *Critical Inquiry* 13 (1987), 371–85, and 'Syllepsis', *Critical Inquiry* 6 (1980), 625–38.

12 P. A. Belanoff, 'Women's Songs, Women's Language: *Wulf and Eadwacer* and *The Wife's Lament*' in *New Readings on Women in Old English Literature*, ed. H. Damico and A. H. Olsen (Bloomington, IN, 1990), pp. 193–203; G. Overing, *Language, Sign, and Gender in Beowulf* (Carbondale, IL, 1990); H. Bennett, 'The Female Mourner at Beowulf's Funeral: Filling in the Blanks/Hearing the Spaces', *Exemplaria* 4 (1992), 35–50.

13 Lacan, 'The Agency of the Letter in the Unconscious or Reason Since Freud' in *Ecrits: A Selection*, pp. 146–78 at p. 174.

14 Foucault, *The Archaeology of Knowledge*, p. 38.

15 K. O'Brien O'Keeffe, *Visible Song: Transitional Literacy in Old English Verse*, Cambridge Studies in Anglo-Saxon England 4 (Cambridge, 1990). D. Moffat, 'Anglo-Saxon Scribes and Old English Verse', *Speculum* 67 (1992), 805–27, criticizes O'Brien O'Keeffe's willingness to give up the idea of the poet as authoritative author. M. Irvine circumscribes the discursive formation for Old English verse differently from O'Keeffe, 'mapp[ing]' a 'hybrid Latin and English grammatical culture' for the ninth through the early eleventh century, based on *grammatica* and the 'semiology' of the Latin manuscript page and its glosses (*The Making of Textual Culture: 'Grammatica' and Literary Theory, 350–1100*, Cambridge Studies in Medieval Literature 19 [Cambridge, 1994], p. 406).

16 Irvine, *The Making of Textual Culture*, pp. 451–3.

17 F. Jameson, *The Political Unconscious: Narrative as a Socially Symbolic Act* (Ithaca, NY, 1981), pp. 82, 20, 77, 95, and 82–3. J. D. Niles, citing Jameson, discusses the 'cultural work' that *Beowulf* performs, identifying the reputations of the Anglo-Saxons' ancestors and of the contemporary Danes as the sites

of conflict ('Locating *Beowulf* in Literary History', *Exemplaria* 5 [1993], 79–109, at 106–7).

18 All citations are from *Beowulf and the Fight at Finnsburg*, ed. F. Klaeber, 3rd edn. (Boston, 1950). See also *Beowulf: A Student Edition*, ed. G. Jack (Oxford, 1994); I cite his gloss for *aglæca* below.

19 M. R. Near, 'Anticipating Alienation: *Beowulf* and the Intrusion of Literacy', *PMLA* 108 (1993), 320–32, discusses oral versus literate modes of expression as a theme in *Beowulf*. His analysis and mine touch on many similar issues but differ in that he evaluates the poem as an oral song recorded in a manuscript, anticipating in its concerns the psychological changes that writing will effect.

20 S. Lerer, *Literacy and Power in Anglo-Saxon Literature* (Lincoln, NB, 1991), p. 174.

21 A. J. Frantzen, 'Writing the Unreadable *Beowulf*: "Writan" and "Forwritan", the Pen and the Sword', *Exemplaria* 3 (1991), 327–57, at 342–4. He also treats writing and story-telling as if they were the same thing, replicating the resolution of difference that the text also attempts to resolve.

9

Old English and
computing: a guided tour

PETER S. BAKER

•

One day, about three years ago, I found myself walking toward the library with a colleague who posed the question whether the computer had produced a theoretical revolution in literary studies or had merely enabled scholars to do more effectively what they had been doing all along. The question seemed an appropriate one to discuss as we strolled through the Academical Village of the University of Virginia, in which Thomas Jefferson so brilliantly wedded his visions as architect and educational philosopher; for Jefferson's phrase 'Academical Village' had recently been adopted as the working metaphor for the University's computer network, suggesting that the network's purpose was not so much to transform our educational and scholarly mission as to realize more perfectly an age-old dream. The question then had – and still has – no obvious answer; but it seems a fundamental one, and the reader should keep it in mind as we tour some of the on-line resources forthcoming or available to students and scholars of Anglo-Saxon England.

The *Dictionary of Old English* and the electronic text

The history of the computer in Old English scholarship goes back to the 1960s, when work began on various computer-generated concordances.[1] By far the most ambitious of these projects was undertaken at the University of Toronto under the direction of the late Angus Cameron, who, as part of a plan for a new *Dictionary of Old English*, proposed to generate an electronic database containing everything written in Old English. In those early days of computing, the approximately 3,000,000 words contained in the 2,000 surviving Old English texts had to be typed by hand onto punch-cards before they could be transferred to magnetic tape; a computer program called Lexico was then used to produce a concordance to Old English prose, glosses, and verse. The result was published in two massive works, *A Microfiche Concordance to Old English* (1980) and *A Microfiche Concordance to Old English: The High-Frequency Words* (1985).[2] These concordances, published on microfiche because publication on paper would have been prohibitively expensive, showed every word with a full sentence of context; for such works as glossaries and interlinear glosses, the Latin word or passage being translated was provided as well. The *Microfiche Concordances* made an immediate impact in the world of Old English scholarship. Previously, scholars conducting word-studies had had to search out data by reading through the texts, often several times (I still have a steel file-box full of 3x5 cards that bring back vivid memories of the process); now, suddenly, readers had at their fingertips a more-or-less complete word-list.

A concordance is simply a text whose words have been rearranged in alphabetical order and printed with cross-references to the original text. There is nothing new about concordances, of course, but it is worth pausing to consider how they transform the way we think about texts. Like an index, a concordance circumvents the sequential organization of the text, allowing the reader to conceptualize it in new ways. But a concordance is a more flexible tool than an index; further, the more inclusive the concordance, the more flexible it becomes. To take a very simple example, the *Anglo-Saxon Chronicle* is arranged chronologically; to find out what happened in the year 854, one needs no special tools. Charles Plummer's classic edition of the *Chronicle* contains an admirable index, mostly of persons and places, but with a few subject headings thrown in (e.g. 'Danegeld', 'relics'). Plummer did not anticipate that readers might want to know about, say, horses in the *Chronicle*, but with the *Microfiche Concordance* one can quickly track down every mention of horses. To take another example, one does not need a concordance to spot the three references to an island in the nineteen-line poem *Wulf and Eadwacer*. If one were interested in islands in Old English literature generally, one could track down all references via the *Microfiche Concordance*, though one would have check more than one word for island (e.g. *ig, igland*) under more than one spelling (e.g. *ieg, eglond*).

These points are obvious, but less obvious are two further points that follow from them: first, the concordance is a more flexible research tool than the index or the glossary because the compiler of the concordance makes fewer assumptions than the compiler of an index or glossary about the queries that readers bring to the work. Second, to the extent that the concordance does not anticipate readers' queries, it also presents its information in relatively 'raw' form. The *Microfiche Concordance*, for example, does not list spellings under headwords as the *Dictionary of Old English* does; one must look for words under various spellings and grammatical forms, and one must be prepared to disentangle different words that are spelled alike (e.g. *ac* 'but' and *ac* 'oak'). The more flexible tool is often the more difficult one to use. The plain text is the most flexible tool of all, but also the most difficult − for every purpose except reading.

The *Dictionary of Old English* project has generously made available the electronic Corpus of Old English texts to interested scholars and institutions; those who are fortunate enough to have had access to it know that an electronic corpus, combined with powerful software for searching the text, opens up exciting possibilities for linguistic and literary analysis. The University of Virginia's Electronic Text Center provides access to the Old English Corpus through a program called PAT,[3] which is capable of conducting nearly instantaneous searches of large corpora and manipulating the results of searches in various ways. Suppose, for example, we were looking for instances of the poetic formula 'heard under helme' and related phrases. The PAT window in fig. 1 shows that we have searched the entire corpus for the principal words of the formula and have found 899 instances of *heard* and 500 of *helm*. Next we have compared the two search results and discovered that the two words occur 'near' (within eighty characters of) each other seventeen times. Finally we have selected just the ten instances of *heard* near *helm* that occur in verse texts. The ten finds are displayed in the box at the lower left of the window (here &a; stands for *æ*, &t; for *þ* and &d; for *ð*); it is far easier to scan these ten finds for the material we want than to look up forms of *heard* and *helm* in the *Microfiche Concordance*. In the University of Virginia system, clicking a mouse pointer on one of these finds starts a program called Lector (shown in fig. 2), which presents the text in more readable form: just a sentence of context, as here, the citation, or the entire work. My sample search yielded no very

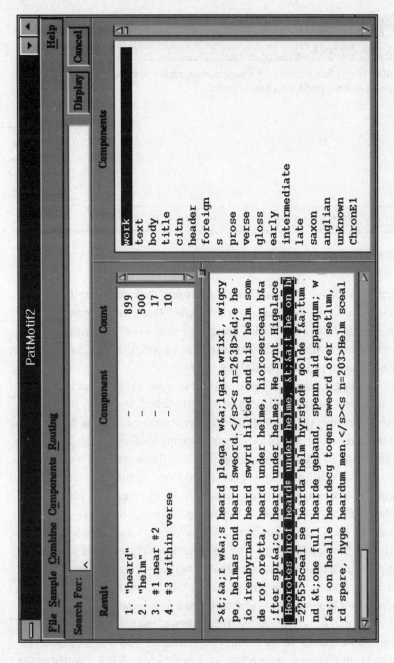

Figure 1 PAT window displaying the result of a search for the formula 'heard under helme'

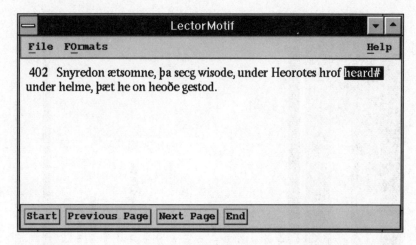

Figure 2 Lector window display of sentence context for 'heard under helme'

startling results: it showed that phrases using the words *heard* and *helm* occurred only in *Beowulf*. More complex searches are possible: one can search individual works, search for one word following another, combine the results of different searches (e.g. *gid, gyd, gied*) into one list for easier manipulation, and so on.

Restricting a search to verse or to individual works is made possible by an aspect of the Old English Corpus called 'markup', that is, the insertion of special 'tags' to indicate the structural features of the text. An ordinary word processor inserts markup to indicate such features as underlining, italics and, paragraph breaks; the markup of a well-made electronic text is both more specific and more useful.[4] The Old English corpus contains tags pointing out titles, short titles, and other useful bibliographical information, registering the approximate date and dialect of texts, and classifying them as prose, verse, or gloss. Within each text, foreign elements and sentences are tagged. It is possible to search any element of the text that is tagged – one can, for example, restrict a search to foreign elements, which are excluded from the *Microfiche Concordance* – and conversely it is impossible to single out any element that is not tagged. The markup of the Old English Corpus is simple, and thus there are things one cannot do with it. At present, for example, one cannot search the works of Alfred, Ælfric, Wulfstan, or any other author because texts are not tagged with their authors' names; one cannot search by manuscript, by manuscript provenance, by genre (e.g. 'homily', 'history'), or by specialized criteria such as liturgical dates, saints commemorated, clause types, metrical features, and so on. Some of these wants will surely be met at some point, but the number of features that might conceivably be tagged is so great that it seems likely that the markup of the Old English Corpus as a whole will remain conservative, while texts with more specialized content and markup will become available as individual scholars create them to serve their own needs. Several interesting projects of this kind are in progress or have appeared: for example, the 'Hidden Corpus' project, coordinated by David Megginson, aims to supplement the Old English Corpus by recording in electronic form the variant readings and emended forms excluded from the Corpus, and Rand Hutcheson has marked up a large body of Old English poetry with data concerning accentuation and rhythmic type.[5]

An electronic text is only as good as the software one uses to access it. The Old English Corpus is too large to load into a word processor, and if it were possible to do so the text would do us little good, for word processors supply only primitive search tools and no analytical tools. The PAT program is a better solution, since it can perform sophisticated searches that take account of the text's markup. But even PAT has its limitations, particularly its inability to deal with variant spellings. If one wished to search for þryþ, for example, one would have to specify separately the spellings þryþ, ðryþ, þryð, ðryð, þrið and so on. Some text-search software, including a few word processors, uses 'regular expressions', a special syntax for specifying search criteria, to allow one to search for words under various spellings. In Microsoft Word, for example, a search for '[þð]r[iy][þð]' would find þryþ under eight different spellings. Unfortunately, PAT does not yet permit the use of regular expressions, so those who wish to use them must make do with less powerful search software.

The limitations of the Old English Corpus and PAT are cited here not by way of complaint, but rather to suggest that despite the rapid advances in computing technology since scholars first started to think about using computers to generate concordances, we are still in the early days of the 'computer revolution'. The Platonic ideal of a combination of electronic text and search software that will answer virtually any need seems very far off indeed. We are very fortunate to have the Old English Corpus; students of no other literary language have so comprehensive a tool available to them. Its quality and usefulness are what make us wish for more.

ANSAXNET: The global conversation

In May of 1995, an extended debate took place among metrists, linguists, and other readers of Old English poetry concerning the evidentiary basis of scholarship on the dating of *Beowulf*. No conference on the subject was held in that month, and this was not an installment in the slow-paced debate that has been going on for more than two centuries in books and articles. The debate was a written exchange among members of ANSAXNET, an electronic community whose messages are carried over a medium called the Internet and posted to a 'list' called ANSAX-L.

Before we proceed, some definitions are in order:

1 The *Internet* is a loosely organized global network of computers communicating over high-speed telephone lines. This network carries text, images, sounds, and videos – anything that can be represented digitally. Originally created for the use of educational and government institutions, it is now open to virtually anyone.

2 Information on the Internet moves between *addresses*. An address is a unique identifier for a computer 'account' (an individual user's access privileges, or a portion of some computer's resources set aside for a particular purpose). A user in Stockholm who wished to send a message to a user in Tokyo would type the recipient's address and the message into a program called a 'mailer'; then, in a process that can take anything from several seconds to several hours, the message would be passed from computer to computer until it was finally deposited as a disk file in the recipient's account.

3 A *list* is a subscription service that operates over the Internet. The computer that operates the list maintains a directory of subscribers' addresses. The list itself has an address; when any subscriber writes to that address, the message is automatically transmitted to every subscriber.

In 1986 Patrick W. Conner of West Virginia University founded ANSAXNET, and it still makes its home (to the extent that it has a geographical home) in a computer in Morgantown, West Virginia, though it is now managed by William Schipper of Memorial University,

Newfoundland.[6] It maintains a file server that stores useful resources, and it sponsors an annual luncheon at the Congress on Medieval Studies in Kalamazoo, Michigan, but its primary function is to promote on-line discussion by Anglo-Saxonists around the world; in doing so it has developed a style different from that of traditional publication and from the kind of free-form discussion that takes place at conferences. Today ANSAXNET is one of the most successful enterprises of its kind in the on-line world, in part because it has always been a well-run list, and also, perhaps, because Anglo-Saxonists are usually the sole representatives of the field in their departments and thus often feel professionally isolated.

Members of ANSAXNET tend to think of the electronic message as an ephemeral medium. As they are not writing for the ages, members generally do not research their postings as they would for publication, though they often draw on their own research. More valuably, members often float ideas for discussion that they would be reluctant to commit themselves to in print. At the same time, members are aware that their postings are all carefully stored in an archive called ANSAXDAT, and this keeps them (mostly) responsible; scrutiny by scholars keeps them honest and the presence of non-academics keeps them intelligible. At its best, then, ANSAX-L is a forum for the testing of new ideas in which immediate feedback from a wide variety of readers helps members to hone their arguments and their presentation.

The possibility that one will read, or participate in, a stimulating exchange among scholars keeps many members on-line. Yet not all of the business transacted via ANSAX-L is of this kind. Many postings are simply requests for information, sometimes from scholars, sometimes from students, sometimes (it must be confessed) from people who seem to have become lost on their way to the sex-chat forum: has anyone come across such-and-such a theme in any Old English poem? what is the etymology of this word? what is the best grammar for the self-taught? what are the best sources for the history of East Anglia? what is this Maldon place, anyway, and why does everyone keep going on about it? The questions can occasionally be annoying, but advanced students and scholars who answer them do a service to others, sometimes by supplying the requested information or pointing out where it can be found, and sometimes by gently suggesting (generally to students writing term papers) that research is part of their educational training and they must not expect others to do it for them. And then, since many members are neither students nor scholars, ANSAX-L is one of the most important connections academics have to the outside world, which is too often ignorant and suspicious of the work we do in the universities.

There is a good bit of disagreement over whether ANSAXNET makes any substantive difference to the professional lives of its members. Since members are generally those who think it does, while those who think it does not tend to steer clear of it, the question can perhaps be allowed to go unanswered. Anglo-Saxonists who value regular contact with interested readers at all levels of expertise will probably want to belong.

Hypertext, the World-Wide Web, and the electronic edition

The Old English Corpus is a collection of sequential texts, a linear arrangement of letters, spaces, and punctuation like a printed text; in the computer age an alternative model of the text – called hypertext – is available. The concept of hypertext is actually much older than the computer, with a lineage that goes back to the 1940s; it was popularized in the 1980s by Apple Corporation's HyperCard program. In a hypertext, various elements of a 'text' (here loosely defined, as it can contain words, images, sounds, videos) are linked to other elements in the same or other texts. The user reads a hypertext on screen via a program specifically designed for the purpose; in a typical program of this kind, one follows a link by clicking the mouse pointer on a highlighted element, and the program displays the linked text, plays the video, and so on. Thus hypertext offers readers an alternative to the sequential organization of the text. A hypertextual narrative, for example, can offer a choice of events, a scholarly text can have 'animated' footnotes, and a dictionary can sound out its pronunciations.[7]

Of course, no medieval writer ever imagined anything like hypertext, a medium that may well strike many readers as inappropriate for thousand-year-old texts; nevertheless, hypertext offers considerable advantages to the modern reader. Among these is its ability to represent the relations among texts (what is currently called the intertext) in a way that traditional printed texts cannot. For example, while annotations in printed editions may contain references to or quotations from sources or related texts, a hypertextual link can lead the reader to the appropriate passage of an entire text, which may itself be annotated with hypertextual links. Thus it becomes a simple matter for the reader to wander through the intertext, and the time required to do so can be reduced from an hour or so in the library to the seconds it takes to press a few keys. A further advantage of hypertext has to do with the extraordinary difference between the medium in which we find medieval texts recorded and that in which we in turn record them. Manuscripts differ from printed books in letter-form, layout, style of illustration, and many other features; more significantly, every manuscript of a medieval text is unique, differing from other manuscripts in spelling, in wording, and frequently in the ordering of sentences, sections, and other elements. The economics of publishing generally force editors to present single texts, either choosing the 'best' manuscript or assembling 'critical editions' from the readings of various manuscripts. Editors who are able to print multiple texts of such works as laws, penitentials, and computi, in which the sections often appear in a different order in the variant manuscripts, must choose between printing some variant texts out of their manuscript order and printing 'parallel' texts that do not run parallel. Because disk space — the medium in which electronic texts are issued — is far less expensive than the printed book, it is now economical to publish variant texts. These can be arranged as a hypertext: passages in which significant variants occur can be linked so that readers can view them in parallel, and parallel passages can easily be called up even when variant manuscripts order them differently. Following an editor's instructions, a sophisticated hypertext program can assemble a critical text out of variant copies (though no computer is yet capable of making intelligent editorial choices): such electronic editions have the potential to make readers active participants in the editorial process by allowing them to intervene in the construction of the texts. Finally, the edited text can be linked to digital images of manuscripts, giving readers better access than ever before to the medium in which texts were originally preserved and demonstrating to students the relationship between manuscript source and edited text.[8]

An elementary application of hypertextual principles can be seen in a pair of drill programs for students of Old English: *Learning Old English* by Duncan Macrae-Gibson and *Beginning Old English* by Constance B. Hieatt, Brian Shaw, and Duncan Macrae-Gibson.[9] Simply put, these programs drill the student in various aspects of the language; they respond to the student's answers by saying 'Well done!' or by offering help in response to a wrong answer. The student has considerable freedom to skip or repeat lessons or to take them out of sequence; thus the drill program, like a hypertext program, presents a non-sequential text. The nature of the material dictates that the drill program must be more rigidly structured than most hypertexts; another group of programs, those that present cultural artifacts and cultural contexts, exploits the possibilities of hypertext more fully.

The best-known and most fully developed hypertext application relating to an Old English text is the *Beowulf* Workstation, a Hypercard application by Patrick W. Conner. The *Beowulf* Workstation presents two windows, one containing a fixed text of *Beowulf* and the other containing a text in which the student can enter notes, translations, and so on, creating a personalized copy of the poem. The fixed text features hypertextual links of various kinds: to manuscript images, to literatim and diplomatic transcripts of the manuscript, to commentary, to images such as one of the Sutton Hoo helmet, to literary criticism, to various translations, and to the student's own notes and translation. In addition, the application contains an abbreviated on-line grammar and a lexicon which the student can search by selecting a word and clicking on a button. The *Beowulf* Workstation supplies a collection of materials that constitute a cultural, linguistic, and scholarly context for the poem; other poems are treated in smaller-scale applications, such as a *Dream of the Rood* hypertext by Judith Weise. An especially ambitious Hypercard application, Project Seafarer by Allen Frantzen, is organized not around a single text, but rather around several texts (the *Life of Ceolfrith*, Ælfric's *Colloquy*, and others) and several topics or 'modules' (e.g. social rank, the monastery), providing a free-form collection of materials that the student can navigate in a number of ways, as interest or research needs dictate.[10]

It might be argued that the *Beowulf* Workstation and most other hypertext applications offer little that cannot be found in the library; indeed, the fact that they do generally draw on copyrighted material that originally appeared in print has prevented the circulation of the most important of these applications outside the institutions where they were developed. However, the aims of the hypertext application go far beyond simply providing a collection of study materials. Rather, it supplies an organized library of materials centered on the computer screen of the individual user, and in doing so changes the relationship between readers and research materials in at least one major respect: before, readers went to the library to find information; in the hypertext model, information comes to the reader.

In the hypertext applications mentioned here, the information available to the student is limited by the amount of storage available on a single computer; even the largest hard disk cannot store the information available in a well-stocked library. Imagine, on the other hand, a text of *Beowulf* that is hypertextually linked not to a limited collection of materials stored locally but rather to a vast collection of electronic materials not bounded by a single computer or a single library. We do not yet have such a text of *Beowulf* or such a collection of research materials, but the technology is in place to create such resources, and there can be little doubt that they will exist soon.

Before going any further we must add one definition to the three offered in the preceding section:

4 The *World-Wide Web* is a method for creating hypertextual resources with links to remote computers accessible via the Internet. With an application called a 'web browser' (the most popular ones, both free, are Mosaic and Netscape), a reader in New York can connect to a computer in Berkeley and read a text stored there; clicking on a 'hot' word, image, or button, just as in HyperCard, may activate a link that takes the reader to a text stored on a computer in London. The World-Wide Web breaks the boundaries of the hypertext and has the potential to turn the global computer network into an immense library. A user of the Web starts a session by connecting to a 'home page', which generally presents a menu of items or categories to choose from. Resources reached by this method may be viewed on the screen or downloaded to the user's computer.

The most ambitious World-Wide Web resource available to medievalists is The Labyrinth, a service developed by Martin Irvine and Deborah Everhardt and based at Georgetown University. Its 'home page' is shown in fig. 3. Resources relating to Anglo-Saxon England available via The Labyrinth include images of the *Beowulf* manuscript, a searchable text of all ANSAXNET messages, the list of texts from the *Dictionary of Old English* project, and a large and growing collection of digital texts. Several major electronic text archives can be contacted via The Labyrinth, though copyright restrictions in place at those archives often prevent access from the Internet. A more specialized and fuller

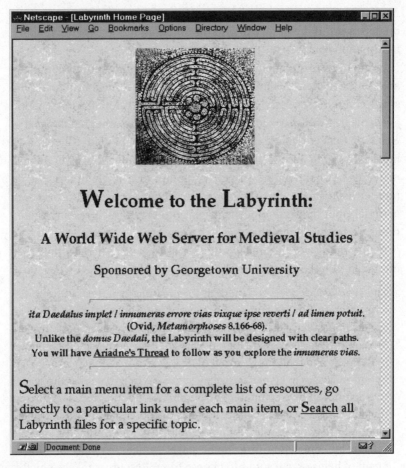

Figure 3 Illustration of Labyrinth 'home page'

collection of materials relating to Anglo-Saxon England is 'Old English Pages', maintained by Catherine N. Ball of Georgetown University, which offers access to an extraordinary range of materials from scholarly publications to diversions and games. Perhaps the most useful of the resources one can locate via 'Old English Pages' are two on-line bibliographies, 'Anglo-Saxon History: A Select Bibliography', by Simon Keynes, and 'Beowulf Bibliography 1979–1994', by Robert J. Hasenfratz. The first of these, equipped with many cross-references and an extensive linked index, exploits the abilities of the Web to the fullest; the second, which updates Hasenfratz's printed bibliography, complete through

1990, shows another aspect of the Web's power, namely that it makes possible nearly instantaneous publication of up-to-date materials.[11] Potentially more significant than any of the resources currently available is the developing interest in computer technology at the British Library, among whose eighteen million volumes is the world's largest collection of Anglo-Saxon manuscripts. Interested readers can find out about the Library's current and projected technological projects via 'Portico', its home page. These projects include on-line access to the Library's catalogue and 'Initiatives for Access', an ambitious plan to make extensive collections available in electronic form. It is unclear at this point how much (if any) Anglo-Saxon material may eventually be accessible via the Internet; the Library's electronic *Beowulf* (discussed below) will be sold on CD-ROM.[12]

A particularly promising use of the World-Wide Web is as a repository for pedagogical materials. Old English teachers (like teachers in all fields) are increasingly making their course materials available via the Web, which thus becomes a means not only of delivering these materials to students, but also of sharing ideas among teachers and promoting Old English studies. Two of the larger collections of materials are by Daniel Donoghue of Harvard University and myself: Donoghue's contains a syllabus, select bibliography, and on-line versions of the texts studied in the course, while mine contains syllabi, 'handouts', select bibliography, and pronunciation exercises. These and other collections may be located via Ball's 'Old English Pages'.

The World-Wide Web, though in its first years of operation, offers an astonishing variety of resources, with more being added daily. It is not without problems, however. One problem is a by-product of the dynamic nature of the Internet and the Web: home pages and other resources come and go, and restless developers frequently move resources from one site to another, with the result that Web links become outdated. It is not at all uncommon to click on a link only to discover that it points nowhere. Such broken links, together with the lack of any central index or catalogue for the Internet, can make locating a particular resource a frustrating exercise. Further, because of the increasing popularity of the Web among a highly diverse group of users, 'cyberspace' has become exceedingly crowded, and long waits to connect to and receive data from remote computers have become the rule rather than the exception at peak hours. These frustrations of using the Web are compounded by the relatively poor quality of Web browsers, which, because of intense competition in the industry, are inevitably released before their 'bugs' have been fully worked out: program and system crashes and generally erratic performance are all too common. A more serious problem than any of these (if less visible) is that the resources available via the Internet are frequently of very low quality. Electronic medieval texts are often transcripts of outdated editions (chosen, in fact, solely because their copyrights have expired); the problem of obsolescence is frequently compounded by that of sloppy transcription. The quality of Internet 'publication' is not controlled by the review procedures common in the publishing industry; thus the user must exercise discretion in choosing and using materials. The problem is not limited to texts available via the Internet; the materials available from repositories such as the Oxford Text Archive are variable in quality, and one of the largest collections, the fabulously expensive 'English Poetry Full-Text Database', is often based on obsolete editions.[13]

Most scholars understand very well that one edition of a text is by no means equivalent to another and that recent editions are generally to be preferred to older ones; however, the matter is likely to be less than obvious to students, who need to be reminded that texts located on-line must be checked against reputable printed editions. Eventually, electronic editions should conform to the scholarly standards that characterize the best printed editions. One notable initiative that aims to achieve exactly this goal is the Society for Early English and Norse Electronic Texts (SEENET), recently founded by a consortium of scholars in association with the University of Michigan Press. This society, modeled on the Early English Text Society, will issue to subscribers texts marked up according to current scholarly standards and subjected to the kind of review procedures that have long been used in the scholarly publishing industry.[14] Projects envisioned by SEENET include a comprehensive edition of the manuscripts of *Piers Plowman* and the British Library's electronic *Beowulf*.

Users of the Internet who have become accustomed to the wealth of free (if sometimes mediocre) material available on-line may resent being asked to pay for it. But the early experience of SEENET suggests that scholars producing electronic resources see considerable economic and professional advantages in their work being issued by publishers, and publishers, for their part, are interested in exploring this new market. As electronic editing comes of age, we are likely to see a growing distinction between free resources and those offered for sale: the former will continue to be largely transcripts of earlier scholarship issued without guarantee as to quality, while the latter will offer original scholarship and will come with the kind of certification that publication by an academic press confers upon a work.

Ready reference: the database

A *database* is any collection of digital information organized in such a way that its components can be recognized and processed by a computer. Understood in this broad sense, the Old English Corpus and most hypertexts are databases. Most computer users understand the word *database* in a narrower sense, as a collection of information organized in the digital equivalent of tabular form, and generally represented on-screen as a table. It is important to remember, however, that the difference between 'text' and 'database' can be arbitrary, being more a matter of the way the computer organizes information than of the nature of the information itself. Many texts can easily be converted into databases, and all databases can be converted to texts; for example, Rand Hutcheson's metrical corpus, mentioned above, exists in both forms.

There are great advantages to organizing certain kinds of information in database form. It is a simple matter to index a database in a number of ways, for example, enabling the computer to display its entries in any order, search it, or link it to information in related databases. One can also submit complex queries to a database. For example, a database of students enrolled in a graduate program can function as a simple directory; but from it one can also extract such information as lists of students from New York State, students who are both teaching and receiving fellowship support, or average exam scores year by year. Many concepts relating to databases are difficult to understand, but once the rudiments are grasped it is easy to imagine many possibilities for organizing information about Anglo-Saxon England. In fact, a number of major database projects are underway.

Perhaps the most ambitious of these is the *Fontes Anglo-Saxonici* project, which aims 'to identify all written sources which were incorporated, quoted, translated, or adapted anywhere in English or Latin texts which were written, or are likely to have been written, in Anglo-Saxon

England, including those by foreign authors'; also 'written sources used by authors of texts written abroad if those authors are certainly or arguably Anglo-Saxons, and by foreigners who were drawing mainly on materials which they had obtained, or are likely to have obtained, in Anglo-Saxon England'.[15] The database is even more detailed in its treatment than this description implies, matching not only works, but also individual passages of works, to their source material. It is in the nature of a database that one can approach the information it stores from several directions, determining not only what sources a particular text used, but exactly where any text was used as a source, and not only what books were read in Anglo-Saxon England, but also what Anglo-Saxon books were read elsewhere.

Other database projects currently underway include a *Corpus of Insular and Anglo-Saxon Illuminated Manuscripts*, which will contain both text and images; *A Thesaurus of Old English*, a subset of the larger *Historical Thesaurus* project, to be issued in both printed and electronic form; a *Directory of Individual Liturgical Sources* by Sarah Larratt Keefer of Trent University; and a *Catalogue Database* of Old English texts and their sources, compiled for the use of the *Dictionary of Old English*, which gathers into a single convenient database information from such standard reference works as the *Dictionary of Old English* list of texts and Ker's *Catalogue*.[16] Once these databases become available to the public, many readers schooled in the use of traditional reference works will find the transition to the use of a database somewhat difficult; but those who persevere will find these to be far more flexible tools than any they have encountered in print.

Digital imaging and the electronic *Beowulf*

The flickering green text-only monitors of early personal computers have little in common with the dazzling monitors now routinely supplied with desktop computers. These normally are capable of displaying 256 colors simultaneously, enough for photographic-quality images. For a relatively small additional investment, the purchaser of a new computer can acquire the ability to display millions of colors; such capabilities will no doubt soon be common. The resolution of monitors has improved along with their ability to display color, and they have steadily become larger and easier on the eyes.

While the quality of the digital display has been improving, the quality of published manuscript facsimiles has been declining. Color facsimiles of manuscripts have never been economical, but until recently two major series — Early English Manuscripts in Facsimile and the Early English Text Society — routinely issued black-and-white facsimiles of such high quality that one could examine them under a magnifier without being able to observe the grain of the photograph. In recent issues of EEMF and recent reissues of facsimiles from EETS one can observe with the naked eye that the photographs are screened — composed of dots of different sizes. A new series, Anglo-Saxon Manuscripts in Microfiche Facsimile, while fast becoming essential to Old English scholars, does not address issues of quality: it neither promises nor delivers high-quality photography.[17] Developments in display technology, together with the decline in quality of the printed photograph, have brought us to the point where a high-quality digital image is better in every respect — resolution, color, and manipulability — than any published photograph. The conclusion is inescapable that the use of digital imaging in the production of manuscript facsimiles is not only desirable, but also inevitable: we will shortly see expensive printed manuscript facsimiles replaced by economical digital ones issued on CD-ROM or other high-capacity storage devices.

As of now, only one project of this kind is underway in Anglo-Saxon studies, but this project, because of its ambitious scope and the importance of the manuscript in question, is likely to become a standard against which other such projects will be measured for some time to come. It is the Electronic *Beowulf*, sponsored by the British Library as part of its Initiatives for Access program and edited by Kevin S. Kiernan and Paul E. Szarmach.[18] The project is intended to supply to scholars a comprehensive record of the evidence on which the text of *Beowulf* is based: it will include a facsimile of London, BL, Cotton Vitellius A.xv, with photographs of the most badly damaged pages under different lighting conditions and details of difficult passages; facsimiles of the two Thorkelin transcripts; and the important early collations of the manuscript. An abridged version will be sold to the general public. Software developed especially for this project will link the various images hypertextually and supply a friendly environment for readers navigating the collection.

The *Beowulf* manuscript and the Thorkelin transcripts have been newly photographed using a high-resolution digital camera capable of recording millions of colors, many more than can be distinguished by the naked eye. The disk files in which such high-resolution color images are stored are very large — about twenty-four megabytes (equivalent to about twenty-four million 'characters' of storage) — but these can be compressed to a fraction of their original size, making distribution on CD-ROM practical. Users viewing these images will find that it is possible to enlarge small details to full-screen size without pixelation (the breakup of the image into visible dots). Because the digital camera records more than the eye can see, the user can (with the aid of image-processing software) manipulate colors to enhance features that are hard to make out; it is not beyond imagining that the computer may one day help us to recover lost readings in this difficult manuscript, though early efforts in this direction have been inconclusive. Perhaps as important as these technical advances, the availability of this and (one hopes) other economical, high-quality facsimiles of important manuscripts promises a dramatic expansion in access to primary source material. Any facsimile is inevitably a compromise; one can never learn as much from a photograph as one can from a session with the manuscript itself. But for those who cannot easily travel to libraries with major Anglo-Saxon holdings, digital imaging will offer considerable advantages over both printed facsimiles and archive microfilm.

Conclusion: back to the beginning

This essay opened by asking 'whether the computer had produced a theoretical revolution in literary studies or had merely enabled scholars to do more effectively what they had been doing all along'. The question is still difficult to answer. One reason for this difficulty is that the computer has, like an underachieving child, not yet fulfilled the promise we know it possesses. For each of the research tools mentioned above that actually exists and is available, such as the Old English Corpus and the Hidden Corpus, several are in progress or in the planning stages; and some kinds of project — especially the scholarly electronic edition — are not even in the planning stages, but exist only as hopes and projections, based on our knowledge of what the computer is capable of doing. Almost all Old English scholars now use the computer, but most use it strictly as a word processor; few are engaged in making or using hypertexts, databases, or digital images, and few have access to the kind of sophisticated search software that one needs to make good use of a tool like the Old English Corpus.

Nevertheless, it is easy to see that the computer is in the process of reorganizing the way we conduct our research. Let me give an example from my own experience. A number of years ago I became interested in the inflection of unassimilated Latin words (those that retain their Latin endings) in the Old English sections of Byrhtferth of Ramsey's *Enchiridion*. It was clear that Byrhtferth was not using the Latin endings that we would expect: for example, he did not necessarily use a Latin dative ending in places where the Old English syntax demanded a dative. I realized that before it would be possible to write anything on this topic it would be necessary to determine whether Byrhtferth's usage was idiosyncratic; but since unassimilated Latin words were generally excluded from the dictionaries, and the one work that treated them in detail did not discuss this aspect of their usage, I put off beginning the project, which would entail months spent searching through a great many Old English texts for unassimilated Latin words. In the meantime, I compiled a list of Latin words in Byrhtferth's Old English prose. After I had lived with the Old English Corpus for a time it occurred to me that it would be a simple matter to search the Corpus for the words on my list, and over a period of a week or so I amassed a considerable body of data concerning not only the Latin words used by Byrhtferth but also many others.

This story gives rise to the following observations: first, the kind of research described here has always been possible, but a great many (including myself) would not have attempted it without the help of a tool like the Corpus. Second, anyone attempting it before the Corpus was available would have organized the labor for the project very differently, centering it on a particular list of Old English texts, not a particular list of words. Instead, having the ability to search all Old English texts at once, I centered my labor entirely on a list of words (which expanded as I encountered others in the passages the search software was turning up) and postponed organizing the resulting collection of quotations by work and author until it was more or less complete. Third, the method I followed in interpreting this data was informed by recent work on loan-words in Old English and other languages, not by the way in which the data had been gathered.[19]

Reflection upon the descriptions offered in this essay of the *wundra fela* of the computer age – electronic editions, databases, digital images, and more – will suggest that my own experience is likely to be far from unique. The computer offers rapid access to unprecedented quantities of information, and such improved access can by itself contribute to a 'theoretical revolution' by encouraging students and scholars to enter previously unexplored territory in their research. Further, because the computer excels at organizing and reorganizing data, it permits us to look at information in new ways, freeing us from the ordering principles we find in our source materials. Yet if the computer can gather information for us, it cannot tell us what information is important; if it can organize information, it cannot tell us how it should be organized. Such decisions remain the province of human thought, and it is from thought – aided but never led by the tools we make – that all theoretical revolutions must arise.

Notes

1 See J. B. Bessinger, Jr., 'Computer Techniques for an Old English Concordance', *American Documentation* 12 (1961), 227–9. Bessinger also coedited *Literary Data Processing Conference Proceedings, September 9, 10, 11 – 1964*, together with S. M. Parrish and H. F. Arader (White Plains, NY, *c.* 1965). In this collection see especially P. H. Smith, 'A Computer Program to Generate a Concordance', pp. 113–27. In collaboration with Smith, Bessinger produced two concordances, *A Concordance to Beowulf* (Ithaca, 1969) and *A Concordance to the Anglo-Saxon Poetic Records* (Ithaca, 1978). See also A. Cameron, R. Frank, and J. Leyerle, eds., *Computers and Old English Concordances* (Toronto, 1970); this book is a record of a meeting on the subject held on 21–2 March 1969.

2 This database contained all texts, published and unpublished, but excluded variant readings. For details, see R. Frank and A. Cameron, eds., *A Plan for the Dictionary of Old English* (Toronto, 1973). The concordances appeared as A. diP. Healey and R. L. Venezky, *A Microfiche Concordance to Old English* (Toronto, 1980) and R. L. Venezky and S. Butler, *A Microfiche Concordance to Old English: The High-Frequency Words* (Toronto, 1985).

3 PAT was developed at the University of Waterloo for the Oxford English Dictionary project. It looks different depending on the platform it is accessed from: there is a version accessible from vt100 terminals (the kind that most dial-up communications programs use), one accessible from X-Windows Unix terminals, and one that works with World-Wide Web browsers. I will describe the X-Windows version.

4 The current standard for the markup of electronic texts is Standard Generalized Markup Language (SGML). A consortium of humanities schol-

ars has developed guidelines for the use of SGML in marking up texts of various kinds; see *Guidelines for Electronic Text Encoding and Exchange* (Chicago and Oxford, 1994); a convenient on-line version of this important document is available at http://etext.virginia.edu/TEI.html. Those who are unfamiliar with SGML should consult especially Part I, Section 2, 'A Gentle Introduction to SGML'.

5 The Hidden Corpus files are available from the ANSAXNET server; members may obtain a list of Hidden Corpus and other files on the server by sending a message that reads 'get ansax-l filelist' to the address listserv@wvnvm. wvnet.edu. Hutcheson's metrical database is currently being prepared for publication.

6 On ANSAXNET, see P. W. Conner, 'Networking in the Humanities: Lessons from ANSAXNET', *Computers and the Humanities* 26 (1992), 195–204; see also his briefer essays, 'Notes from ANSAXNET', *Old English Newsletter*, 22.2 (Spring, 1989), 23–4, and 'Notes from ANSAXNET, Again', *Old English Newsletter*, 24.1 (Fall, 1990), 32–35. To subscribe, send a message to listserv@wvnvm.wvnet.edu; the message should read simply 'sub ansax-l'. After that, a message sent to the address ansax-l@wvnvm.wvnet.edu will be distributed to the ANSAXNET membership.

7 For the concept of hypertext, its history, and its application in literary studies, a convenient guide is G. P. Landow, *Hypertext: The Convergence of Contemporary Critical Theory and Technology* (Baltimore and London, 1992). Hypertextual reference works have recently become popular in the home computing market: good examples are the Microsoft Bookshelf (including an encyclopedia, a dictionary, and a thesaurus) and Compton's Interactive Encyclopedia: both contain images, sound, and video as well as text.

8 For a convenient overview of problems and opportunities in the electronic editing of Old English texts, see M. Deegan and P. Robinson, 'The Electronic Edition' in *The Editing of Old English: Papers from the 1990 Manchester Conference*, ed. D.G. Scragg and P. E. Szarmach (Cambridge, 1994), pp. 27–37. For a discussion of the dynamic display of textual variants and a description of a model program for displaying texts with variants, see P. S. Baker, 'The Reader, the Editor, and the Electronic Critical Edition' in *A Guide to Editing Middle English*, ed. D. Moffat and V. McCarren (forthcoming, Ann Arbor).

9 *Learning Old English*, 3rd edn. (1984, with computer program added in 1988) is published by the author. *Beginning Old English* appeared as *OEN* Subsidia 21 (Binghamton, NY, 1994). For these and other language-learning programs, see P. W. Conner, M. Deegan, and C. A. Lees, 'Computer-Assisted Approaches to Teaching Old English', *OEN* 23.2 (Spring, 1990), 30–5.

10 See P. W. Conner, 'The *Beowulf* Workstation: One Model of Computer-Assisted Literary Pedagogy', *Literary and Linguistic Computing* 6 (1991), 50–8. Conner reports that development of the Workstation has now stopped,

as the technology on which it is based has recently been overtaken by Internet-based hypertext applications (see below). The *Dream of the Rood* and Seafarer projects are described from brochures and ANSAXNET postings. Neither project has been released or published.

11 The URL ('Universal Resource Locator', an address to be typed into a web browser to connect to the home page) for the Labyrinth is http://www. georgetown.edu/labyrinth/labyrinth-home.html. The URL for the Labyrinth's collection of Old English texts: http://www.georgetown.edu/ labyrinth/library/oe/oe.html. For 'Old English Pages': http://www. georgetown/edu/cball/oe/old_english.html. For 'Anglo-Saxon History: A Select Bibliography', which updates Keynes's *Anglo-Saxon History: A Select Bibliography,* 2nd rev. edn., *OEN* Subsidia 13 (Binghamton, 1993): http://www.wmich.edu/medieval/rawl/keynes1/home.html. For '*Beowulf* Bibliography 1979– 1994', which updates Hasenfratz's *Beowulf Scholarship: An Annotated Bibliography* 1979–1990 (New York, 1993): http://spirit.lib. uconn.edu/Medieval/beowulf.html. After the completion of this essay, another important bibliography became available on the Web: Janet Bately, *Anonymous Old English Homilies: A Preliminary Bibliography of Source Studies* (Binghamton, 1993): http://www.wmich.edu/ medieval/rawl/ bately1/cover.html.

12 The URL for Portico is http://portico.bl.uk/. Interested readers may now consult a similar home page being developed by the Bodleian Library, Oxford: http://www.rsl.ox.ac.uk/welcome.html.

13 Cf. the disclaimer published on the OTA home page (http://ota.ox.ac.uk/ ~archive/ota.html): 'OTA texts come from so many different sources and are held in many different formats. The texts also vary greatly in their accuracy and the features which have been encoded. Some have been proofread to a high standard, while others may have come straight from an optical scanner, Some have been extensively tagged with special purpose analytic codes, and others simply designed to mimic the appearance of the printed source. The Archive does not require texts to conform to any standard of formatting or accuracy.' Neither, it appears, does the Archive require literacy of those who write its on-line materials. The 'English Poetry Full-Text Database' is issued by Chadwyck-Healey Inc., 1992–4. The same company is currently issuing an electronic version of the *Patrologia Latina*. More modern editions of patristic texts are available in the CETEDOC *Library of Christian Latin Texts* (Turnhout, 1991), a CD-ROM version of most of the texts published in the series *Corpus Christianorum*, along with a number of others; CETEDOC comes with search software.

14 For further information on SEENET, consult the World-Wide Web page http://jefferson.village.virginia.edu/seenet/home.html.

15 D. G. Scragg, 'An Introduction to *Fontes Anglo-Saxonici*', *OEN* 26.3 (Spring, 1993), Appendix B at p. 2.

16 For the manuscript Corpus, see T. H. Ohlgren and M. O. Budny, 'Corpus of

Insular and Anglo-Saxon Illuminated Manuscripts: Statement of Goals and Organization', *OEN* 26.2 (Fall, 1992), 27–9. For the latest report on the *Thesaurus*, see J. Roberts, 'Report on A Thesaurus of Old English', *OEN* 27.3 (Spring, 1994), 23–4; L. Grundy, 'The Structure of A Thesaurus of Old English Database', ibid., 25–7, and C. Kay, 'From HT to TOE (or vice versa)', ibid., 28–9. For the *Catalogue Database*, see N. Speirs and L. Cipin, 'The Catalogue Database of the Dictionary of Old English', *OEN* 25.1 (Fall, 1991), 44–53.

17 *Early English Manuscripts in Facsimile* has been published by Rosenkilde and Bagger in Copenhagen since 1951; readers interested in tracking the decline of photographic quality in this series might compare an early volume, such as *The Thorkelin Transcripts of Beowulf*, ed. K. Malone, EEMF 1 (Copenhagen, 1951), with the very useful recent volume, *Old English Verse Texts from Many Sources: A Comprehensive Collection*, ed. F. C. Robinson and E. G. Stanley, EEMF 23 (Copenhagen, 1991). The two major facsimiles of Old English manuscripts issued by the Early English Text Society are *The Parker Chronicle and Laws*, EETS os 208 (London, 1941) and *Beowulf. Reproduced in Facsimile from the Unique Manuscript, British Museum Ms. Cotton Vitellius A. XV.*, 2nd edn. rev. N. Davis, EETS os 245 (London, 1967); compare the first issues of these books with the reprints of 1973 (*Parker Chronicle*) and 1981 (*Beowulf*). Anglo-Saxon Manuscripts in Microfiche Facsimile, gen. ed. P. Pulsiano (Binghamton, NY, 1994–), issued by Medieval and Renaissance Texts and Studies, issues facsimiles taken mostly from archive microfilms. Two volumes have appeared so far.

18 On digital imaging of the *Beowulf* manuscript, see K. S. Kiernan, 'Digital Image Processing and the *Beowulf* Manuscript', *Literary and Linguistic Computing* 6 (1991), 20–7. On the Electronic *Beowulf*, see K. S. Kiernan, 'Digital Preservation, Restoration, and Dissemination of Medieval Manuscripts', in *Scholarly Publishing on the Electronic Networks: Gateways, Gatekeepers, and Roles in the Information Omniverse*, ed. A. Okerson and D. Mogge (Washington, DC, 1994), 37–43. This essay was also published as a World-Wide Web presentation (http://www.uky.edu/ ~Kiernan/welcome.html), and in revised form as 'Opening the "Electronic *Beowulf*"', *OEN* 27.1 (Fall, 1993), 35–40.

19 For the result of this research project, see 'The Inflection of Latin Nouns in Old English Texts', forthcoming in *Words and Works: Studies in Medieval English Language and Literature in Honour of Fred C. Robinson*, ed. P. S. Baker and N. Howe.

The following suggestions for further reading supplement the work cited in the notes to the individual chapters and are offered as an aid to future study. For a comprehensive bibliography of work in Old English consult: S. B. Greenfield and F. C. Robinson, *A Bibliography of Publications on Old English Literature to the End of 1972* (Toronto and Buffalo, 1980) and the annual bibliographies in *Anglo-Saxon England* and the *Old English Newsletter*.

Comparative literature

For general discussions of comparative method see: A. O. Aldridge, *Comparative Literature: Matter and Method* (Urbana, IL, 1969); D. W. Fokkema, 'Cultural Relativism Reconsidered: Comparative Literature and Intercultural Relations' in *Douze cas d'intéraction culturelle dans l'Europe ancienne et l'Orient proche au lointain* (Paris, 1984), pp. 239–58, and 'Comparative Literature and the New Paradigm', *Canadian Review of Comparative Literature* 9 (1982), 1–18; F. Jost, *Introduction to Comparative Literature* (Indianapolis, IN, 1974); S. S. Prawer, *Comparative Literary Studies: An Introduction* (London, 1973), pp. 54–5; R. Wellek, *Discriminations: Further Concepts of Criticism* (New Haven, CT, 1970). In addition to the studies cited, for comparative work in Old English and Anglo-Latin see: M. Lapidge, 'The Present State of Anglo-Latin Studies' in M. W. Herren, *Insular Latin Studies: Papers on Latin Texts and Manuscripts of the British Isles: 550–1066* (Toronto, 1981), pp. 45–82; and his 'Aldhelm's Latin Poetry and Old English Verse', *Comparative Literature* 21 (1979), 249–314; see also M. Irvine, 'Medieval Textuality and the Archaeology of Textual Culture' in *Speaking Two Languages: Traditional Disciplines and Contemporary Theory in Medieval Studies*, ed. A. J. Frantzen (Albany, NY, 1991), 181–210. For illustrations of comparative studies of Old English and other vernacular languages see, for example: Ute Schwab, 'The Battle of Maldon: A Memorial Poem', in The Battle of Maldon: Fiction and Fact, ed. J. Cooper (London and Rio Grande, OH, 1993), pp. 63–85 (Old High German); for Old Irish see C. D. Wright, The Irish Tradition in Old English Literature (Cambridge, 1993); for Old English and Old Norse see, variously, Thomas D. Hill, 'Tormenting the Devil with Boiling Drops: An Apotropaic Motif in the Old English Solomon and Saturn I', JEGP 92 (1993), 157–66, and Seth Lerer, 'Grendel's Glove', ELH 61 (1994), 721–51; for Japanese see Michiko Ogura, 'An Ogre's Arm: Japanese Analogues of Beowulf', forthcoming in Words and Works: Studies in Medieval English Language and Literature in Honour of Fred C. Robinson, ed. P. S. Baker and N. Howe.

Sources and analogues

For collections of sources see: Sources and Analogues of Old English Poetry: The Major Latin Texts in Translation, trans. M. J. B. Allen and D. G. Calder (Cambridge, 1976); A. S. Cook, Biblical Quotations in Old English Prose Writers (London, 1898) and Biblical Quotations in Old English Prose Writers, Second Series (New York, 1903); M. C. Morrell, A Manual of Old English Biblical Materials (Knoxville, 1965); J. D. A. Ogilvy, Books Known to the English, 597–1066 (Cambridge, MA, 1967); 'Addenda and Corrigenda', Mediaevalia 7 (1981 [1984]), 281–325. For specific studies and approaches see: J. M. Bately, 'Evidence for Knowledge of Latin Literature in Old English', in Sources of Anglo-Saxon Culture, ed. P. E. Szarmach with the assistance of V. D. Oggins (Kalamazoo, MI, 1986), pp. 35–51, and 'Old English Prose Before and During the Reign of Alfred', ASE 17 (1988), 93–138; P. Clemoes, Interactions of Thought and Language in Old English Poetry, Cambridge Studies in Anglo-Saxon England 12 (Cambridge, 1995); J. E. Cross, Latin Themes in Old English Poetry (Bristol, 1962), his 'The Literate Anglo-Saxons – On Sources and Disseminations', PBA 58 (1972), 3–36, and 'Towards the Identification of Old English Literary Ideas – Old Workings and New Seams' in Sources of Anglo-Saxon Culture, ed. Szarmach, pp. 77–101; M. McC. Gatch, Preaching and Theology in Anglo-Saxon England: Ælfric and Wulfstan (Toronto and Buffalo, 1977); T. D. Hill, 'Literary History and Old English Poetry: The Case of Christ I, II, and III', Sources of Anglo-Saxon Culture, ed. Szarmach, pp. 3–22; C. D. Wright, The Irish Tradition in Old English Literature (Cambridge, 1993). For discussions of method and theory see: C. Chase, 'Source Study as a Trick with Mirrors: Annihilation of Meaning in the Old English "Mary of Egypt"' in Sources of Anglo-Saxon Culture, ed. Szarmach, pp. 23–33; T. D. Hill, 'Introduction' to Sources of Anglo-Saxon Literary Culture: A Trial Version, ed. F. M. Biggs, T. D. Hill, and P. E. Szarmach with the assistance of K. Hammond (Binghamton, NY, 1990), pp. xv–xxix; K. O'Brien O'Keeffe, 'Source, Method, Theory, Practice: On

Reading Two Old English Verse Texts', *Bulletin of the John Rylands University Library of Manchester* 76 (1994), 51–73, and published separately by the Manchester Centre for Anglo-Saxon Studies; D. G. Scragg, 'An Introduction to *Fontes Anglo-Saxonici*', *OEN* 26 (1993), Appendix B, 1–8.

Philology and linguistics

For general reference: K. Brunner, *Altenglische Grammatik (nach der angel-säschischen Grammatik von Eduard Sievers neubearbeitet)*, 3rd edn. (Tübingen, 1965); A. Campbell, *Old English Grammar* (Oxford, 1959); D. Donoghue, *Style in Old English Poetry: The Test of the Auxiliary*, Yale Studies in English 196 (New Haven, 1987); B. E. Dresher, *Old English and the Theory of Phonology* (New York and London, 1985); H. Gneuss, 'The Old English Language' in *The Cambridge Companion to Old English Literature*, ed. M. Godden and M. Lapidge (Cambridge, 1991), 23–51; R. M. Hogg, ed., *The Cambridge History of the English Language. Volume 1: The Beginnings to 1066* (Cambridge, 1992) and R. M. Hogg, *A Grammar of Old English. Volume 1: Phonology* (Oxford and Cambridge, MA, 1992); R. Lass, *Old English: A Historical Linguistic Companion* (Cambridge, 1994); B. Mitchell, *Old English Syntax*, 2 vols. (Oxford, 1985); E. C. Traugott, 'Syntax' in *The Cambridge History of the English Language. Volume I: The Beginnings to 1066*, ed. Hogg, pp. 168–289. For general discussions of work in Old English language see: M. Blockley, 'Old English Language', *ANQ* ns 3 (1990), 45–8; A. diPaolo Healey, 'Old English Language Studies: Present State and Future Prospects', *OEN* 20 (1987), 34–45. On linguistic means of dating see: A. Crandell Amos, *Linguistic Means of Determining the Dates of Old English Literary Texts*, Medieval Academy Books 90 (Cambridge, MA, 1980); J. Bately, 'The Compilation of the Anglo-Saxon Chronicle, 60 BC to AD 890: Vocabulary as Evidence', *PBA* 64 (1980), 93–129. On meter see: A. J. Bliss, *The Metre of Beowulf*, rev. edn. (Oxford, 1967); T. Cable, *The English Alliterative Tradition* (Philadelphia, 1991); R. D. Fulk, *A History of Old English Meter* (Philadelphia, 1992); B. R. Hutcheson, *Old English Poetic Metre* (Woodbridge, Suffolk, 1995); C. B. Kendall, *The Metrical Grammar of 'Beowulf'* (Cambridge, 1991); G. Russom, *Old English Meter and Linguistic Theory* (Cambridge, 1987). For discussions of philology, old and new, see: C. T. Berkhout and M. McC. Gatch, ed., *Anglo-Saxon Scholarship: The First Three Centuries* (Boston, 1982); R. H. Bloch, 'New Philology and Old French', *Speculum* 65 (1990), 38–58; J. Culler, 'Anti-Foundational Philology', *Comparative Literature Studies* 27 (1990), 49–52; P. de Man, 'The Return to Philology' in his *The Resistance to Theory*, Theory and History of Literature 33 (Minneapolis, 1986), pp. 21–6; S. Fleischman, 'Philology, Linguistics and the Discourse of the Medieval Text', *Speculum* 65 (1990), 19–37; A. J.

Frantzen, *Desire for Origins: New Language, Old English, and Teaching the Tradition* (New Brunswick, NJ, 1990); S. G. Nichols, 'Introduction: Philology in a Manuscript Culture', *Speculum* 65 (1990), 1–10; L. Patterson, 'On the Margin: Postmodernism, Ironic History, and Medieval Studies', ibid., 87–108; M. Rissanen, 'On the Happy Reunion of English Philology and Historical Linguistics', in *Historical Linguistics and Philology*, ed. J. Fisiak (Berlin and New York, 1990), pp. 353–69; C. Watkins, 'What is Philology?', *Comparative Literature Studies* 27 (1990), 21–5.

History and historicism

W. Benjamin, *Illuminations*, ed. H. Arendt (New York, 1969); J. N. Cox and L. J. Reynolds, eds., *New Historical Literary Study: Essays on Reproducing Texts, Representing History* (Princeton, 1993); A. J. Frantzen, *Desire for Origins: New Language, Old English, and Teaching the Tradition* (New Brunswick, NJ, 1990); F. Nietzsche, 'On the Uses and Disadvantages of History for Life', in *Untimely Meditations*, trans. by R. J. Hollingdale (Cambridge, 1983), pp. 59– 123; L. Patterson, 'On the Margin: Postmodernism, Ironic History, and Medieval Studies', *Speculum* 65 (1990), 87–108; H. White, *Tropics of Discourse: Essays in Cultural Criticism* (Baltimore, 1978), pp. 101–20; K. Popper, *The Poverty of Historicism* (London, 1986; first published 1957); E. W. Said, *Orientalism* (New York, 1978). For resources in Anglo-Saxon history see the bibliography by Simon Keynes: *Anglo-Saxon History: A Select Bibliography*, 2nd rev. edn., *OEN* Subsidia 13 (Binghamton, NY, 1993); for an accessible compilation and translation of documents see D. Whitelock, *English Historical Documents, Volume I: c. 500–1042*, 2nd edn. (London, 1979). The following suggestions are samples of approaches: P. W. Conner, *Anglo- Saxon Exeter: A Tenth-Century Cultural History* (Woodbridge, 1993); R. Frank, 'The *Beowulf* Poet's Sense of History', in *The Wisdom of Poetry*, ed. L. D. Benson and S. Wenzel (Kalamazoo, MI, 1982), pp. 53–65; R. W. Hanning, '*Beowulf* as Heroic History', *Medievalia et Humanistica* ns 5 (1974), 77–102; N. Howe, *Migration and Mythmaking in Anglo-Saxon England* (New Haven, 1989); M. Irvine, *The Making of Textual Culture: 'Grammatica' and Literary Theory, 350–1100* (Cambridge, 1994); C. Kendall and P. S. Wells, eds., *Voyage to the Other World: The Legacy of Sutton Hoo* (Minneapolis, 1992); U. Schaefer, 'Alterities: On Methodology in Medieval Literary Studies', *Oral Tradition* 8 (1993), 187–214; D. Townsend, 'Alcuin's Willibrord, Wilhelm Levison, and the *MGH*', in *The Politics of Editing Medieval Texts*, ed. R. Frank (New York, 1993), pp. 107–30; P. Wormald, 'Bede, *Beowulf* and the Conversion of the Anglo-Saxon Aristocracy' in *Bede and Anglo-Saxon England*, ed. R. T. Farrell, *British Archaeological Reports* 46 (1978), 32–95.

Oral tradition

For general background, in addition to the citations in the notes, see: R. Frank, 'The Search for the Anglo-Saxon Oral Poet', *Bulletin of the John Rylands University Library of Manchester* 75 (1993), 11–36; D. H. Green, 'Orality and Reading: The State of Research in Medieval Studies', *Speculum* 65 (1990), 268–80, and his *Medieval Listening and Reading: The Primary Reception of German Literature 800–1300* (Cambridge, 1994); for theoretical and comparative approaches to oral traditional literature see the following works by J. M. Foley: *Oral Tradition in Literature: Interpretation in Context* (Columbia, MO, 1986); *The Theory of Oral Composition: History and Methodology* (Bloomington, IN, 1988); *Traditional Oral Epic: The 'Odyssey', 'Beowulf', and the Serbo-Croatian Return Song* (Berkeley, CA, 1990); *Immanent Art: From Structure to Meaning in Traditional Oral Epic* (Bloomington, IN, 1991); and J. M. Foley, ed., *Oral-Formulaic Theory: A Folklore Casebook*, Garland Folklore Casebooks 5 (New York, 1990). See also J. Opland, *Anglo-Saxon Oral Poetry* (New Haven, CT, 1980).

Textual editing

For general background in textual editing see: L. E. Boyle, 'Optimist and Recensionist: "Common Errors" or "Common Variations"?' in *Latin Script and Letters A.D. 400–900: Festschrift presented to Ludwig Bieler*, ed. J. J. O'Meara and B. Naumann (Leiden, 1976), pp. 264–74; D. C. Greetham, *Textual Scholarship: An Introduction* (New York and London, 1992); P. Maas, *Textual Criticism*, trans. B. Flower (Oxford, 1958); P. L. Shillingsburg, *Scholarly Editing in the Computer Age: Theory and Practice* (Athens, GA and London, 1986); G. T. Tanselle, 'Classical, Biblical, and Medieval Textual Criticism and Modern Editing', *Studies in Bibliography* 36 (1983), 21–68. For studies of editing in Old English see: M. Godden, 'Old English' in *Editing Medieval Texts: English, French, and Latin Written in England*, ed. A. G. Rigg (New York and London, 1977), pp. 9–33; M. Lapidge, 'Textual Criticism and the Literature of Anglo-Saxon England', *Bulletin of the John Rylands University Library of Manchester* 73 (1991), 17–45, and published separately by the Manchester Centre for Anglo-Saxon Studies; E. A. Levenston, *The Stuff of Literature: Physical Aspects of Texts and Their Relation to Meaning* (Albany, NY, 1992); B. Mitchell, 'The Dangers of Disguise: Old English Texts in Modern Punctuation' in *On Old English* (Oxford and New York, 1988); K. O'Brien O'Keeffe, 'Texts and Works: Some Historical Questions on the Editing of Old English Verse' in *New Historical Literary Study: Essays on Reproducing Texts, Representing History*, ed. J. N. Cox and L. J. Reynolds (Princeton, 1993), pp. 54–68; D. G. Scragg and P. E. Szarmach, eds., *Editing Old English* (Woodbridge, Suffolk and Rochester, NY, 1994).

Feminist criticism

In addition to the bibliographical material in the notes, the *Medieval Feminist Newsletter* is an essential source for both bibliography and special issues, for example E. A. Matter, ed., 'Gay and Lesbian Concerns in Medieval Studies', *Medieval Feminist Newsletter* (Spring, 1992), 1–15; and 'Multiculturalism in the Middle Ages and the Renaissance', *Medieval Feminist Newsletter* 16 (Fall, 1993), 3–40. For general theoretical background see the following: H. Bloch, *Medieval Misogyny and the Invention of Western Romantic Love* (Chicago and London, 1991); J. Flax, *Thinking Fragments: Psychoanalysis, Feminism, and Postmodernism in the Contemporary West* (Berkeley, Los Angeles, Oxford, 1990); E. Fox-Genovese, *Feminism Without Illusions* (Chapel Hill and London, 1991); R. Hennessy, *Materialist Feminism and the Politics of Discourse* (New York and London, 1993); J. Kristeva, *Powers of Horror: An Essay on Abjection*, trans. L. S. Roudiez (New York, 1982) and her *Tales of Love*, trans. L. S. Roudiez (New York, 1987); L. Irigaray, *Speculum of the Other Woman*, trans. G. C. Gill (Ithaca and London, 1985) and her *This Sex Which Is Not One*, trans. C. Porter (Ithaca and London, 1985); T. Lovell, ed., *British Feminist Thought: A Reader* (Oxford, 1990); E. Marks and I. de Courtivron, eds., *New French Feminisms: An Anthology* (New York, 1981); T. Moi, *Sexual/Textual Politics: Feminist Literary Theory* (London and New York, 1985); G. R. Overing, *Language, Sign, and Gender in 'Beowulf'* (Carbondale and Edwardsville, 1990).

Post-structuralist criticism

On post-structuralist theory generally see: R. C. Davis and R. Schleifer, *Contemporary Literary Criticism: Literary and Cultural Studies*, 3rd edn. (New York, 1994); *The Johns Hopkins Guide to Literary Theory and Criticism*, ed. M. Groden and M. Kreiswirth (Baltimore, MD, 1994); D. G. Marshall, *Contemporary Critical Theory: A Selective Bibliography* (New York, 1993); *Redrawing the Boundaries: The Transformation of English and American Literary Studies*, ed. G. Gunn and S. Greenblatt (New York, 1992); *Structuralism and Since: From Lévi-Strauss to Derrida*, ed. J. Sturrock (Oxford, 1979). For work on Anglo-Saxon studies and critical theory see: A. J. Frantzen, *The Desire for Origins: New Language, Old English, and Teaching the Tradition* (New Brunswick, NJ, 1990); J. P. Hermann, 'Why Anglo-Saxonists Can't Read: Or, Who Took the Mead out of Medieval Studies', *Exemplaria* 7 (1995), 9–26; R. M. Liuzza, 'The Return of the Repressed: Old and New Theories in Old English Literary Criticism' in *Old English Shorter Poems: Basic Readings*, ed. K. O'Brien O'Keeffe (New York, 1994); see also the following selected studies on Old English using post-structuralist theory: A. N. Doane, 'Oral Texts, Intertexts, and Intratexts: Editing Old English' in

Influence and Intertextuality in Literary History, ed. J. Clayton and E. Rothstein (Madison, WI, 1991), 75–113; J. P. Hermann, *Allegories of War* (Ann Arbor, MI, 1989); M. Irvine, *The Making of Textual Culture: 'Grammatica' and Literary Theory, 350–1100*, Cambridge Studies in Medieval Literature 19 (Cambridge, 1994); M. R. Near, 'Anticipating Alienation: *Beowulf* and the Intrusion of Literacy', *PMLA* 108 (1993), 320–32; K. O'Brien O'Keeffe, *Visible Song: Transitional Literacy in Old English Verse*, Cambridge Studies in Anglo-Saxon England 4 (Cambridge, 1990); G. Overing, *Language, Sign, and Gender in 'Beowulf'* (Carbondale, IL, 1990); C. B. Pasternack, *The Textuality of Old English Poetry*, Cambridge Studies in Anglo-Saxon England 13 (Cambridge, 1995); various essays in *Speaking Two Languages: Traditional Disciplines and Contemporary Theory in Medieval Studies*, ed. A. J. Frantzen (Albany, NY, 1991), including Frantzen, 'Prologue: Documents and Monuments: Difference and Interdisciplinarity in the Study of Medieval Culture'; G. R. Overing, 'On Reading Eve: *Genesis B* and the Readers' Desire'; C. A. Lees, 'Working with Patristic Sources: Language and Context in Old English Homilies'; M. Irvine, 'Medieval Textuality and the Archaeology of Textual Culture'; essays in *Vox Intexta: Orality and Textuality in the Middle Ages*, ed. A. N. Doane and C. B. Pasternack (Madison, WI, 1991), including J. M. Foley, 'Orality, Textuality, and Interpretation'; W. Parks, 'The Textualization of Orality in Literary Criticism'; U. Schaefer, 'Hearing from Books: The Rise of Fictionality in Old English Poetry'. For studies of deconstruction, in addition to works cited, see: J. Derrida, *Of Grammatology*, trans. G. C. Spivak (Baltimore, 1976); C. Norris, *Deconstruction: Theory and Practice*, rev. edn. (London, 1991). For semiotics and textuality, in addition to works cited, see: R. Barthes, 'From Work to Text', in *Textual Strategies*, ed. J. V. Harari (Ithaca, NY, 1979); *The Kristeva Reader*, ed. T. Moi (New York, 1986) for Moi's introductions as well as selections, especially 'Stabat Mater'; R. Scholes, *Semiotics and Interpretation* (New Haven, 1982). For psychoanalysis, in addition to works cited, see: T. Brennan, *History After Lacan* (London and New York, 1993); H. Cixous, 'The Laugh of the Medusa', *Signs* (summer, 1976), repr. in *New French Feminisms*, ed. E. Marks and I. de Courtivron (New York, 1980), pp. 245–64; J. W. Earl, 'The Role of the Men's Hall in the Development of the Anglo-Saxon Superego', *Psychiatry* 46 (1983), 139–60; *Feminine Sexuality: Jacques Lacan and the Ecole freudienne*, ed. J. Mitchell and J. Rose (New York, 1982); L. O. Fradenburg, '"Be not far from me": Psychoanalysis, Medieval Studies, and the Subject of Religion', *Exemplaria* 7 (1995), 41–54; T. Moi, *Sexual/Textual Politics: Feminist Literary Theory* (London, 1985) for discussions of Lacan and Kristeva; J. P. Muller and W. J. Richardson, *Lacan and Language: A Reader's Guide to Ecrits* (New York, 1982).

INDEX

Note: Titles of works follow all other subheadings after the author's name.